LANGUAGE HUNTING IN THE KARAKORAM

LANGUAGE HUNTING IN THE KARAKORAM

BY

E. O. LORIMER

GYAN

Published by

GYAN

Gyan Publishing House
5, Ansari Road
Daryaganj, New Delhi-110002
Phone: 011-47034999, 9811692060
E-mail: books@gyanbooks.com

Distribution Network
gyanbooks.com
India, USA, Canada, UK, Australia, France

ISBN : 978-81-212-9994-7 (PB)
First Published, 1939

2nd Impression 2021

Printed at: Gyan Press, Delhi.

Language Hunting in the Karakoram
Author: E. O. Lorimer

LANGUAGE HUNTING IN THE KARAKORAM

by

E. O. LORIMER

George Allen & Unwin Ltd

40 Museum Street

London

Hunza River at Aliábád (winter). Middle distance, Hasanábád Nullah debouching from right. Background, Rakaposhi, 25,550 ft.

(*See pp.* 138–9)

To

DL

Ubi tu Caius ego Caia

'Tis yours to judge, how wide the limits stand
Between a splendid and a happy land.

GOLDSMITH: *The Traveller*

NOTE

THIS is not a serious book. Comparative philologists hoping for news of Burushaski, anthropologists interested in the highly civilized though materially primitive life of the Burusho of Hunza, ethnologists curious as to their origin, the scientifically-minded of every sort, are once for all referred to the published and to the yet unpublished books and articles of my husband, Lieutenant-Colonel D. L. R. Lorimer, late of the Indian Army and the Foreign and Political Department of the Government of India, hereinafter referred to as David or DL.

I have been concerned merely to set down our personal day-to-day experiences—they do not merit the name of adventures—and our first impressions of the delightful people who for fourteen months in 1934–35 were our neighbours and our friends.

The journey to and from Hunza and the semi-camp life there had at an earlier period been the commonplace, all-in-the-day's-work life of ourselves for four years (1920–24), as of a long series of other Political Agents and their wives both before and after us. The only thing that lent a spice of adventure to this last tour was our delightful freedom from all official responsibility, and our age. Changes of climate and altitude, shortages of food and sleep, fatigues of travel, at which one smiles at forty present a graver challenge to fifty-five.

The triumph of our elderly excursion lies not alone in the sheaves carried home by DL, but in the fact that we both came back more than a little battered, it must be confessed, but still smiling; and treasuring memories which are worth incomparably more than the price exacted.

My excuse for writing so superficial—perhaps worthless—a book at all must be that it has made me happy to recall this silver honeymoon spent in the Karakoram and to pay a tribute to our hospitable and beloved Hunzukuts as they were in 1935, as they must have been for uncounted generations in the past, as they may be for generations yet to come, if the poverty and inaccessibility of their country happily keep them safely quarantined against "the sick fatigue, the languid doubt," the unrest and fear and hustle of our civilization.

For the map I am indebted to DL; the illustrations are my own.

E. O. LORIMER

UNIVERSITY WOMEN'S CLUB

April 1938

CONTENTS

CHAPTER PAGE

NOTE 5

Part 1. Preliminary

1. THE HUNT IS UP 15
2. GILGIT APPRENTICESHIP 17
3. PRACTICAL VALUE OF VERNACULARS 22
4. AT HOME 25
5. A DREAM COMES TRUE 28
6. EAST AGAIN 31
7. HALT IN KASHMIR 34

Part 2. The Journey

8. OFF AT LAST 41
9. ENTERING GILGIT AGENCY 48
10. TOWARDS GILGIT 56
11. THE LAST LAP 66

Part 3. Life in Hunza

12. SETTLING IN 77
13. HOUSEKEEPING PROBLEMS 83
14. FIRST WALKS ABROAD 93
15. ILLNESS CALLS A HALT 104
16. HOME LIFE AT NO. I 114
17. LAND AND HOUSES IN HUNZA 120
18. SEPTEMBER HARVEST 133
19. HARVEST THANKSGIVING 143
20. HUNZA BABIES 153

CONTENTS

CHAPTER | PAGE

21. HUNZA CRAFTS 163
22. MARRIAGE IN HUNZA 179
23. WINTER AND THE "GREAT COLD" 194
24. BARLEY SOWING AND "STARVATION SPRINGTIME" 221
25. LEARNING AN UNKNOWN LANGUAGE 248
26. DIGRESSION TO YASIN 263
27. THE FIRST OF THE HARVEST 282
28. FINALITIES 297
INDEX 307

LIST OF ILLUSTRATIONS

Hunza River at Aliábád (winter) *Frontispiece*
Middle distance, Hasanábád Nullah debouching from right. Background, Rakapóshi, 25,550 ft.

PLATE *Facing page*

I. 1. Trout-fishing in Kargah Nullah near Gilgit 20
2. Looking up Gilgit River from maize field in Gilgit 20

II. 1. Part of ruined temple of Martand 36
2. Backdoor Gossip in Kashmir 36

III. 1. Mail-runners' Refuge on Burzil Pass (summer) 48
2. Junction of Gilgit (left) and Indus Rivers 48

IV. Looking up the Hunza River gorge, half a march from Aliábád. The Road (see Plate V) runs round face of right-hand cliff 64

V. Cliff Road with three horsemen 72

VI. 1. Old Fort-Village of Aliábád with beacon tower. Background, Rakapóshi 80
2. Old Mosque at Aliábád, with Hurmat seated in verandah 80

VII. Group on roof of No. 1 watching passers-by in street below. Small boy is carrying baby on his back of whom nothing is visible but tiny fists on brother's shoulders 88

VIII. 1. Grandfather minding Baby Faqér 96
2. Baby Worship. Naját standing in field 96

IX. 1. Threshing 112
2. Winnowing. Foreground, Afiato and Yaman 112

LIST OF ILLUSTRATIONS

PLATE		*Facing page*
X.	1. Dumping manure	114
	2. Afiato Ploughing	114
	3. Aliko Sowing. Small boy interrupted in game of "foot-polo"	114
	4. Party of women weeding	114
XI.	Hunza Fields. Background, Raka in cloud	118
XII.	1. Street Scene. Children carrying new-born lambs and kids in their arms to display them to us on our return from Yasin	128
	2. The Dála, typical road cum water-channel, flanked by field wall	128
XIII.	Young Friends:	
	1. Nímo and sister with the baby	144
	2. Dádo with Akíl Sháh, aged two	144
	3. Zulfi	144
	4. Kháno with baby sister, Guláb	144
XIV.	Household of No. 8:	
	1. Bibi Anjír (left) and a Neighbour	160
	2. Hérul Nisa with baby-niece (the first grand-child)	160
	3. Ustád Nadíro and Hérul Nisa	160
XV.	1. Little girl barely five taking baby brother of two for a ride. Madat, the elder boy, watches the experiment with some anxiety	176
	2. Fetching firewood in a shoulder basket	176
	3. Gúlo and friends working mud into "cakes like those Mother makes." A wish-fulfilment of Starvation Springtime	176
XVI.	1. "The Merry Widow," just about to be re-married: "And I'm in great demand, I can tell you," she said	184

LIST OF ILLUSTRATIONS

PLATE		*Facing page*
	2. Washing a homespun cloak	184
	3. Brother and Sister	184
	4. The "Cheshire Cat" of No. 4 with small sister	184
XVII.	1. Gohir Nímo of No. 9, reaping	224
	2. Family Group of No. 1A. Aliko (seated in background) watches Sóni proudly rocking his first grandson	224
XVIII.	Mir's Fort at Báltít, 600 years old. Mountains in background 23,000 ft. concealing the great glacier that waters all the oases of central Hunza	240
XIX.	Old Fort at Áltít, centre of ancient ceremonial	256
XX.	1. DL taking photo of Mir Muhammad Nazím Khán on the mountain side at Báltít	272
	2. View of Áltít Fort from the same spot, lookup Hunza River	272
XXI.	The road cum water-channel on which our nearest neighbours lived	280
XXII.	1. Rakapóshi in summer from Aliábád. Apricot trees in foreground	288
	2. The sole type of wheeled vehicle in Hunza, a barrow used only in levelling fields	288
XXIII.	1. Children watching water-hole (centre) to close it with the mushroom-plug (right) at given signal from father	304
	2. Two small Hunza Princesses with pet puppy	304
	3. Khalífa Farághat teaching his son to read the Persian scriptures	304
	Map of the Karakoram	*at end*

PART I

Preliminary

Chapter 1

THE HUNT IS UP

It was in 1920 on a summer afternoon in Ziarat, the little hill station in Baluchistan, where various civil and political officers of the Government of India have their hot-weather bungalows at 8,000 feet among the barren but juniper-scented hills. David was at the moment away in Quetta conferring with colleagues, and I had to go alone to an afternoon tennis party at the Summer Residency.

David had had five or six gruelling months in Loralai, and I knew that he was finding thoroughly unsatisfactory to a man of his particular temperament and previous experience the unending office work, blent of law, revenue, and red-tape, that prevented his freely getting out to travel on horse or on foot and learn to know the people of his district—the first duty, as he saw it, of a political officer. All his earlier posts, military and political, had been actually on the frontier, or beyond it, in the Tochi or the Khaibar, in Persia, Arabia, or Mesopotamia, where human relationships were of more importance than office files and where senior officers were sufficiently distant to let the man on the spot get on with his job.

We were deep in a well-contested four when I saw the Chief advancing with a sheaf of papers. We finished the rally before I turned my head and responded to an imperious call. "Should you be willing to go with your husband to Gilgit?" was barked at me, in a tone which said plainly to the bystanders: "Of course, being a woman she'll prefer to stand in his way." The Chief's attitude to wives always challenged me, and I barked back: "I'm willing to go with my husband to HELL." This unconventional, not over-courteous, outburst provoked a milder: "Then I may wire him and say you'll have no objection?" "It will be a waste of time. He knows." We resumed the interrupted game, but my head was joyously humming at the thought of escape, escape to Gilgit; for me my first sight of great mountains, for David the open road again—people—the work he loved.

He returned from Quetta, overjoyed at the unexpected prospect of a transfer to Gilgit, a place he had always longed for, though—true to his principle of never clamouring for or pulling wires to get a coveted job—he had never applied for it. I had a suspicion that it was not thus that most of his colleagues nursed their careers. His only misgivings about Gilgit were that it might be rough on me: "It'll be lonely, and I shall be most of the time on trek, and you won't always be able to come." That didn't worry me. I asked only one question: "What language does it mean?" "I've been asking; there are four or five more or less unknown vernaculars, but the chiefs and headmen all talk a certain amount of Hindustani, and the Political Agent carries on in that." "And shall you?" He smiled without waste of words, and I knew we were for it. Gilgit offered few amenities, a hard life and constant travel at all temperatures; it offered the tangled politics of seven different provinces; it offered possible opportunities—if there were time—for mountains and big game (his favourite hobbies as a boy; some of his trophies still hung in the Guides' mess, some of his records were still holding a place in Rowland Ward); but above all, it offered "four or five more or less unknown vernaculars."

Chapter 2

GILGIT APPRENTICESHIP

THERE followed four glorious years in Gilgit. The seven districts or provinces under David's supervision gave him plenty of official work and lots of incident, of which in another time and place I should love to write. One, the district of Chilas in the Indus Valley, was directly under a British Officer, Assistant to the Political Agent. Lying on the borders of the restless, untamed democracies of the independent territories of Darel and Tangir (casually lumped together in ordinary speech as Yághistan—"The Home of Rebels") it had, unlike the rest of the Agency, an unenviable record of serious crime, including from nine to fourteen murders a year. Gilgit itself was then administered by Kashmir officials with all the paraphernalia of Wazír-i-Wazárat, Revenue officers, and law-courts. With these two districts the Political Agent was less directly concerned, though his official headquarters were in Gilgit, the only really prosperous oasis of any size in the Agency. Then there were the four political *iláqas*, small states ruled by Government-appointed governors, Punial, Yasin, Kuh-Ghizr, and Ishkoman, and finally the two semi-independent kingdoms of Hunza and Nagir, with their own kings, or Mirs, hereditary chieftains whose families (or family, since the two Mirs are descended from a common ancestor) have held sway in their present territories for at least six hundred years, since the days of our earliest Edwards. Since the famous Hunza Nagir Campaign of 1891 the two Mirs have been our trusty and faithful allies.

It was David's job to be the friend and counsellor of governors and chiefs; to keep a sharp eye out for tyranny or oppression; to be at all times, whether at headquarters or on the road, immediately and easily accessible to humble folk with real or imaginary grievances; to ensure that slave-trading, arms-traffic, or foreign intrigue did not disturb the peace of the hardy peasant populations that were wringing a livelihood from the rocky mountain sides of what must be one of the highest and most inhospitable inhabited regions of the earth. This entailed constant travelling. He visited each district at least once a year, and most of them twice. Each tour entailed four or six days' travelling out and again four or six days back, up or down one river or another, for travel is only possible amongst the mighty mountains of the Hindu Kush and Karakoram where a river has contrived to cut its way. In summer he would push out beyond the inhabited oases to the great passes that form the gates of entry to British India from Afghanistan and Central Asia or the links with Chitral.

The spacious, if oddly planned and straggling, bungalow in Gilgit that was our home, with its English garden and valuable fruit and vegetable supplies, saw him only for a few weeks at a time between these ever-recurring tours on which I joined him when possible, but by no means always, for I could not feel it fair to nurse and baby to leave them too often alone. On the longer tours, moreover, during which David traversed every inch of the Gilgit frontier and crossed some unknown internal passes, difficulties of supply and transport which would impose burdens on isolated hill communities where the barest necessaries of food and fodder are cruelly scarce, debarred me from adding two extra mouths—mine and my pony's—to the party.

During those eventful and yet peaceful years David worked steadily and unremittingly at mastering and recording the local languages.

Obviously the first language to attack was Shina, and in this he accumulated over 400 foolscap typed sheets of texts, with ample notes, recording current folk-lore and superstitions, local history, customs, etc., and worked out the skeleton of a practical grammar to be amplified later into a more detailed, more scientific one, and collected a comprehensive vocabulary.

While he thus worked systematically I would sit by, knitting woollies for baby, mending the family socks and absorbing as much as I could of what was passing between David and his informant. Then, as I went my daily rounds with the servants, weighing in firewood, or issuing stores, packing away woollen clothes to protect them against moth or what not, I would enquire the Shina for all I saw, and listen to the servants' talk amongst themselves, jotting everything in my notebook to memorize it later, until by degrees I could substitute Shina for my sketchy memsahib's Hindustani. Not frequently but sometimes a phrase or word or form which I thus caught on the wing proved useful to supplement DL's much wider-flung enquiries.

Next came Khowar, the language of Chitral, of which David had made a preliminary study during nine months as Political Agent there during the War. To my bitter grief I had not been allowed to accompany him, and so had missed his first steps in Khowar. Though by listening I learnt enough for typing and indexing purposes, I always felt this delightful language something of a step-child compared with Shina, and I never attempted to speak it. The "Royal Families" of Yasin and Punial are descendants of the Chitral Khushwaqts, who had conquered parts of the Agency two hundred years ago. They retain their native language and have, to a certain extent, imposed it as a second language on the upper strata of their subjects. Throughout the Agency it is therefore regarded as a polite language, meet for chiefs. In the same way as for Shina, DL collected texts, notes, vocabulary, and all the data for a scientific grammar to supplement his considerable material from Chitral, noting how very trivial were the differences between the two varieties of Khowar.

Not until the end of our third year in Gilgit was he able to devote himself to the infinitely more thrilling task of acquiring Burushaski. Now Shina and Khowar are both members of the Indo-Iranian family of languages—possibly taking off from the parent stock before the Indian and Iranian branches were fully differentiated—and are therefore related to Hindustani, Persian, Pashtu, and each other, as for instance Icelandic to Rumanian, or Dutch to French. There was therefore nothing sensationally new about their structure, and a large number of their words had for a scholar recognizable kinship with Sanskrit or Avestan roots. They might, in fact, be styled relatively "easy."

Burushaski was another matter. Here was, it would seem, a language entirely unrelated to its neighbours, or to any other known form of human speech, alive or dead. If, as Sir George Grierson conjectured, it was the survival of an aboriginal language spoken perhaps over the whole of northern India before the Sanskrit-speaking Aryan invaders pushed their way southwards across the mountain barriers into India (some two or three centuries before Christ?), it had been driven ever further and further up into the inaccessible mountain valleys of the Karakoram, where it is preserved almost pure among the sturdy peasants of Hunza, somewhat contaminated by Shina amongst their Nagir neighbours across the river, and subject to independent development across the ranges in Yasin, where the peasant people speak what they call Burushaski, though the Khowar-speaking upper classes dub it Werchikwar.[1]

The fact that the structure of Burushaski is utterly non-Indogermanic, non-Semitic, non-Turkish, non-Mongolian, non-anything-known, and that—with the exception of a few Persian-Arabic loan words which have filtered in with the coming of Islam—its vocabulary is entirely its own, awaking no echoes in the mind to aid the memory, makes it a difficult language to tackle. Though British officers have been regularly associated with Hunza and Nagir since 1891, and less regularly for some years before, the only one who had attempted to work on it was that fine old sportsman, Colonel Biddulph—who had published in 1880 twenty-two octavo pages of grammar, our of sentences and texts, and twenty pages of vocabulary. Leitner, of the Educational Department, published a *Hunza and Nagyr Handbook* in 1889, which contains a considerable amount of material in unsystematic form. Both

[1] In the language of Chitral, -wár means "speech" and -ík "the people of a country." Their own language Kho-war is the "speech of the Kho people" and Werch-ik-war "the speech of the Weresh (= Burush) people," the earlier, if not necessarily aboriginal, dwellers in Yasin, at the time of the Chitrali conquests.

1. Trout-fishing in Kargah Nullah near Gilgit

PLATE I

. Looking up
Gilgit River
rom maize
ield in Gilgit.

these pioneers deserve the greatest credit for their work, and had to wait for forty years to find a successor.. They had worked chiefly on the Nagir form of Burushaski, and had not, of course, distinguished the Shina elements in it, and they had to work wholly through interpreters, which accounts for much misunderstanding and inaccuracy. David therefore thought it wiser to start from scratch, as in the case of Shina and Khowar. Here, again, with infinitely greater labour, he amassed texts, notes, and vocabulary.

When we eventually bade a sad farewell to Gilgit in 1924 to go "on leave, pending retirement," we were comforted by knowing that we need not relapse into bath-chairs in Cheltenham or Camberley to bewail the good old times, the decay of the British Empire and the shortcomings of the young, nor to shout "koi hai?" to an unresponsive world, but had enough material in manuscript and typescript to keep us happily employed for the rest of our joint lives.

Incidentally David had snatched fleeting opportunities to collect also some Wakhi material, though not on the same scale as the other three languages. Wakhi is spoken in the higher levels of Hunza by immigrants from the Afghan territory of Wakhan, who have established themselves at the non-apricot-growing heights—often 10,000 feet and more—which the Hunzukuts proper consider barely habitable. Wakhi is a language of Persian descent, and was of particular interest to DL who, during many years in Persia, had made himself an authority on several unrecorded dialects of Modern Colloquial Persian, and while in Chitral had done what work he could on the Persian dialects of Madaglasht and Badakhshan.

Chapter 3

THE PRACTICAL VALUE OF VERNACULARS

It must not be imagined that the value of DL's work on these local languages of Gilgit Agency was merely scientific. His colloquial knowledge of them was turned to advantage every day. As he rode along from stage to stage, the fact that he greeted the villagers in their own tongue instead of Hindustani, and chatted with them about their crops; the fact that even if he used an interpreter in complicated discussions about ownership, inheritance, or water-rights, he was following the petitioner's speech himself and interpolating questions or comments in the vernacular gave pleasure and evoked confidence as well as surprise. In another respect, too, he created a precedent. At the Annual Jalsa in Gilgit it was the custom for the Political Agent to make a speech in English to the assembled chiefs and their retainers, which was then repeated in Hindustani by the Indian Assistant. At his first Durbar a few months after our arrival, DL followed, of course, the usual routine; at the second he made a short speech in Shina; at the third in Khowar; and at the fourth in Burushaski. This last effort came as a complete surprise. David had given much care and thought to the speech, and rehearsed in private with a good informant, but no rumour of it had got about even within the household.

Sitting on the dais behind him I saw with amusement an electric shock go through the Hunza Nagir ranks in the usual place of honour on the right of the large audience: bodies tautened and leaned forward, eyes brightened, faces smiled; there was no mistaking the amazement and delight with which the Burushaski speakers heard their language for the first time on the lips of a white man. Every syllable rang out clearly, every word was followed with rapt attention, and when ceremonies and presentations were over and the Political Agent had ridden off in state, the Mir of Hunza came over to me, radiant, to shake hands and offer congratulations. "Was it all right? Could you really understand?" "Every word and every sentence was perfect," he said, "far better than I or Nagir could have done it, for you know we don't ever attempt public speaking." His sincerity was transparent and his congratulations were presently reinforced by the Mir of Nagir. But the happiest moment of a happy afternoon still awaited me. After greeting the various other chiefs, I mounted as quickly as I might and trotted full speed uphill to the Agency House to see that tea and drinks were all in order for the informal gathering that always followed the Durbar. I rode round to the back verandah and made straight for the pantry to cast a final eye on boiling samovars and trays of cakes. All was well in train, but the place was buzzing with unwonted excitement. All our best servants were Hunza men, and the head-boy, Nazar, came forward, seized and kissed my hand with tears in his eyes: "Mother, dear Mother, we didn't know that it was possible." A chorus of appreciation echoed from the other Hunzukuts, standing respectfully about. This humbler tribute delighted me, I need hardly say, even more than the Mirs', and I noted with pleasure that Nazar's emotion had betrayed him into this unwonted form of affectionate address—little suspecting that the respectful "Mother, dear Mother" of Hunza would one day become so familiar, though never to the point of losing its thrill for me.

. . . . .

When we had settled into our own house at home and at last got books and papers sorted, and a study—woefully small after the spaciousness of Eastern rooms—into working order, the question was where to begin the long task of hammering all this material into shape. It was clear that Burushaski, being far the most difficult and "foreign" of the languages we had been working on, would also be the easiest to forget, and it was wise to set to work while the sounds of it were still fresh in our ears, if by no means fluent on our tongue. Also, it would be the most interesting to the comparative philologist, and possibly when all David's data were available some scholar with a wider range might discover the affinities—if any—with perchance the Munda languages of southern India, which had been driven to the south by the same wedge of invasion as had (by hypothesis) pushed Burushaski up into its remote asylum in the Karakoram; or conceivably with the languages of the Caucasus; or better still, with some hitherto undeciphered language rescued from the dust-heaps of Central Asia by the archaeological zeal of Aurel Stein, Lecoq, or Sven Hedin.

His task would not be easy. For even if Burushaski *had* blood relations surviving anywhere, it had developed in isolation on its own lines for at least five thousand years, and in the absence of any record of its form at any point in that long stretch of time, relationship could not be superficially easy of detection. If there were no history, no literary records, no intermediate language-links, it would be "some" philologist who could now prove the identic origin of *cow* and *beef*, of *quick* and *vivus*, or the kinship between the Gaelic of the Scotch Highlands, the Greek of modern Athens, and the language of Bengal. Anyhow, all this was other people's job; ours the more modest one of throwing the bone for them to blunt their teeth on.

In writing "we" and "our," let me make it clear from the outset that while I was always vividly interested in David's work as he went along, and while I picked up enough of this and that to save his time by acting as amanuensis, I did no serious research of my own. This may seem feeble. To myself in retrospect it does. But I was pretty well occupied with the house and the nursery, with humble questions of clothes and linen, with keeping the "godowns" stocked with fuel, oil, food supplies, and wine, with supervision of the servants, the household accounts, the entertainment of passing travellers, the occasional outbursts of official hospitality entailed by Christmas, the King's Birthday, the Annual Jalsa, with routine family correspondence and business letters of various kinds—the thousand and one distracting but essential jobs which are the natural work of what the Census reports describe as "the unoccupied woman": the mere wife.

Chapter 4

AT HOME

THE language material amassed in the four Gilgit years was by no means in such coherent form as to be immediately available for other scholars. The final process of reducing it to order was not less but more laborious than the original collection. In Burushaski alone DL had some hundreds of pages of foolscap type-written texts carefully correlated by reference numbers with the original notebooks from which they had been copied, and in addition eight fat quarto notebooks full of notes in small writing on every imaginable subject. His first task was to make a careful, literal translation of the texts, aided by his own manuscript notes made at the time of recording; the second to work through these and the notes of every sort, card-indexing every word as it occurred with all its inflected forms and the reference to each place of its occurrence. This being done, he was able to begin to work out the grammar. For the paragraphs about the noun, for instance, 1,800 cards had to be taken out, examined, sorted, the results analysed and tabulated till the four gender-like categories and the thirty-eight possible plural forms of Burushaski were reduced to order. The subtle and complicated Burushaski verb eventually revealed its secrets —or the bulk of them—only to an examination of hundreds of cards, each packed full of recorded forms. The commonest and most everyday verbs gave—as every dictionary maker will understand—incomparably more trouble than the rarer ones.

Then the texts had to be edited with the necessary explanatory notes and a key-translation to help the potential student, for whom a free translation in more polished English would be less useful. Finally, the Vocabulary, or Dictionary, had to be drawn up with examples of the uses of the words.

The Burushaski material which had been collected in the leisure of one short year, while DL was continuing work on Shina and Khowar, took four and a half years of steady desk work to prepare for press, and resulted in three stout volumes of 464, 418, and 545 large printed pages. The typing for the printer was, of course, nearly concurrent with the manuscript draft, and when this was completed the next question was to find a publisher.

The prospect looked none too bright, and we gloomily predicted that some German or Russian would anticipate David's work on Burushaski, when an unexpected letter came from Professor Georg Morgenstierne, himself a professional philologist and a pioneer worker amongst Central Asian languages, asking whether DL would care to submit his Burushaski work for consideration by the Norwegian Institutet for Sammenlignende Kulturforskning (Institute for the Study of Comparative Human Culture) with a view to its possible publication by them at their expense. The offer was too generous to refuse. We felt sad, homesick as it were, that Oslo, not Oxford, should stand on the title-page; but if Norway with scientific endowments could face what unendowed English publishers could not, national pride had to give way before the practical consideration that if the work was to be of use to scholars it must first be printed, and if it were not speedily printed it might be anticipated. David therefore gratefully accepted for his Burushaski the honour of a place in the Institute's distinguished series of learned publications. We found later, to our surprise and pleasure, that the Institute having once undertaken a scientific book, undertake also that nothing shall prevent its reaching the right public, and are prepared to send copies to almost *any* person interested enough to want them—a generosity which no ordinary publishing firm could emulate. It will be remembered that when Hooker was bringing out his great *Flora Indica*, his publishers expressly stipulated that no copy was to be given free to anyone who could possibly require the book!

So the typescript went to Oslo in 1931 and work began on the proofs, the reading of which was even more laborious than we had anticipated. In spite of the most generous co-operation of Professor Morgenstierne, many sheets had to be read seven or eight times, the first two volumes eventually appearing in 1935 with Messrs. Williams & Norgate as the English agents of the Institute; and the third, the Vocabulary, in 1938.

Chapter 5

A DREAM COMES TRUE

THOUGH happily occupied with his other language work, David was pondering sadly on how much Burushaski there was yet to learn; how many questions of custom, beliefs, etc., he had not been able to pursue; how many knotty problems could only be resolved by a visit to Hunza and a study of peasant life on the spot. We toyed with the idea; it haunted us; it lured us. But a military pension in a post-War world, with a daughter still at school, could not by any arithmetical juggling be made to finance a private expedition to the Karakoram. Then luck took a hand. An elderly maiden aunt in Scotland, whose very existence David had almost forgotten, on whom we had no claim and from whom we had no "expectations," came to die, and left a small legacy. Prudence might suggest investing it, but what is the annual income from a couple of hundred pounds, which may at any moment be "converted" into even less? Common sense pointed out that this was not nearly enough for so long and expensive a journey and a lengthy stay. It wasn't. Then luck once more took a hand. One day we read in *The Times* of the new Leverhulme Research Fellowships for advanced workers, who lacked means or opportunity to complete a piece of research already begun. Not for some days did the idea dawn on us that perhaps David might come into the category of possible "fellows."

We pooh-poohed it to each other. The research would need to be on the line of pulverizing atoms, or curing cancer, or curving space, or liquefying air, or adding another span to already useless lives; it could hardly cover research into the speech and life of the Burusho of Hunza. Yet while laughing at the thought that our work could seriously engage the attention of the Leverhulme Trustees, DL decided to lay his programme and his financial problems before them. We could hardly believe our eyes or ears when we found that he was one of the first seventeen fortunate workers to be awarded a fellowship for which there had been four hundred applicants. We wasted some sympathetic philosophizings on the 383, and then began to think. There was a lot to think of.

It would take time to make preliminary arrangements, and while these were going forward DL attended lectures on Anthropology at London University, since clearly the anthropological approach to our task would be the most helpful, though his interest was primarily linguistic. We were both reasonably widely read in the subject, but in Professor Malinowski's lectures and seminars at the London School of Economics he got encouragement and stimulus, as well as new and useful points of view, and made many valuable acquaintances. In the interval various negotiations were proceeding. Would the Government of India permit an ex-Political Officer to return and settle for a year or more unofficially in his successor's bailiwick? Would the present Political Agent have enough faith to raise no objection? Would the Mir of Hunza, firm friend though he had always been, welcome the proceeding? The suggestion was entirely unprecedented. Retired officials do not come back.

> Our sons inherit us, our looks are strange,
> And we should come like ghosts to trouble joy.

Obviously an indiscreet ex-Political Agent might raise all kinds of trouble. Could all these parties be convinced that DL's interests were wholly scientific? Could they believe that he would show tact and detachment enough to cause no disturbance in the happy but always delicate relations between the Mir and his people, the Political Agent and the Mir?

To everybody's credit—not least, perhaps, to the memories of goodwill and understanding that DL had left behind him—Government opposed no objection, while the Mir and the Political Agent, Major Gillan, offered a cordial welcome; but all this varied correspondence took time.

We were grateful for what was ultimately accorded: permission to go at all; to use the Government rest-houses *en route*, subject, of course, to the prior claims of officers travelling on duty; to draw supplies on payment from depots of the Indian Army Service Corps (more familiarly known to us by its original name of the Supply and Transport Department); to bring in kit and equipment duty free. This was a very great deal.

I seem perhaps to be dwelling rather sordidly on money matters, but despite the generosity of the aunt and the Leverhulme, we were going to have to exercise the utmost economy at every step if we were to avoid bankruptcy. A minor deficit we might hope to make good by spartan retrenchment on our return—though our normal way of life left little room for more spartanism—but a major deficit would be a disaster. And the expenses ahead were impossible to estimate.

Chapter 6

EAST AGAIN

We knew, of course, that it would not be possible to ride over the snow passes into Gilgit before June or July, but we had no wish to incur the heat of the Red Sea or the Indian plains in May. We therefore sailed on March 1st (1934), a slack shipping season, for few people return to India just before the hot weather if they can help it. After an uneventful journey out, with an unprecedentedly dull lot of fellow-passengers (or were we ourselves grown old and dull? we didn't feel it. We felt like a pair of school children who had snatched an unexpected holiday and were off on a wild adventure), we found ourselves back in the familiar clammy dampness of Bombay. We made it our first business to pay a courtesy call on the Russian scholar, Professor Ivanow, with whom DL had had correspondence from time to time. We thought of no practical advantage beyond the pleasure of the great man's personal acquaintance. Professor Ivanow is, of course, one of the leading authorities on the doctrines, practices, and literature of Ismailism, the Muslim sect to which the Hunza people belong. But the Hunza peasant would know as little about these esoteric mysteries as the nominal Church of England peasant aboutt he homoousian or filioque controversies or the detail of the Thirty-nine Articles.

It happened, however, that the Professor was in touch with some Hunza people in Bombay, more especially with a small deputation which had just come down—on foot through the winter snows—to pay their respects and their annual "Peter's Pence" to His Highness, the Agha Khan, the spiritual head of the Ismailis, and to them God's vice-regent upon earth, whether his headquarters be Paris or Monte Carlo or the racing stables. They came to see us—a cheery, pleasant group of wholesome mountain people—oddly out of place in the lounge of a Bombay hotel. They were naturally eager to get home as quickly and inexpensively as possible, and we were able to annex two. One, Daulat Shah, was willing to act as personal servant and factotum, though untrained in such work and more familiar with plough and spade than artificial European needs. Throughout the whole of our stay in Hunza "Dádo" was our trusty, loyal friend. God bless him! Secondly, a well-educated man of the Wazir's family, distantly related to the humbler, peasant-proprietor Daulat Shah, one Qudrat Ullah Beg, who proved an invaluable language-informant, and worked well for David to the end. He was not capable of the same whole-hearted devotion to us and our affairs as Dádo, and never stirred our affections to the same degree, but his knowledge of Persian and Hindustani was considerable; he could write as well as speak them both, and he possessed an interest in and a knowledge of his own language that proved unique. Under David's tuition he ultimately became in fact a fine philologist, and took the greatest delight in every new revelation about Burushaski that their joint work afforded. He was the kind of man that would have been an ornament to any Oxford Senior Common Room, and like the don of fiction was somewhat conceited, very self-centred, and little use in practical affairs.

It was incredibly cheering—within forty-eight hours of landing in Bombay—to have acquired two Burushaski speakers as travelling companions.

Dádo began his duties at once, took charge of our kit on the railway, and performed such shoe-cleaning, bed-making services as he could, with intelligence and will. Easter Saturday, 1934, saw us driving up the famous poplar avenue into Srinagar, and by teatime next day happily and most comfortably installed on a jolly little boat, aptly called the PAX. It was Easter Sunday, but luckily the Kashmiri does not observe our pagan festivals.

We moored our boat at the side of the main river, well upstream from the picturesque but highly septic city, quite near the Residency, the European Club, the Post Office, and the major shopping centre—the Band. To get to our boat we had to cross the river in a shapely little shikára, a cross between a punt and a canoe. We drew up alongside and stepped straight in to our drawing-room.

Our reach of the river ran roughly east and west, and caught the light of rising and setting sun and the reflections of sky and cloud in the most entrancing way. The left bank was irregularly but amply lined with willows and tall, thin poplars; the right with immense chenars—a particularly lovely type of maple—of untold age; both had barges, native boats, and European houseboats packed tight along them.

Walking down our tiny gangway and climbing a few feet of sandy, muddy beach we were at once in a little willow wood with rough grass underfoot. Going straight through it and up a bank which is the base of a fine row of poplars, we looked out over a sea of bright yellow mustard with occasional willow hedges, across the valley to a huge range of glorious mountains, the Pir Panjal, averaging 10,000 to 15,000 feet, the lower half of which took every possible shade of blue, violet, and purple while the top half was still covered in snow. Close behind us in the other direction were small mountains (only 8,000 to 9,000 feet!), bare, rugged and seamed, drenched in the loveliest, ever-changing colours; these foothills screened from us the giant Karakoram.

We had some months to put in before the passes would be open, but we were able to live more economically than at home, and with our two Burusho retainers housed on the cook-boat next door we were able to work our fill—and did. After the fatigue of the last months at home, anthropologizing, buying equipment (cameras, exposure meter, cine-cam, etc.), packing kit, clearing the house for our tenants, and so forth, the peaceful Jhelum days and all the beauty round us gave us a deserved and needed rest. We were on occasion hospitably entertained by Colonel Lang, the British Resident in Kashmir, and Mrs. Lang, and by Colonel Colvin, the Maharajah's Prime Minister, and by an old friend of Gilgit days, Captain Wreford, now Food Controller for the Kashmir Valley, and his wife.

Chapter 7

HALT IN KASHMIR

BEFORE leaving home I had with some temerity approached *The Times* to ask whether I could perhaps, if opportunity offered, act as their amateur correspondent during our travels. I was met with the greatest kindness and courtesy, given some hints as to what sort of articles or news might prove acceptable, and provided, to my amused elation, with "cable facilities" for occasional use. This gave me a right—or at any rate the shadow of a right—to introduce myself to various departments and officials, whom as a private individual I should have hesitated to molest, and added greatly to the interest of our enforced halt. Colonel Millar, of the I.M.S., the Principal Medical Officer in Kashmir, allowed me access to his files, and demonstrated the immense progress that has of late been made in securing a trustworthy supply of drinking water for the city, in introducing vaccination, combating epidemics, fighting tuberculosis and venereal disease—a record of which the State has every reason to be proud.

Captain Wreford most generously gave a whole forenoon to showing us over his Food Control Department, and allowed us to wander at any time through the gardens and take photographs at will.

A visit to the State granaries was a most refreshing experience. Forty great containers, each capable of holding close on four hundred tons, are dotted about in an ex-royal garden with grass walks and stately trees and rows of willows. They are built of local wood, to a locally evolved design, by local workmen, and fit into the landscape as no ferro-concrete silos could. So perfect are the arrangements for turnover of stocks, extermination of vermin, etc., that the total loss from all causes is less than two-thirds of one per cent. With further grain stores in the city, the department is able to hold stores of over twenty-two thousand tons, which amply guarantee the valley against fear of famine, and help to stabilize general prices in times of scarcity.

With Sir Ivo Elliott, the inspiring spirit of the new Kashmir Constitution, we enjoyed motor drives to places of interest in the Kashmir Valley, which we had not been able to visit on previous fleeting visits to Srinagar, and which without his hospitable car would have been beyond our range.

In striking contrast to India, Kashmir has been jealous of her past and diligent in recording it, and the historian has stores of native material for the basis of his research. The early Hindu dynasties who held sway until the middle of the fourteenth century left their records not only on the written page but in magnificent stone temples, which not all the iconoclastic zeal of their Muhammadan successors was able wholly to blot out. There remain lovely ruins of cut limestone, dating from the third to the eighth century, to demonstrate that the ancient Kashmiris fully deserved the name by which the Indians knew them—"The Architects." Their architecture is their own, entirely distinct from the Buddhist and Hindu architecture of India, and to a Western eye no less impressive and incomparably more beautiful. It owes to Greek influence its pediments, its fluted columns with base and shaft and capital—learnt, probably, from the Bactrian Greeks of Kábul. The priceless possession of plentiful timber, as well as stone, permitted the Kashmiris to adapt Greek forms to Buddhist and Hindu ritual and to a climate of winter rain and snow. Their pillars were spaced farther apart than the Greek, their pediments pitched higher and their temples crowned with pyramidal roofs tapering to a single lotus blossom, while the interior walls were enriched with deep reliefs. Here their multifarious deities were depicted: the three-faced, eight-armed Vishnu, the river goddess Ganga with her crocodile and the rest, along with many real-life figures of lovers in balconies, ascetics, huntsmen, and dancing-girls, many rich designs of bird and beast and flower, interwoven with geometric patterns of great intricacy and beauty. Much excavation and restoration has been done under the direction of Sir John Marshall and his worthy Kashmir disciple, Mr. Ram Chandra Kak, author of *The Ancient Monuments of Kashmir*. The best preserved of these stone temples are at Awantipura and Martand, both within easy motoring distance of Srinagar.

Mr. Kak's excavations of the site of Herwán have brought to light another style of Buddhist architecture immensely more primitive and yet apparently contemporary with the dressed-stone buildings of Martand. These are temples whose mud walls are beautifully faced with a diaper of pebbles, or of smooth boulder slabs framed in a setting of pebbles and small stones, their floors paved with self-coloured baked tiles bearing interesting reliefs and arranged in ingenious mosaic designs. India has, as yet, shown no other examples of this primitive yet beautiful building.

These refreshing distractions only added zest to the steady slogging at Burushaski. As time drew on we had to give more and more attention to preparation for our long ride to Hunza, the repacking of our kit in mule-trunks and small cases for pack transport, the purchase of saddles and camp gear of every sort, and homespun clothes for ourselves on the road.

My own riding outfit required some thought. I had come out to the East in 1911 with an expensive regulation side-saddle and habit which I never wore, and which, of course, had to be scrapped when we started on our 350-mile ride to Kerman fron the coast at Bandar Abbas. I had then substituted for it a dirzi-made divided riding skirt of the length and fullness that in 1912 seemed "suitable for a lady" when the mere idea of riding astride (the only non-suicidal thing to do) was a sufficiently dashing innovation. By 1920 women's fashions had become saner, and I adopted riding breeches like David's, with brogues and puttees and a Norfolk jacket for everyday, and smart riding boots and long, well-fitting white coat and white breeches for more ceremonial occasions. I rather fancied myself in this gear in 1920. But regretfully studying in the glass the more matronly figure of 1934, I decided to revert to the divided skirt (of more rational length and width than

1. Part of ruined temple of Martand.

2. Backdoor gossip in Kashmir.

1912's), and the capacious pockets of a Norfolk jacket. I had no reason to regret this. It proved an eminently practical and comfortable get-up, yet neither unsightly nor unseemly (at least so I imagined).

As always, we laid in a stock of Kashmir *chapplis*, well-fitting sandals with soft leather socks ankle-high, and well-nailed soles. These are safer and more serviceable for walking than any European shoe. The inner sock fits snugly and keeps out sand and pebbles, and when these creep in above the sandal sole they are easily ejected by gestures of the toes.

As the road to Hunza has rest-houses at convenient stages (which we had official permission to use) we were saved the necessity of carrying tents.

PART 2

The Journey

Chapter 8

OFF AT LAST

MINDFUL of age and infirmity we knew that we must not attempt the passes till they could be *ridden* over. As June approached, with their official "opening," due on the 15th, we made such enquiries as were possible from occasional down-coming travellers. Their reports were not reassuring. There had been an abnormal late snowfall, and the passes would be slow to clear. My *Times* cabling had introduced me to the kind-hearted and obliging telegraph master, and he promised to keep us informed. One day we heard with joy that he had learned by telephone from Minimarg (the last telegraph station on the Kashmir side of the Burzil) that the pass was entirely clear of snow on the southern side.

We paid off our Kashmiri cook and boatmen, who, being over-paid and over-tipped, characteristically bade us a surly and injured good-bye. The better friends you are with a Kashmir servant, the more generously you treat him, the more he regrets on parting that he has omitted to squeeze more out of you. It is a well known but unlovable trait, and does the Kashmiri less than justice, for he is essentially a kindly, willing, even affectionate fellow, and these grudging farewells spoil your kindly thoughts of him. They mean nothing, however; he greets your return with radiant face.

We mobilized and started in the highest spirits on June 12th, comparing with amusement and no regret the very modest houseboat that bore us down the Jhelum and across the Wular Lake with the more sumptuous barges that the Political Agent of other days had commanded. We even welcomed the lesser luxury as proclaiming to ourselves and others our complete freedom from the ties of officialdom.

At the other side of the Lake—growing less attractive with each year as its water surface shrinks and its mud-flats extend—we found our flock of pack animals awaiting us, and spent the night as the guests of Major Rice, of the I.A.S.C., in his bungalow at Sonawain, a couple of miles above the landing-place at Bandipur. He had already shown us much thoughtful kindness in Srinagar by placing a large storeroom in his depot at our disposal for the re-packing and assembling of our kit: cameras, photographic supplies; typewriters and eighteen months' stationery; reference books and lighter literature; carpenter's tools; Aladdin lamps; first-aid requisites, and all sorts of odds and ends that experience had taught us would be worth gold three hundred miles from shops; and, of course, the usual kitchen and pantry paraphernalia. Our own personal kit was a minimum, though we could not leave evening and "Sunday" clothes behind, as we should have liked to do, since we might have to turn out on occasion as civilized folk. Luxury stores, such as tinned meat, fruit, and vegetables, wines, or spirits, we took none: our only alcohol was one bottle of cognac for medical emergency. When emergency came we both forgot to use it, and David eventually drank it by thimblefuls out of a measuring glass (since we had no wine-glasses) during the last fortnight in Hunza to avoid the bother of re-packing it. We had always eschewed the use of tinned foods ourselves, though in official days we had had to keep a goodly store of them, as of wines, for entertaining. So our "Europe stores" were confined to soap and baking powder, tea, coffee, and Quaker Oats, a little cornflour and arrowroot, and a few pots of marmalade, with some tinned milk and butter for the road.

We owed to Major Rice the supply of transport animals and all arrangements for their due payment in the regulation instalments. His kindness greatly simplified our upward journey as far as Gilgit.

Kashmir had been warming up; we had been painfully toasted in the sun-facing parlour on the boat coming down river, so we were not sorry to leave behind the sun-baked flats of Bandipur and climb through scented pine-woods towards the Tragbal rest-house, some 6,000 feet above the lake. It was a glorious day of radiant sun as we mounted to begin the 200-mile preliminary ride to Gilgit, and it was a delight to feel a horse between the knees again. Looking back as we breasted the hillside we could see the whole fertile Kashmir plain outspread below us like a patchwork quilt in pastel colourings, silver-seamed by innumerable waterways, and dotted by dark green clumps of the magnificent chenár trees that Kashmir owes to her Mughal conquerors.

All the far horizon was enclosed by the jagged, snow-clad peaks of the Pír Panjál, the mighty range that separates Kashmir from the torrid plains of the Punjab. This middle and further distance formed a delicate study in water-colour under a pale blue sky, while the immediate foreground was a contrast in strong oils: spur after spur of pine-fledged ridges plunging abruptly into the plain like giant cliffs guarding a wide sea-coast.

Next day we rode up and ever upwards, still through pine forest, till we emerged on the great exposed plateau of the Tragbal itself, commanding a matchless panorama to north and west and east, of crowded snow-crowned peaks, conspicuous amongst them the sharp twin teeth of Haramuk on our right, and far ahead, beckoning us on, the glorious mass of Nanga Parbat.

Even on such a perfect summer day it was easy to realize how deadly this wide smooth plateau can be to bewildered travellers in mist or driving snow.

A long, slow descent—the first mile or two through unpleasant stretches of half-melted, slushy snow which our ponies emphatically did not like, then over easy grassy slopes—led us through forest to the wooded banks of the river, where our next rest-house nestled amongst pines at the junction of two mountain torrents.

Soon after us some of the caravan got in, and we looked forward eagerly to lunch—breakfast seemed to belong to a distant past—but still no sign of Shafi (the cook). We got hungrier and hungrier, and I began to be afraid that he had sprained his ankle and David that some accident had happened to the balance of the kit. This seemed improbable, for it was as easy a stretch of road as we were ever likely to see. Presently Shafi came hurrying in on foot (happily unharmed) thinking of dinner—for lunch-time was long since past. He brought gloomy news. The ponymen had let their ponies cluster too close to drink at one of the little streams that crossed the track; two started a scrap, and one had contrived to fling his double load spinning down a steep hillside. Both boxes were smashed to smithereens, and Shafi had dutifully stayed behind to see that the men retrieved as much as they could of the scattered contents. We were not far ahead when it happened, and—oh!—if they had only called us back to superintend the salvage! The worst loss was one of the two new Coronas. It was spewed out from the nest of cushions and eiderdowns into which I had so carefully lashed it, out of its own travelling case, and smashed into three independent bits, with all its delicate arms and legs twisted and bent—a sorry sight. As well as this, all our precious stationery for a year and a half was scattered over half a mile of hill. Picture ten thousand index slips of different colours, ten reams of typing paper, boxes of carbon paper, dozens of file-covers and folders, quires of blotting paper, a ream of "shelf paper" for scribbling, envelopes of every sort and size, and two dozen nice large different-coloured note books and as many little ones, luggage labels, pins, paper clips, rubber bands—all scattered sheet by sheet and pin by pin like the track of an insane giant's paper-chase. It must have looked quite funny though we might not have seen the jest. To improve matters there came a heavy thunder shower to drench the mess. The poor ponymen, full of contrition over an inexcusable piece of carelessness, gathered up everything—including, alas! twelve unrolled typing ribbons—higgledy-piddledy into handkerchiefs, blankets, saddlecloths, and whatnot, and presently brought in these dripping bundles. It was inky dark; there was nothing to be done that night unless we had buried it darkly with a lantern dimly burning—as we should have liked to do. We went to bed and bitterly thought of the morrow. Just as we had got into a mournful sleep one end of David's wooden *charpai* collapsed, and he spent the rest of that ill-omened night upon the floor.

Next day took us through the loveliest stretch of river and wooded hill country that even the Kishengunga can boast, and we gave ourselves up to the delight of the day's march. Happily a day's halt was due in Gurés. The rest-house is extra roomy, designed to house two parties at need; there was no one else there, so we had plenty of space. We got all the damp stuff dumped in a wide, sheltered verandah and started opening the unappetizing bundles. It was a grim sight.

We roughly sorted note books from papers, and papers from envelopes, etc., and carried bundles in and spread them on big kitchen tables (part of the most valuable equipment of every rest-house) and roughly wiped off the worst of the most obvious mud, and then spread things out on the grass to dry. Happily there are large rough lawns around the house, and by great luck there was no wind. We toiled all that afternoon till sunset; then carted everything into a big room and lit a fire and went on. Early next morning (the day that was to have been a rest) we were at it again—wiping, sorting, spreading, gathering, tying up and smoothing out—it was quite the dismallest and most fatiguing eighteen hours' work I have ever done at a stretch. You can't conceive how much ink lives in twelve typing ribbons, nor how much dye in the cover of a note book, nor how much gum in the flap of a manila envelope, nor how many sheets are in a ream, nor how many slips to a thousand till you have tried a job like this. Dádo and the others helped all they could, and we despatched a couple of ponymen to see whether they could anywhere raise a couple of packing-cases. There were none in Gurés, but seven miles ahead there was an S. and T. depot (why placed so far from where any traveller could want it, we never discovered), and after many formalities and the signing of documents and a promise to hand the boxes back to the depot in Gilgit, we succeeded in procuring four dirty, smelly kerosene oil cases without lids, which after some work with saw and hammer served well enough to pack the revolting stuff into as it was ready. How disgusting it looked I cannot tell you. All the file covers were cobbled and distorted; all the smart note-books had their covers smeared, defaced, and bent; every single sheet of every one was smudged with ink or grass or mud or dye or gum or a mixture of them all; every sheet of paper, every index slip the same; the flap of every envelope was firmly stuck on to something else; almost everything would after a fashion be useable and must be used, for it would take too long to replace them from home. But to think of taking all our notes and writing all our writes on this revolting paper! However, it might have been much worse; it might have been the cameras and chemicals. On the other hand, if these precious ponymen could do this in the easy Kashmir country, what might they not do on the precipitous cliff roads ahead!

We cabled for typewriter ribbons and went to bed with aching backs and legs and hearts.

The next march was a short one to the hillside bungalow at Peshwari. We halted there a day to let the animals graze and to rest ourselves. The jolly little bungalow, clinging to the hillside above the Burzil river, was haunted more than any of the others we had passed, by memories of baby—in particular of her arrival there one pouring afternoon. The Willesden canvas cover of her doolie that should have completely sheltered her, had begun to leak in places, and as the willing coolies rushed the cradle up the last steep bit of hill we noticed that the faithful Alipo, who had voluntarily marched beside it every foot of the way from Bandipur, had stripped off his own homespun cloak and flung it over to keep Missie Baba dry. Good, smiling Alipo, wet to the skin! We could see him vividly again, and we gratefully remembered.

To-day there was no rain. It was the first time we had ever seen Peshwari without, and a very pleasant little spot it is in sunshine. Peasants were ploughing tiny fields below us, the grass of the slopes above was lit with big blue cranesbill, Siberian wallflower, hellebore, and spikes of blue larkspur, and a lovely yellow "weed" with flowers in feathery balls, over which armies of butterflies were hovering: tortoiseshells, painted ladies, half a dozen kinds of fritillaries and tiny blues, and one magnificent pair of swallowtails. We spent a happy, lazy day, strolling out to get a few photographs of this lower section of the Burzil Valley in the intervals of working at Gurezi Shina. The hillsides on our bank of the river were wholly bare of trees but covered with rich grass and grazing herds, while on the steeper-faced cliffs opposite us triangular masses of spruce and pine rushed uphill, vertically striped by pencil lines of muddy waterfalls.

As we rose and rose during the next day's march, through scenery that grew bleaker and wilder at every step, as we noticed the snows above us creeping lower and nearer, and as we saw the lines of fretful waterfalls now paralysed into silent impotence, our faith in the telephonist from Minimarg grew every moment less. We saw the village itself lying across the river in a bay of valley to our right, just below the present snow, magnificent snowpeaks towering over it; we turned the last corner and high above us saw the snow stretching right down to the last rest-house some 2,500 feet below the pass.

This was a blow. Pensively we climbed the steep hill to the bungalow of Burzil Chauki. The last half mile was soft and soppy, alive with water and carpeted thick with short-stalked primulas, mauve, purple, white, and glorious pink, masses of a starry waterflower like a huge white king-cup, quaint little bushes with yellow feathery tufts, and a thousand other lovely things only a botanist could name. There could be no waiting for the pass to clear; it would be a matter of weeks, and on these journeys you hope at such uninhabited stages to find at most one day's supply of fuel and fodder. The *chaukidár* (caretaker) agreed that by day the sun would make the snow impossible: there was nothing for it but to cross by night.

Chapter 9

ENTERING THE GILGIT AGENCY

CHILLUM CHAUKI
June 22, 1934

AT this point the two passes were safely behind us, and we had had amazing luck in having perfect weather for both. Anxiety had haunted me about them before we left home in the early hours of many a morning (when it is very hard to be a hero). I greatly feared that DL might crock on one of these passes and I be helpless to get help in time, or that I might crock and be a nuisance to him. Those spectres were now laid. We were over, and, though stiff and tired, apparently not a penny the worse. We were pleased to find in Kashmir that we were still able to fling a leg over our ponies (small pack animals only, not the officers' chargers of earlier days), and that the height of the Tragbal (close on 12,000 feet) didn't worry either of us. In fact, we had never trekked together in better spirits than those first days. The scenery and the smell of the sun-drenched pines were glorious. We were thankful to get away at last from Srinagar and the cramped quarters of the houseboat, and barring the accident to the stationery the journey to Burzil Chauki at the foot of the pass was leisurely and uneventful, but as I have explained, our "intelligence department" had failed us badly.

We had pushed on in good faith that we should be able to ride to the top of the Burzil Pass. We both admitted that it was unlikely that we could, either of us, *climb* at any altitude, and we had sat patiently two and a half months in Srinagar to avoid all risk of having to do it. At Peshwari we were passed by a cheery young couple, Wing Commander and Mrs. Somethingorother, who had been up for three weeks' shoot-

III

1. Mail-runners' refuge on Burzil Pass (summer). (*See p.* 53)

2. Junction of Gilgit (left) and Indus Rivers. (*See p.* 61)

ing; they reported an abnormal amount of snow which was walkable only, and walkable only by night. There would, however, be a good moon from sunset till one-thirty.

After a picnic lunch at Burzil Chauki (11,100 feet) we consulted with the ponymen. They averred, quite truly, that the snow would be too soft till after midnight—so the precious moon was a washout. We agreed to start at twelve, and turned in to get what prophylactic sleep we could—which was little: partly height, partly uncertainty about the coming adventure. The caretaker of the rest-house assured us that there was a well-trodden riding track to the top, 13,775 feet according to one, 13,900 feet according to another reckoning. At ten-thirty we dined—or breakfasted?—and dear Shafi, instead of giving us plain hen and potatoes, outdid himself to produce a three-course meal, adding soup flavoured with rancid fat and birch-wood smoke, and finishing with "fritters" of dried apricots, fried in the same rancid grease, followed by gritty, smoked coffee. He meant kindly, and we did our best to do justice to his intentions, but we mounted our ponies with heavy tummies and some foreboding.

What moon remained had disappeared behind the mountains. Steep above us rose two fine snow peaks on the top of which squatted respectively the Great Bear and Cassiopeia, both looking oddly hunched up and accessible. In the snow-filled trough between lay our Pass, out of sight to the left, some 2,600 feet above and about six miles distant by the normal, well-graded, zigzag road, which we had ridden four times before in perfect comfort, but which was now smothered in snow and indiscernible. It was a beautiful, clear night with heaps of stars; our valley was darkened by the moon's shadow, and brightened only by the faintly starlit snow. Dádo led off on foot with a lantern, which it is true revealed immediate pitfalls but was otherwise nothing but a blinding nuisance. We followed on horseback, and behind came Qudrat Ullah leading Dádo's pony. A specially engaged "tiffin-coolie" carried two ferrostats of tea and a basket of sandwiches for future use. The laden caravan was to follow, lit by the remaining lanterns.

We zigzagged comfortably for about 200 feet, then all trace

of track disappeared and there was nothing but a wilderness of steep snow slopes. The ponies refused to set hoof on the untrodden snow as long as we were on their backs. You couldn't blame them; the extra ten or twelve stone made all the difference to their feet going through—into what?—and they took the safety first line. So we set out on foot. We had nail-studded *chapplis*, and each a long staff with an iron point.

Dádo, of course, is mountain bred; and DL, without being a mountaineer, had always loved mountain sides and heights and spent leave big game shooting in Tibet. He had at least the memory of the right muscles in his legs and the right wind in his lungs. But in my lady-like Victorian childhood the mildest exercise was enough for any girl, and never in my absurd life, overfilled with futile examinations, had I walked ten miles at a stretch or climbed 1,000 feet even at sea-level. Anyhow, whatever we had once been able for, we were both out of training and getting on in years. The others led on silently, and I followed carefully—even I silent for once—learning to prod my stick horizontally into the snow slope beside me. It was all rather thrilling and romantic.

The lantern only obscured larger issues, so we banished it behind us, while David and the hill-wise Hunzukuts chose routes and slopes keeping an eye on the general direction. It would have been easy to climb futilely up and down and reach an impasse every time. Now we swung left to avoid too steep a rise, now hastily veered right to escape an involuntary slide down unseen slopes at the base of which we could hear the torrent crashing below its crust of ice and snow. You would have been sure of an icy bath and a dislocated or broken limb. Woefully soon my wind gave out and I had to stop and blow. The slopes were about 65 degrees, and you could lean almost upright against them. The heat of my body would melt the snow under me, which then refroze, so I had always to tug myself free, wondering with amusement whether each stage of my progress would be marked by little tufts of fair-isle wool. David was unspeakably patient with me, urging me to go slow and take my time, and assuring me, in answer to gasping apologies, that the compulsory halts were equally necessary for him (which was only partially true, for his early training was standing him in good stead).

So on we plodded, my halts getting longer and more frequent. It was the queerest experience. You felt quite active and vigorous when suddenly every muscle and sinew turned into vermicelli, your head got a centrifugal whirl inside it as if your skull and eyes and eardrums might fly up at any moment to join Cassiopeia and the Pleiades, and a deadly sea-sickness took hold. No amount of resolution could induce another step and you had to flop again against the sloping snow. Then for a second or two you felt as if you could never move again, while your body heaved involuntarily from head to foot with the deepest deep-sea breathing I have ever known. I could feel the wind whizzing in under my toe-nails. After a bit your head eased up and you could deep-breathe less violently, but still leaned paralysed till quite suddenly your muscles braced again and you set out full of new hope and vigour, only to collapse once more a few yards on. This effect of altitude was interesting and by no means wholly unpleasant; relapsing half vertically against the gentle snow, there came a delicious sense of powerlessness and utter, abandoned weariness, like the onset of a pleasing anaesthetic. At those instants I should have asked nothing better of life than in an ecstasy of self-surrender "to cease upon the midnight with no pain."

My mind restlessly toyed with relevant and irrelevant quotations from the poets (do other people, I always wonder, keep a first-aid outfit of this kind with them?)—"My eyes are closing and my lute is dumb, slower and slower go my songs to sleep—Geometria una et aeterna est in mente Dei refulgens—Because he finds his egg contain, green, hungry, horrible and plain, an infant crocodile—De l'enfer il ne sort que l'éternelle soif de l'impossible mort—For the wind has blown into my body and blown away my soul . . . in the pine-trees' top and dallies with the wind and scorns the sun—Der Dichtung Schleier aus der Hand der Wahrheit—and perchance the coming night is full of stars—Heureux ceux qui n'ont jamais vu la fumée des fêtes de l'étranger—and God have pity on the sadder folk who travail without hope—sie zu verscheuchen hab' ich dann gepfiffen die frechen Reime eines Spottgedichts . . . —forest-tribute, sombre sightly"—miles and miles of forgotten poetry reeled through my head. I battled with the all too vivid memory of Shafi's fritters; I laughed inwardly (having no wind to spare for outward laughter) to think of starting mountain climbing at fifty plus; I wondered with a quiet chuckle whether David would have the nerve and wisdom to slide a vacated body down the hill and let Nature deal with it; I knew that even if he had the sense he couldn't do it before witnesses, and the thought of cumbering him at such a moment with an unmannerly, unhandsome corpse revived my will; I thanked whatever gods there be for his unconquerable soul.

The coolness of the air was like a draught of icy water on a hot-weather day. When after laboured gasping you were again able quietly to breathe your fill, there came an intoxication unlike any other delight I have ever known. David would constantly offer a hand to pull me upright or an arm to help me on; each time I gratefully refused it; reckoning that he might need all his own strength to reach the top. I could not, however, prevent his plunging his long alpenstock into the snow below my feet and standing guard for fear of an accidental skid.

At first an alluring boulder projecting from the snow occasionally tempted me to choose it for a prop, but as I took a step towards its reassuring firmness I plunged shoulder deep in softened snow. I was so green as not to know that the heat accumulated in the stone by day would have half melted the snow beside it! One lives and learns.

By day the melting snow had cut deep furrows for itself, whose ridges were as sharp as the teeth of a giant comb. Their graceful sweeps followed the curves of the mountain side as the natural waves of a woman's hair follow the lines of her head (a fact the "perm" forgets—a murrain on it!), but they flowed at an angle to our course and made progress infinitely laborious. These little trenches, only perhaps a foot across and eight inches deep or so, which any intelligent beast stepping from crest to crest could have negotiated easily, put the wind up our ponies, who gathered their four feet together—

like the chamois, in sudden short spasms on the brink of deep chasms—then leapt as if competing in a steeplechase and landed plunging and frantic in the bottom of the next trough. At one point of these winter sports Dádo's pony escaped from Qudrat Ullah, and an anxious hide and seek in the dark followed till he was recaptured.

About three-quarters up we gleefully recognized the mail-runners' shelter—a tiny hut that projects on wooden stilts above the 40 feet of winter snow and looks so otiose in summer time. Its legs were still buried knee deep in snow.

Inch by inch we crept up till we were within a couple of hundred feet of the top, and I was very, very near the end of my tether. Suddenly the rise grew extra steep again. If we had had to do it unaided (except by the poets) at my then rate of progress, we should be there still. By great good luck the snow here was harder and the slope straighter, and we struck a snow furrow running for once in the right direction. A reluctant pony was induced to walk in the inconvenient narrow trough; kind hands boosted me into the saddle and towed me to the top. So with bumps and jerks and springs and plunges I thankfully and ungallantly rode the remaining feet. Just then a dazzling star showed above a bend in the mountain to our right; I gasped out a query as to what planet it could be. David said it was the Morning Star, and right enough there was a slight glow all round, not coming, as for a moment I had thought, solely from the star. For the next few minutes you were conscious not so much of the coming of light as of the silent, mysterious disappearance of the stars. Then dawn crept on, and just as we landed on the brow of the Pass a first streak of gold caught the highest crests of the white-grey snow, and one tiny pipe of one tiny bird greeted the double event. The three direct miles had taken us just five long hours.

We jerked onwards to the four-roomed shelter that crowns the Pass and sat down in the verandah. It was dirty enough, but inside was unspeakable. I don't suppose it is ever cleaned, and generations of weary beasts, including man, have refuged there. Though cold, the night was windless and not bitter. Eight feet of snow lay round the shabby, welcome hut. The sun's daytime heat echoing from the walls (a phenomenon I now thoroughly understood) had melted a wide, steep-sided moat all round it, and it stood there in comic isolation. The prudent Hunzukuts had brought some wood and invited us to a blazing fire. It was eminently cheering, but as we were well clad and warm and they had only cotton trousers—in spite of a generous gift of rupees "to buy warm clothes," which we suspect they had spent on gaudy rubbish!—we presently withdrew and called them in to cluster round it. I noticed with pride in them that they called the Kashmir sweeper to come and share the warmth. To the true Muslim, not contaminated (as so many Indians are) by Hindu caste-prejudice, all believers are men and brethren, whatever their occupation. It warmed my heart to see Sheikha, as they called him, treated as an equal and a friend.

So we sat awhile, paralysed with weariness, but happy and glad to be alive, and watched the gold creep down the peaks, and lovely lights and shadows flow across the basin of snow in which we sat. We saw our bird, who was neither a phoenix nor a simurgh as he should have been, but an impish, dingy, indomitable Cockney sparrow. I swear it was a sparrow. David had other theories, but could not supply a name. Anyhow it was the only bird in sight. Then we got up and tried to photograph the unforgettably lovely scene; but we could make no guess as to what exposure would record the grey, the white, the gold, the pale blue of the sky, and the meter was in a knapsack miles away. We lingered perhaps an hour, till the growing light, welcome as it was—for the relief from the impotence of darkness was very great—reminded us of snows softening below us and the thirteen miles that still separated us from Chillum.

The sandwich-coolie offered us his wares at the top, but we were too dead weary to eat just then, and waved him on: "Not just now; a little later." The caravan came up and toiled bravely past us, not daring to halt, and presently we started the descent. It was too steep to ride, but now gravity (*pace* Einstein) was with us, and we stepped out manfully. Soon we passed from softening snow into a welter of treacherous slush and marsh and mud, and by the time we reached dry land again the sun was fiercely hot. We called for a little food, but the tiffin-coolie (despite the most explicit instructions) had streaked on and we found him innocently waiting for us at the next rest-house! We felt not only hungry but ashamed that our excellent *bandobast* had broken down. Only very inexperienced travellers incur unnecessary starvation. We peeled our outer wrappings, which were many and various, but we could not so easily rid ourselves of more intimate woollies, and that last seven miles was as hot a ride as I remember.

The triumph of that memorable night was wholly David's, for he had not only done the climb himself but by silent moral suasion enabled me to do it too. The joke was, of course, that our mighty feat would have been nothing to younger folk in training—a fact to which we were fully alive, but it was a feat we had very definitely done our best to avoid performing. The weather had been perfect. In wind or mist or driving snow there would have been a different tale to tell—and we should not have been the tellers.

Beyond being full of half a hundred aches and rather off our grub and off our sleep, with heads still somewhat dazed and buzzy, we did not seem seriously the worse. Neither of us would willingly have missed that Morning Star, that dawn, that piping sparrow, nor I my first experience of mountain sickness. Though I vow it was not the height but Shafi's meal of grease and birch-wood smoke that accounted for my nausea.

Chapter 10

TOWARDS GILGIT

After the fertility of the wooded and grassy Kashmir valleys, the bleak grandeur of the first Gilgit marches, familiar though it was, was finely impressive. Chillum rest-house looks out over a great delta of grey high-piled boulders, flowing down from the Burzil, with a few storm-tormented birches sparsely scattered on the rocky mountain sides. Gradually you descend with the waters. The rare villages are built still somewhat in the Kashmir style, mainly of logs plundered from the rare pines, but already their lower walls are stone. The landscape grows in patches more genial, where pine and fir succeed to birch.

The women in their tiny terraced fields—which seem at this height to grow only barley and broad beans—wear woollen bonnets like a cloth bag with brass ornaments at the back, and in front Salvation Army peaks with a row of brass circles along their upper edge.

About five miles beyond Godai we came to a lovely well-remembered village with a real polo ground, levelled and well cared for, shaded by rows of tall, spreading poplars (the kind that do spread). Where every inch of levellable ground is priceless, it is touching to see, as from now on you do, the best piece always set aside for polo; no English heart can resist this silent appeal. From here we knew we must look for our first full peep at Nanga Parbat above the bleak and barren foreground hills. And there in fact she was, but before cameras could be snatched from knapsacks she had swathed herself, as she loves to do, in veils of flying cloud.

Soon after, you turn almost at right angles into the Astor Valley, and the crystal clear waters of the Burzil-Chillum torrent are cut across by the muddy flood of the Rupal Nullah bringing the drainage from the northern glaciers of Nanga. The two unite to form the wild, mud-laden Astor River, flowing between steep earthen cliffs. Gurikot is a beautiful and large oasis, the more lovely for the arid desolation round: some miles of poplars, walnuts, willows, and fields of barley, wheat, and beans, the two latter sown and reaped together.

The next two marches are tiring, for the road dips from its average level of 9,000 feet or so right down to the river-bed many hundreds of feet below, where glorious stretches of tamarisk-bearing sand invite a lovely canter (if you have a beast that isn't a pack pony), and laboriously up again. The picturesque village of Dashkin, perched on a crag, bears an unenviable reputation for leprosy, and its rest-house is invariably (in our experience) stiff with flies. After it, came a well-remembered mile or two through a belt of shady, scented pine forest, the last glimpse of natural vegetation we were to see for many a day, and we were out again on the bare mountain side. From the crest 10,000 feet or so which towers above Doian—a tiny settlement of small fields, clinging incredibly to precipitous rocks 2,000 feet below—we looked down into the utter and unredeemed desolation of the Indus Valley. It is the most awe-inspiring view I know, and reduces man to his true stature of a fidgety intrusive insect.

Immense mountains in every direction fold, project, retreat, hemming in the plain below, their browns and chromes, sepias and khakis indistinguishable from the colours of the boulder-strewn sands of the plain, and these again from the muddy flood of the Indus between the railway-cutting of its barren banks. And for all the miles the eye can see from this lofty eyrie, there is not one blade of grass, not one tree, not one human habitation, no sign of man or beast or bird. The only touch of hope is the line of jagged snow peaks in the far distance, whose tips contrive to peep over the dun-coloured nearer mountains. Without map and compass-bearings we could not distinguish which was Rakaposhi, which Haramosh, and which the guardian peaks of Hunza.

In the tiny Doian rest-house we met Major and Mrs. Gillan

on their way down to Kashmir. He was the outgoing Political Agent, and we owed it to his non-obstructiveness that we had obtained the Government of India's consent to our coming. They hospitably gave us tea and dinner, and we then retired to bed to snatch a few hours' sleep before another midnight start. By all that was unlucky, having had unexpectedly late snow on the Burzil, we were now plunging into a record heat-wave. The Fates clearly do not approve of *revenants*! A mile or so beyond the Ram Ghat defile the road crosses the Devil's Gorge, and the bridge across it had been carried away some years before, so that travellers have to make a long detour up the rocky sides of the ravine to find a possible ford. The torrent was now in full spate under the late June suns, and could only be attempted—with luck—at dawn, when the stream after the coolness of the night would be at its minimum. Hence we had to brace ourselves for another midnight start. The air of the Doian heights was deliciously bracing and cold, but the 4,000 feet drop of the next march would land us in the stifling heat of the Indus Valley. If you could sail down on a tea tray it would not be more than three miles to river level, but the graded road is full ten miles, now interminably criss-crossing the steep face of the Hattu Pir, where it seems impossible that a road should cling (and in fact it often slithers quietly downhill and has to be coaxed into place again), now along a rock-shelf where the left cliff almost overhangs the track and the right falls sheer 800 feet into the river below. The fact that you hear no murmur from the full, raging torrent at the bottom adds awe to the sense of height. Then another endless, precarious zigzag brings you down to the deafening roar of the Astor River as it plunges through the rocky narrows of the Ram Ghat defile to fling itself and its glacier mud into the Indus.

We crossed Ram Ghat, still in the dark, by the steel suspension bridge and duly reached the Devil's Gorge just before dawn. A day or two before I had had the bad luck when tramping downhill to crash—from carelessness or sheer fatigue—full weight with my left knee on a spiky rock, and the pain of that night's walk was an ugly nightmare. I welcomed the relatively level rock-shelf where I could mount again, for though the cramped position with foot in stirrup was hardly less painful, it was a change of pain. With instinctive chivalry Dádo leapt off his own pony and without a word led mine, knowing that with the wounded knee I could have no effective grip; and on these rock *peris* one slip may send horse and rider to certain—but not necessarily immediate—death. At any time this march is a somewhat racking one, but, with a treacherous moon throwing inky shadows where you most wanted light, it was even less luxurious than usual.

Having left the Astor torrent behind us we climbed up a rough track to the so-called ford, marked by the ruined piers of a dead bridge (one of many, for this ill-famed gorge is unkind to its bridges), bitterly grudging the extra miles entailed by some arm-chair official's economy campaign that had left the broken bridge unreplaced, and found that we ourselves were just able to cross three-quarters of the stream on two long tree trunks. Dádo insisted on going before us backwards and piloting us across; we both have steady heads, and slightly resented being treated as babies, but there was no doubt that his bare feet had a better grip than our *chapplis*, and his intentions were noble. A belt of swirling water still lay between us and the farther bank. The Hunzukuts, plunging in to their armpits, coaxed the riding horses over, then Dádo returned and insisted on carrying us over shoulder high. Again we should have preferred to take our own ducking as he had his, but one could not wound the sporting fellow by insisting.

The next two hours were anxious ones. We stood and watched the sturdy Kashmir ponymen, seconded by our resourceful Hunza people, post themselves on vantage points of steady boulders amidst the tossing, foaming waters. One man chased a reluctant pony in, the next caught it, steadied it, and pushed it on, and so, like the chain of buckets at a fire, the animals were herded safely over one by one. At every moment some precious box threatened to take a header into the maelstrom, where it would infallibly have been dashed to pieces. Would it be the cameras or the chemicals, the reference books or the one surviving typewriter? But luck this time was with us. All loads, of course, were thoroughly splashed, but none were soaked or lost, and tin-lined cases and double waterproof wrappings guarded the most perishable stuff from harm.

During this anxious transit Shafi, the cook, provided some comic relief. He was a Hunza man we had picked up in Srinagar, and his main qualification for the job was the fact that he was a Burushaski speaker—we did not want to import language and racial distractions by taking on a Kashmiri. Secondly, he had served for some time as "cook's mate" in a Rawalpindi hotel, and he presumed he could "carry on." He did. It was we who nearly perished. Meantime, in contrast to his fellow-countrymen, he was a frail little creature, who had deteriorated physically in India. He insisted, however, on "helping." He kept mounting on rickety boulders and falling off and having to be rescued from a watery grave, causing endless agitation and delay. Again and again the others fished him up and with perfect good humour and much laughter redumped him on a steady rock. We shouted to him from the bank to leave the pony work, ride ahead, and put the kettle on; but either the roar of the water drowned our voices or he was fanatically determined to be a hero. Nothing would induce him to quit. We found out afterwards that—apart from his cooking—he had learned other evil things, including drug-taking, in India. He left Hunza again, for his country's good, soon after our arrival, heartily unregretted.

At last, after two hours of struggle, the crossing was accomplished without casualty to man or beast or kit, but the sun was now well up and there remained for us seven miles of red-hot riding over burning rocks and stones and sand to the thrice-accursed oasis of Bunji—hot enough at any time, but in summer a foretaste of Hell. The only vegetation in all the hateful Bunji plain was the great octopus of the caper plant, with its rubber ha'pennies of leaves and bold white flowers whose yellow stamens and pert pistil give a gay and insolent turn to its expressive face.

When we had scrambled out of the steep gorge and up on to the plain, we were rewarded by a magnificent early-morning view of the whole Nanga Parbat range blocking the valley to the south, for once entirely free from cloud, dazzlingly white against the burning blue. The German party were on their way there. We tried to spy out their probable route, but it is never easy to tell among all those mighty peaks which is officially "the top." If they were blessed with such weather. . . .

We vainly tried to sleep through the hot day (100° and anything in the shade), and midnight saw us again quitting Bunji by a treacherous moon—I'm sorry to be always so rude to the moon—riding through a desolate waste of rocks and sand, in imminent danger of losing the semi-invisible track and having to plunge wearily up and down the countless gullies which seam the plain and which the "road" skilfully circumvents. The valley is shut in on both sides by giant hills whose surfaces of stone breathe out with interest the heat absorbed by day, and the hot air throbbed against our cheeks like the blast from a baker's oven.

The worst of night-marching (which in great heat is necessary for the animals) is that you can get little sleep in one-storey sun-steeped bungalows, thronged by flies despite their wire doors. Tents are, of course, infinitely worse, and the rest-houses on the Gilgit road are a most welcome mitigation both of heat and cold.

Seven miles out from Bunji we reached the river, flung ourselves full length on soft sand between the boulders and breathed deep of the cool river-borne air, then halted as we crossed the great bridge of Partab Pul to look down for a moment into the unplumbed muddy depths of the Indus. Swift, silent, and stealthy she flowed below us, terrifyingly still, hypnotizing and paralysing you with a sense of resistless latent power, like a great wild beast crouching to spring. No ripples, no waves, no sound. She might have been dead and motionless but for the quivering of her tawny hide and pitiless tiny whirlpools gleaming like a tiger's eyes.

As we turned from the Indus into the almost equal barrenness but lesser monotony of the Gilgit Valley, having seen "our" river noiselessly swallowed up by hers, we felt a delightful sensation of nearing home. At the mouth of the Gilgit River the mountain side wildernesses of stone and boulder are extraordinarily varied; no doubt a geologist could read their riddles. Some are of grey granite, some a dark chocolate colour, some the shade of golden sand. At one place for a hundred yards or more the cliffs and their boulder offspring are deep chocolate streaked with cream in the pattern of fantastic Swiss rolls.

On the two marches between Bunji and Gilgit there are many precipitous cliffs, *peris* as they are locally called, across the face of which the road rises and falls in flights of hairpin bends, where a false step at any turning will plunge you 50 or 100 or 200 feet into a rocky ravine. Even by day these ask for careful riding, but in quivering moonlight and pitchy shadow, when your eye can scarcely distinguish the narrow, grey path from the grey of the river far below, they strain your tired attention to breaking point. Whatever snatches of sleep I might have got by day had been banished by my aching knee, and at moments I nodded so helplessly on my pony that David would grow alarmed, and when we came to a flattish bit of ground would gently help me to dismount and lay me out between the boulders for a ten-minute snooze. It was luxury to stretch the aching leg and ease the nagging toothache in the joint, but I was never sure whether the temporary relief was not too dearly bought by the agony of mounting and dismounting. On the other hand, the tiny bouts of sleep enabled me to go on again with less risk of dozing in the saddle, which might have been final. As on the Burzil I felt apologetic for adding to a husband's anxieties.

After another sleepless day in Pari we passed the two welcoming oases of Minór and Seker,[1] and soon after daybreak were toiling slowly up the interminable, rock-strewn delta of Jutiál, but with the knowledge that invisible beyond the crest lay the glorious three miles of Gilgit cultivation.

On the brow we suddenly spied two horsemen who instantly dismounted to come towards us. It was two dear old retainers: Sar Faráz and Jemadár Kasír, less changed by time than we, whose happy faces radiated welcome, and who flung forward to cover our dust-stained *chapplis* with their kisses.

[1] Not "Mináwar" and "Sequár" as British officers tend to dub them.

We were profoundly moved, for such demonstrations of personal affection are not offered to the official. They had nothing now to hope for from us, and we nothing now to grant; but man to man they were glad to see us back, and came to say so. It was worth the Burzil and the heat to know that we were remembered after all the ten long years with this disinterested affection. Riding between the prosperous fields where golden wheat was waiting to be reaped or was already stooked, where young rice was showing four inches of brilliant green, and purple lucerne bespoke a wealth of fodder; to the tinkle of flowing water—what a sound in arid lands!—and in the shade of willow hedges, we beguiled the way with eager question and answer; we enquiring for other Gilgit friends, they asking wistfully after Missie Baba, now a strapping, tennis- hockey-playing schoolgirl of fifteen. It appeared that this was the second morning they had ridden out and waited, for we had been expected yesterday. Everywhere peasants in the fields stopped their work to wave a greeting, more and more old friends joined our escort, and as we entered the gates of our old home, the Agency house (which the absent Political Agent had most graciously placed at our disposal), we were given a royal welcome, all the more impressive that it was not complicated by flags or guns or guards presenting arms.

We had indeed come home. Flowers in familiar vases stood everywhere that flowers could stand; dishes of lovely garden fruit were on the tables; tea was brought in cups we knew of old and drunk as we lounged in dear old chairs, while the very carpets smiled an old-time welcome. Our faithful new friends, Dádo and Co., looked on, half proud that we should be so popular, half perhaps a little jealous while older friends unwound our putties and carried off our dusty sandals.

We halted ten days in Gilgit, and no long-lost parents could have been given so much glad service and assistance on every hand. Unfortunately the heat-wave gave us 105° in the shade, and sandflies offered unwelcome company, so that our rest was less refreshing than we had hoped. David, who had held out on the journey so much more manfully than I, succumbed to an ominous bout of fever, and from his bed made the necessary arrangements for paying off our Kashmir ponies and engaging local ones for our further journey. Meantime my knee obligingly mended itself, and in a few days DL rallied. We bade a regretful farewell to our staunch old friends, left the rich crops, the trees, and the English gardens of Gilgit not unwillingly behind, crossed the fine Gilgit bridge, passed the new landing-place for aeroplanes on a jutting windswept promontory at the junction of the Gilgit and the Hunza rivers, and turned north into the great barren gorges that lead to Hunza Nagir. After the first march—seventeen miles of sheer and utter desolation—the scenery gains in grandeur and shakes off the suggestion of wasteful, wanton chaos that haunts the Indus marches.

One of the inevitable economies that had hit us rather hard was the lack of our own good riding ponies. They would have entailed the wages of two extra men and extra fodder, so in Bandipur we had just chosen the two best of the pack ponies and made them do. They were stout, sure-footed beasts enough, with whom, however, it was impossible to establish human contact. They treated us as packs—of awkward shape and tiresome habit—and jogged steadily their wonted two and a half miles per hour, refusing to be cajoled or coerced into varying the pace. This meant that a twenty-mile stage which we had always ridden in three and a half hours would take us eight. Every traveller knows that it is not the distance covered but the number of hours in the saddle that measures the fatigue of each day's trek. Sometimes, as the cold bit through our wraps, or we raced the relentless rising of the sun, we thought fondly on Mohawk and Black Beauty, Ginger and Habshi, who had so gallantly carried us of old. But now we had exchanged the secure if uninspired Kashmiri mounts for two rickety old screws from the Gilgit bazaar—the only beasts available. David's white one was like a starved rocking-horse, whose legs needed to be better screwed in and whose back had been disjointed and badly set; while my brown was about the size of a mouse or a fairy cycle, and weak though willing. Occasionally in a sandy stretch he would just lie down, but allowed himself to be lifted inertly to his legs, till next time.

Looking up the Hunza River gorge, half a march from Aliábád. The road (see Plate V) runs round face of right-hand cliff. (*See p. 67*)

PLATE IV

Thus mounted, we rode sorrily to Chalt, a wind-swept open plateau at the meeting of three gorges. Here we were able to procure slightly better ponies, and thankfully paid off the two Gilgit toys. From the Chalt rest-house through lovely fields, round a bold spur, over a fine suspension bridge into the Hunza Nagir gorge, where a magnificent view of Rakaposhi greeted us and a terrific *peri* led us into the large Nagir settlement of Sikandarábád. This had grown out of recognition in the intervening years, a fine oasis that owes its development to the enterprise of the present Mir of Nagir, Sir Sikandar Khan, after whom it is appropriately called.

High above the rocky river-bed the alluvial fans on our side (we were now in Nagir on the left bank of the river) are dotted by the green oases of Nagir, watered by the inexhaustible glaciers of Rakaposhi. On the opposite, sun-scorched, south-facing, waterless Hunza cliffs there is not a blade of grass to be seen. We passed through occasional villages, separated by roads slung between heaven and earth, fearlessly grazing the face of nightmare precipices, saw again the chorten at Thol, reminder of ancient Buddhist days, rode over the Nilt gorge, famous in frontier history, and dismounted as always to pass on foot at Ghulmit the ultra-sacred shrine of Saiyyid Shah Wali, making the halt an opportunity for tea under a magnificent chenar. The villagers gathered round us, goitrous, friendly, not too intelligent, and grinned broadly at David's chaff about the mean way in which they had stolen the holy relics from their neighbours. He thus made his first public appearance as a Burushaski speaker, only to find after this mental and moral effort that though they understood Burushaski we were still in the Shina-speaking area. His change-over to Shina caused further merriment. Between Sikandarábád and Nilt we recognized a jolly little orchard with grass and apricot trees and running streams and enclosed by low stone walls. We had drunk tea there ten years ago, when we never hoped to see this country again except in dreams. We *had* to get down and drink tea in it once more, as a sort of thanksgiving. This time the trees were laden with golden fruit. On we rode to our next halting-place at the fertile oasis of Minapin.

Chapter 11

THE LAST LAP

ALIÁBÁD REST HOUSE, HUNZA
July 17, 1934

MINAPIN was delightfully cool—we had, of course, been climbing steadily since Gilgit—and we were able to sleep indoors with comfort. After we had said "Start at five," we almost thought it was foolish and unnecessary to be quite so early—for a mere eleven miles. When Dádo came at quarter to four and we were drunk with sleep, we thought so more than ever. We remembered, however, that the road is vertical rather than horizontal most of the way, and once we were off we were thankful to have made an early start. You can't imagine anything quite like it. I wish I had kept the aneroid at hand to verify how high the various climbs were. (I always vowed to take it next time, only my pockets were already so full of filters and exposure notebooks, penknife, and bits of string, spare hairpins and what not.) So I am frankly only guessing, but I think I am minimizing rather than exaggerating, for with these stupendous mountains all round, cliffs look small that would create a sensation at Dover.

Like most human habitations in the Karakoram, Minapin is on a fertile shelf some hundreds of feet above the river. We plunged straight over the lip of a cliff and down a steeply-graduated slope from the Minapin fan to the "beach" of the river—700 or 800 feet. Since our last visit the treacherous cliffs had suffered many landslides. High above us we could see the shattered revetments of the road we used to ride, and several of its predecessors. Our new track scrambled painfully through and over masses of new-fallen boulders, or through miles of loose soft sea-sand. For one short stretch the rocks were all a dark sinister crimson and gave out a suffocating smell of sulphurous gas. Our men urged us to "press the pace," for the friable, forbidding cliff face above looked as if it were not nearly done with shedding boulders. There is assuredly no myth more misleading than that of the "everlasting hills."

From river level we could see the pin-scratch along the cliffs on our right, some 600 or 800 feet above the river, and, often as we had ridden the road before, it seemed incredible that it could be possible to round it. The cliffs on our left bore similar scratches, representing the Hunza road between the two oases of Mayun and Hindi. Poor starved-looking little places they seem in contrast to the rich Nagir ones. We chaffed our Hunzukuts that obviously the Nagir road up the gorge was the better one since Government had chosen it for the regular route. They rose at once to the bait: the Hunza road was really the better and well kept up—which we could quite believe since the Mir always travels it himself, not to trespass on Nagir territory more than he can help—it had only one slight drawback: there were seventeen places between the two oases where "shoots" were apt to carry it away.

As we scrambled our way along through the riverside boulders we noticed dozens of discarded millstones, some broken, some apparently perfect. Not that people bring their old millstones here to cast away! The opposing cliffs at this point happen to provide the best type of stone for mills, and, oddly, those on the Hunza side make the better nether millstones and those on the Nagir side the better upper ones (or it may be *vice versa*. David will have it accurately noted). When you want a new millstone you travel your ten or twenty miles or more to these cliffs, choose what seems the most promising boulder for your purpose, and with a rough bit of iron hack and chip it into a circle of the radius and depth required. You then bowl it home your ten or twenty or more miles like a child's hoop, up ravines and across gorges to your mill. If it hasn't broken as you fashioned it, which it frequently does—this explains the number of discarded millstones that here strew the countryside—it may very likely break on the rude road home. If so, you just go back and carve yourself another.

A note of bitterness crept into the Hunza voices. Whereas Hunza permits the Nagirkuts to cross the river and help themselves free to Hunza stones, the Nagir people levy a tax on all stones taken from their side. So our folk averred; but very probably we should hear the tale reversed if we spoke to Nagir millers on the subject. For the Burusho of Hunza and Nagir, though they speak the same language, are of different race and mentality, and understand each other as little as the Saxon and the so-called Celt, and the rivalry of centuries divides them. At one point they both professed the Shiah faith, but since the Hunzukuts some four or five generations ago adopted the Ismaili (or "Maulai") heresy religious differences have added to their ever-wakeful mutual hostility.

Quitting these contentious subjects, we essayed some photographs by the water's edge and turned sharp to mount a side-gorge and reach the level of the cliff road above, by the steepest thing calling itself a path you ever saw. The new Minapin ponies were happily sturdier than the rocking-horses, and managed to climb almost vertically for 600 feet or so. A brisk torrent, which is most of the time a waterfall, pours down the gorge, the sides of which are lined with trees and grass, and the track runs right through a most picturesque little village called Tishót. The stone houses are almost indistinguishable from the rocks against which they are built, one here, one 20 feet above, just wherever they can be got to stick. The ponies took the four-foot steps from boulder to boulder as if they had been taught circus riding up and down the Great Pyramid. I never professed to be a horsewoman, and I don't know the orthodox way of staying in the saddle when my pony's back is perpendicular, so I shamelessly wound my right hand in his flowing mane, pressed the stirrups back, and lurched triumphantly to the top. When we emerged on to the fan above we felt so virtuous after the climb that we halted to drink tea, though we had only done four miles and had not really deserved it. Our usual routine on these slow marches was to divide the day's ride into three: have thermos tea at one-third and lunch at two-thirds the distance, and thus let Shafi get well ahead to be preparing the evening meal.

From here we saw the fine granite piers of the old Tishót Bridge, the one we always used to cross by. It had stood for thirty years, and then was wrecked one day by a hurricane; wind can be fierce and powerful in these gorges. But the fact that it *had* stood thirty years proved that the chosen site was a good one. There was firm rock (not the crumbly kind of everlasting hill) on both sides at a considerable height above the river, well out of reach of summer floods. The obvious thing would have been to replace the bridge and use again the unharmed granite piers; but some engineer decided otherwise, and we had to stay on the Nagir side and ride on to the new bridge. The cliffs on each side here rise anything from 2,000 to 3,000 feet, and the road round them is a little ledge a few feet wide, some 800 feet above the river-bed. When it is a ledge of firm rock all is well, but, as I have already said, the mountain sides are mainly crumbly masses of stones, boulders, and sand, and there often seems no good reason why the road should not just slide down to join the other debris (and so often it does, especially after rain). Sometimes even where there is a firm rock ledge it isn't wide enough for a laden pony. Then if the inhabitants can find a couple of firm rock spikes below they throw a tree trunk across and build up a loose wall of unmortared stones on that till they get it to road level. If there are no natural spikes, they bore holes in the rock, and drive in a few pegs to take their tree trunks.

This is the method they have to use to revet the faces of their fields and the sides of their aqueducts, which are often carried eight or twelve miles round the face of the most impossible-looking precipices, so they are experts in the art. Accidents happen often enough to the road-makers, but are almost unheard-of amongst road-users. The look of the road might make your hair stand on end, but it is far safer than our murderous motor roads at home.

At last we got off this gallery business and out on to another fan, and we saw the new bridge on our left, quite fairly near, but the cliffs were steep and high and crumbly and there was no direct way of reaching it, so we had to overshoot it by a mile or two before the road turned down. And such a road!

It was the steepest spiral you can conceive, about 2 feet wide and just one welter of soft dust like flour or french polish. There seemed nothing on earth to keep the path in place except a tiny wall of stones that rested on the dust. Still it did stay. Of course you could not ride it, so we slithered down on foot, over ankles in flour-like dust, and opposite, across the river, we saw the famous hot springs of Murtazábád. They say you can cook a chicken in them or wash your clothes, but clothes or chicken smell ever after of sulphur. We saw only dark red splashes on the face of the cliff. Having got down some hundreds of feet or so of floury slide, we had to ride back to the wretched bridge through tiring sea-sand. The bridge was the usual handsome steel-cable suspension bridge, but only a few feet above the summer water level; I wonder will it last the thirty years of its predecessor? I doubt it. Having crossed it, we set foot on Hunza soil (July 16th). The ascent from the river to Murtazábád was steeper and higher than the spiral we had just come down, but a shade firmer and less dusty, and the zigzag was better graduated; but we rose 1,000 feet as steeply as it was humanly possible, and I again had to take refuge in my pony's mane.

The view was magnificent: the tiny bridge, the gorge, and Raka—looking her very best. We never normally dismount in awkward places (which makes you ride many a time when you would feel happier on foot), for it gives trouble to the men behind, who for courtesy must dismount too and have to take charge of two loose horses. But it was the chance of a lifetime to register this view; you might ride the same stretch a hundred times and never again get the same lighting and the freedom from cloud. So I hopped off and had a shot. DL was too far ahead for me to ask him kindly to read his "wonder-working" exposure meter (one of these glorious electric cell things which we had gratefully bought from the Leverhulme grant); so I blazed away by guesswork, and remembering that the amateur always tends to under-expose, I gave it a 25th at F8. It should have been about a 200th! The result is not too bad, but the negative is as black as ink and it takes hours to print, and is, of course, not nearly so delicate in tone as it should have been. With heartfelt apologies to Dádo and Co., imperturbably good-tempered as they steadied the ponies on their hind legs on that criminal slope, I hurried to catch up the advance party. As we got higher and higher we began to meet fields and trees. Never were there such "fields." There would be a stone wall 15 or 20 feet high, beautifully built of loose stones packed most skilfully like pieces of a jigsaw puzzle, so that though no mortar or mud is used to bind the walls they are nevertheless perfectly firm. On top of this a strip of ground not 3 feet wide and perhaps only 10 or 12 feet long, holding a tiny ditch for water and outside that a row of of poplar saplings and inside a strip of grass not as wide as a stair-carpet. There are staircases and staircases of "fields" like this with willows, apricots, poplars, grass, lucerne, and even barley or wheat. But they don't usually plant the two latter unless the field is at least the size of a hearthrug! Silly that in English we have only one word for "field." Burushaski, of course, has a dozen, to differentiate the various sizes and the steepness of the hillside on which they are and the height of the revetting walls.

There was water trickling carefully from one staircase to the next, not a drop being wasted, for it is a great deal more precious than gold. At last we got out on to a bleak, hot, sunny bluff, where we were met by two grandsons of the Mir, who apologized that their elder brother (the heir after his father) was not with them, but he was down in Gilgit training with his Hunza Scouts. I ought to have said sooner that we were met in Minapin by a son of the Mir of Nagir, a pleasant, gracious lad, whom we had known long ago as a small boy. He rode with us to the top of the Nagir cliff and there bade us good-bye, conveying polite messages of welcome from his father.

The two Hunza princes were very charming, the younger a little shy; it was, I fancy, his first serious grown-up appearance on one of these ceremonial meeting-parties. We dismounted to rest the animals after the long pull up, and sat for a few moments in some rather inadequate willow shade beside a tiny stream. The Mir had sent the kindest messages, and we enquired after all the Royal Family and exchanged the usual compliments. Then I remarked hopefully: "Aliábád is quite near now, only four miles isn't it?" "Oh yes, only four miles." I noticed David quietly smiling. We rode about ten yards when I saw (what he remembered but I had quite forgotten) that the great torrent from the Hasanábád glacier cuts in here to join the Hunza River, and we had to go down some 500 or 600 feet to cross it and then up again to get out on to the Aliábád fan. It was exactly the same sort of business as crossing the main river all over again, except that the Hunza roads, however steep and difficult, are better designed and better kept than Nagir ones. Hasanábád village lies on both banks of the torrent, and climbs up the farther side to its own excellent polo-ground. The fields were being reaped, and I marvelled at the neat, tidy rows in which the cut barley was laid out. Everything the Hunzukuts do is beautifully done, and their methods are in the greatest contrast to the slovenliness of Nagir; you notice this everywhere, down to the tinest detail; it may be merely because water is scarcer and life harder that their fields are more scrupulously level, their walls more ingeniously perfect, their cut swathes more exactly aligned, but I incline to think that the cause lies deeper; in the difference of race and temperament already suggested.

Just beyond the wooden bridge which took us over the torrent, we were met by a good-looking elderly man whom we both remembered but could not immediately identify. He was almost in tears as he greeted us. I was puzzled to think why he was so moved. As soon, however, as he had paid full tribute of politeness to us, he bolted on and flung himself on Qudrat Ullah's neck. The whole cavalcade, about forty of us by this time, burst into sympathetic laughter, and poor Qudrat Ullah looked radiant but sheepish as he returned his father's embraces. Going up the steep hillside with so large a following was, as usual, not at all funny. You dare not stop to let your pony breathe without holding up the rest whose horses would be at some most inconvenient turn.

We got up at last, however, and found a fine deputation of all the Hasanábád elders drawn up to greet us on the polo-ground

PLATE V

Cliff Road with three horsemen. (*See p.* 69)

outside the House of Assembly (the Maulai kind of meeting-house that has superseded the Shiah mosque). As we neared Aliábád, riding through rich, flat, large fields, and past walled orchards we heard the local band burst into the familiar "welcome music." Presently we came to an open steeply sloping space near the half-ruined Sarkari Fort, and here was a whole party from the capital (four miles away), including Prince Ghazan Khán, the eldest son, and heir of the Mir,[1] and father of the two young princes who had met us earlier. The band changed the time to the "arrival tune," and we all walked on together to this bungalow. We passed a smart set of new little buildings which are the dispensary, built by the Mir. There is a resident Assistant Surgeon here, an Indian with a certain amount of medical training, who is able to render first aid and keeps a stock of simple drugs.

We found chairs set out in the rest-house verandah, and while we and Ghazan Khán talked of old times and the latest Hunza news, the rest of our train grouped themselves on the steps, and all the small boys of Aliábád gathered under the trees along the neighbouring watercourse to see any fun that might be going: a jolly, cheery, intelligent crowd they looked, not a moron or cretin among them; again in a marked contrast to Nagir, where both abound. Presently a tray with teapot was brought, and we thankfully turned to the "doctor" (the afore-mentioned compounder) whose gift it was. Tea was what we were just dying for after the hot climb; but when I poured it out I found it was a tepid mixture of tea, milk, sugar—and cinnamon. David and Ghazan Khán dealt bravely with it; I unobtrusively hid my cup.

[1] He succeeded our good friend his father, Sir Muhammad Nazím Khán, in July 1938.

PART 3

Life in Hunza

Ill fares the land, to hast'ning ills a prey,
Where wealth accumulates and men decay:
Princes and lords may flourish, or may fade;
A breath can make them, as a breath has made;
But a bold peasantry, their country's pride,
When once destroyed, can never be supplied.

A time there was, ere England's griefs began,
When every rood of ground maintained its man;
For him light labour spread her wholesome store,
Just gave what life required, but gave no more;
His best companions, innocence and health;
And his best riches, ignorance of wealth.

(GOLDSMITH, *The Deserted Village.*)

Chapter 12

SETTLING IN

July 1934.

THIS Aliábád bungalow is a good deal bigger than the ordinary rest-house, for it was enlarged to make room for a resident Assistant Political Agent (whose post after a year was found unnecessary), and then two further rooms were added on to accommodate on occasion the Political Agent himself (who never stays there). There is a good-sized dining-room, with pantry behind; a double bedroom with a bow window; two single bedrooms; three bathrooms of the primitive dak-bungalow variety of course (one of which we at once ear-marked for a "dark-room"), and a really handsome sitting-room with another bow window; finally—an unexpected and welcome luxury—a store-room with plenty of good shelves where we could stack our modest supply of stores and all our spare stationery. At the back there are the usual kitchen, servants' quarters, "stables," and what not. Everything was most scrupulously clean when we arrived, and for this we had to thank the forethought of our good friend the Mir. It happened that our old "head-boy," Nazar (already mentioned), was up from Gilgit on leave at his home in Aliábád, and the Mir bade him take charge and get the house ready as he thought we should like it.

He gladly took over for a few days from Dádo, whom we sent off to see his people. The poor boy came back to find that his mother and his grandmother had died during his absence. This hit him hard, and when we stammered our sympathy he murmured: "It is God's will." We were glad to hear that he has a wife and baby boy to cheer him. To show how much we appreciated his devotion on the journey up—which had far exceeded any normal "duty"—David gave him a good silver watch. (Our equipment, of course, had to include suitable objects for various presentations.) As a special testimonial from myself—for without his constant kindness I doubt if I should ever have got here—I added my own Guide knife, with its corkscrews, awls, etc. I missed it dreadfully, so I was glad I gave it; but I often had to borrow it back for a moment when doing odd jobs about the house.

We then got down to the business of making the house habitable for a longish stay. We unpacked and arranged things as well as we could; David went round with his carpenter's tools and in a short time made a wonderful difference to our comfort (yet some women marry men who can't drive a nail or turn a screw!); he assembled the Aladdin lamps and fixed up the brackets to hold them and got them into working order, and lovely things they are. Meantime I fished out cheap curtain materials picked up in Gilgit, the cuphooks and spring rods brought from home, and quickly ran up curtains to give us some privacy. Most of the doors and windows are wired against flies, but not, of course, the two big bow windows that are most needed. Whoever designed them had put bolts, etc., in the most inconvenient places and made them open *out* instead of *in*, so that it wasn't easy to drawing-pin mosquito netting over them; still with a little ingenuity it was contrived, though the job didn't look as neat as it should have done. Rings on a few travelling rugs let us sling up heavy curtains when necessary against the sun (which poured unfortunately straight into our bedroom all the afternoon so as to stoke it up for the night). Then we put our two kitchen tables in position, and with dark rugs to hide their ugly surfaces they served excellently to work at. Our own four camp easy chairs had come through unbroken, and soon with books and papers strewn about, the room looked extremely homely and Lorimerish; I think any friend would have guessed it was ours if he had come in without knowing we were there.

Two or three days got all this done, and the household routine working smoothly, and our next duty was to ride over to Baltit and make our formal call on the Mir, our host.

Our chief lack at first was shelves and cupboards, but as soon as we had seen what was most needed and what could be accommodated David got busy with rulers and squared paper and drew up detailed specifications, which he sent to the Divisional Engineer's office in Gilgit. They were able to make us the skeletons and send them up in such form that we needed only to screw them together. I then nailed cloth over the back of the cupboards and hung curtains over the front so that we no longer needed to live in the misery of half-unpacked boxes.

The bow window of the study where we sat to smoke and take tea looked out on to a jolly little watercourse (about 2 feet wide) which chattered merrily along. On its farther bank is a row of apricot and mulberry trees which, if they break the view a bit, also provide some welcome shade. From the foot of the trees terraced fields fall away, down, down, down to the top of the great cliff—some 500 feet or so—that forms the right bank of the river. We looked right across the gorge (the river, of course, is entirely out of sight, and nothing would lead you to guess its existence if you hadn't just had to cross it) to stark, magnificently seamed mountains, with tiny fans of green here and there, which are other villages similar to Aliábád on the Nagir side.

The nearer side of our little stream was one of the main highways; and all the life of the place went on in full view of our window. People passed by all day, laden with green fodder for their beasts, or carrying baskets of ripe apricots to dry. The nearest field of lucerne had just been reaped, and then below it the barley field, and we watched them stack the barley and make a circular threshing floor on which to deal with it. They flooded a patch of the newly reaped field, built a little circular wall of mud about four inches high round it, then flooded it twice more, and then when it was nearly dry a whole family, from grandfather down to the small boys and girls, systematically tramped it down with their bare feet till the surface was as smooth and level as a hard tennis court.

Jolly youngsters of all sizes romped in the new-cut fields, snowballed each other with clods of dry earth, tripped each other up, chivvied their lambs and kids about by chucking stones skilfully to turn but not to hit them, and half a dozen noisy scamps would jump to and fro over the watercourse in competition.

Between us and the river bank were groups of poplars, willows, and fruit trees with quaint cube-like stone houses dotted about in between, and right above this delightfully restful patch of green (which you could not properly appreciate if you had not had days and days of barren bleakness before you reached it), in the great triangular space between the barren mountains of Nagir and those of Hunza which rose around and behind us, there towered up the great mass of far the loveliest mountain on earth: RAKAPOSHI.

She is 25,550 feet high, and the top 10,000 feet which we saw from our window is a conical series of triangles, cliffs, precipices and peaks all covered in dazzling frozen snow—a never-ending joy to watch. At this time of year she was usually clear, escaping the skirts of the monsoon which are apt to catch on Nanga Parbat; and the clear sky behind changes from the palest blue at dawn to the brilliant burning blue of midday and then to delicate shades of pink, green, violet, and orange towards sunset. Ruskin could write volumes on the ever-changing shadows and colours that delighted us: I must leave them to the imagination. From our beds we could see Raka when we first woke and bid her good-night before we fell asleep. It is a wonderful thing when beauty such as this becomes part and parcel of your daily life.

It was still pretty hot in Hunza in July, in spite of our 7,600 feet. We had it up to 95° in the shade of the verandah outside, but were able to keep the study ten degrees cooler by closing doors and windows in the morning before the sun got up. Out in the sun the heat is all the fiercer for the altitude, a point stay-at-home travellers seldom realize. Another odd point is that in cloudless, dustless air like this, granted equal apparent brightness, photographic exposures need to be *longer* than lower down—at least this is David's experience.

The people round were from the first unbelievably friendly; we could run out quite informally at any moment and join

PLATE VI

1. Old fort-village of Aliábád with beacon tower. Background, Rakapóshi. (*See p.* 123)

Old Mosque at Aliábád, with Hurmat seated in verandah. (*See p.* 132)

them in the fields and ask what they were at, and why, and what their various implements were called. They were quick to understand what we tried to say, and except when several of them talked at once we could usually make out most of their replies. They often started amusing arguments among themselves, not agreeing about certain words, just as at home you can set a discussion going in any company about "apple dumplings" or "pies."

I had a most entertaining half-hour my second afternoon. Some women and little girls were beating a pile of green stuff on the threshing-floor just below, whacking it with a sort of wooden mallet. So I ran out (with pencil and notebook), greeted them, and sat down beside them on the nice dry ground and watched the whole performance. The crop was a small lentil or purple pea, and the heap was a pile of plants, stalks, roots, pods and all. They just beat and beat till all the pods had burst open, then piled pods and seeds into a big sieve and tossed it till most of the seeds were shaken out. Next they transferred it into a big flat tray and shook it to and fro till they could skim the pods off the top. Everyone was taking a hand, and after I had jotted down all the words I could conveniently collect, I took the various articles in turn and caused much amusement by saying carefully: "This is a sieve, I toss the lentils," "This is a tray, I shake it to and fro," etc. I felt rather like a star turn at a variety show, and brought down the house at the end with: "This is a little thorn bush, I sweep up the threshing-floor."

It is a sort of improved Berlitz method of teaching yourself. I found that when my Burushaski ran out I could still delight them by chattering on in English in a friendly way. They felt the goodwill, and they didn't know I was saying: "You're a nice-looking little minx, but you'll look better when you wash your face." I got most of their names written down, and then when they began to get ready to go home I had a romp with the small ones, who ran off squealing when I tried to catch them, just like English kiddies of the same age. I hadn't had such fun since our own youngster was small enough to romp with.

It was at once clear that there was not going to be any initial hostility or distrust to overcome, even amongst the women. This is rather remarkable when you think that not one of them has ever been more than five or six miles away from her home village, and that they have never seen a white woman at close quarters before. They are a fine, healthy, good-looking crowd, and always appear cheery and good-tempered. Undoubtedly the short-cut to the women's hearts was to make much of their youngsters. In a superstitious place this would be dangerous; they would be terrified of the Evil Eye; but we noted with thankfulness that these entirely non-Oriental people were as free from inhibiting superstitions as we ourselves. This promised to make our work immensely easier.

Chapter 13

HOUSEKEEPING PROBLEMS

Before we could really settle down to the business of life there were several practical problems to clear up. Water was naturally the first item. The jolly little stream just in front of our rest-house did not run by any means all the time. It brings water from the great glacier behind Báltít; the actual aqueduct channel is some twelve miles long, and represents an amazing feat of engineering. It was made about three generations ago—before which the "New Settlements" of Aliábád and her outliers did not exist—when iron was still practically unknown in Hunza. The excavations and the galleries on which it is piloted so skilfully over gorges and along impossible cliff faces were all made with wooden shovels and picks tipped with ibex horn. The people had—and have—no instruments of precision, no theodolites, nor levels. Against this they have some hereditary instinct that we lack, and an inherited or traditional common sense that enables them to adjust the necessary downward gradients exactly right. You never hear of anyone making a false shot in laying out a water channel, and you never hear of any "labour" difficulties. When a new work is undertaken for the public good it is supervised by the Mir, or his Wazir acting for him, and it is carried out by communal labour, of which everyone recognizes the justice and necessity. The Dála, which will frequently recur in my story, is the main aqueduct that supplies Aliábád, but it has to feed other villages *en route*, and our stream, which was its last section, was therefore only in action at certain times. These are, however, known to everyone, and our people drew water enough when they could get it to carry on for the day or half-day when it would be cut off.

It was beautiful, soft, pure water which gave delightful baths, but heavily silt-laden and supposed not to be fit to drink. We were luckily able to get half a dozen big petrol drums from Gilgit (left behind empty by the R.A.F.), and we stored it in these and let the silt settle. This water served us for washing and for photography.

About two miles away there was a spring of clear but hard water that issues from the foot of a cliff down near river level. This was recommended for drinking. So we took on a special man, Sagi by name, as water-carrier and general washer-up, to help in pantry and kitchen. He was a nephew of our old friend Nazar and a good fellow, though for some reason a little less cheery in appearance than our other men. Twice a day he would walk the two miles, climb down and up the 500 or more feet, and bring water for our tea, etc., and for making up the photographic solutions. We paid him the princely sum of about a pound a month, and he was delighted, while his brothers divided amongst them the extra work at home.

Considering the labour involved, it made us feel rather pigs to drink tea half a dozen times a day and expect a daily bath. When two of us were photographing hard and perpetually wanting to wash negatives and prints in eight or ten changes of water, my heart rather bled for Sagi. One day that had been particularly severe I said as he appeared with more and more water buckets at the door of the dark-room: "Poor man, I'm afraid our photographs give you a lot of extra work and trouble." His usually quiet face lit up with a peculiarly charming smile: "Nay, Mother dear, it is a pleasure, not a trouble. The work and trouble are yours."

The next thing in importance was food, and we found that we could, without apparent hardship to the people, buy a daily hen. There are a couple of officials whose job it is to see about supplies for travellers, and they arranged to get the fowls now from one village and now from another, so that our demands might not press too heavily on anyone. The Hunza hen is an athletic bird. You may see her fly like a lumbering, over-weighted pigeon 15 or 20 feet across a gully, and so we were not surprised to find her wing muscles well-developed.

Still she provided us with hen-water soup, and we varied our diet by having the wings for lunch and the legs for dinner, or vice versa. When the cold weather came and the flocks had returned from the mountain grazing grounds, we were sometimes able to vary her with mutton—athletic mutton.

Shafi, the camp cook, had one major fault—he could not cook for nuts. A minor one was that when anything went wrong he lost his head completely (as in the crossing of the Devil's Ford) and immediately did the wrongest thing that was possible. But he was willing, and no doubt did his best. Soon after we got in he went sick and we committed him to the care of the Compounder, who soon got him round. But we did not feel that we could face his food again. While he was ill, one Zaidu was announced who had come to pay his respects. Who was it but an old friend of Gilgit days who had been with us for four years as general underling! He had helped the cook and used often to cook for the nursery, so he was not without some elementary ideas. We offered to try him and he accepted with joy. His family could gladly manage the extra work at home, and hailed with pleasure the prospect of sharing his wages. We never thought of these jolly men as "servants" in any ordinary sense of the word. They were peasant proprietors in a tiny way, but though they had enough to eat and to wear, they were absolutely without cash, and were willing to do any honest work to get some. Zaidu looked much more flourishing and fitter than in Gilgit days. He was then rather young, and I suspect that the older servants put upon him a good deal, but now he had been living an independent life again and had got back his natural dignity and self-respect. His pleasure at the thought of working for us again was disarming. So we took him on, and though he was no chef he did us well. He was ingenious in devising new ways of cooking the half hen, and his scones were light and eatable, a pleasant change from Shafi's paper-weights. Moreover, he was willing to learn.

We were able to get white flour up from Gilgit for cakes and biscuits, but we found that native bread-flaps made from the local stone-ground wholemeal wheat were more appetizing than white bread in any form. They are made without yeast and cooked on a griddle, like small, thin pancakes. Zaidu made them as of course, since they are the normal local food, and we had a few fresh for every meal (they are horrid stale). Their great merit is that they can be eaten without butter or jam. This was a great advantage, for butter was a problem. The tinned butter we brought with us for the road all went bad—you could not blame it in that heat—and butter in our sense of the word is unknown in Hunza.

There was fortunately a little cow's milk to be had, but the cows get so little to eat that their milk has not much butter-content. A really good Hunza cow yields at most a quart of milk a day after she has fed her calf, and she only gives milk at all for a month or two after the calf is born. So milk is no part of the regular local diet. The people normally milk into a gourd, which makes an excellent jug, but has the drawback that there is no ready way of cleaning it. Where fuel is so scarce no one could boil water merely to scald milk-vessels, and the method is to hold the gourd over the smoke of the fire. This seems to be perfectly wholesome, but it gives a gruesome taste to the milk, already sufficiently tainted with memories of yesterday, last week, last year. So we would send one of our people with a clean aluminium bucket and get the cow milked straight into that. In this way we procured as much as we needed for tea and coffee and puddings, but of course not enough to make butter from, as we had been accustomed to do in Gilgit. Fresh butter proved to be an unattainable luxury. The local butter, which they call *maltash*, is much prized; there is so little of it that it is kept strictly for feast days and great occasions. Their chief chance of making it is from the goats' milk when the men have the animals up at the summer pastures. They make it day by day, a little at a time, and when they have collected about two pounds they shape it into a ball, wrap it in birch-bark, tie it up with strips torn from the roots of juniper, and then bring it home to store. With luck one good she-goat will provide two balls of *maltash* per season. It is then stored in a tiny stone larder under the nearest water-channel to keep it damp and cool, and thence produced when wanted. Even when quite fresh it tastes very "high" from the unwashed smoky gourds, and it gets more and more tasty the longer it is kept. The tastier it grows the more they value it, "nice and peppery" they say. But the taste for *maltash* must be acquired, and it was too late for us to acquire it.

When Dádo was going off for his few days' leave, his last words were: "I'll bring you back some nice fresh butter; I'll bring enough for a month; it shall be my gift, and you shall be my guests." He was only away two days, and he must have drained all the cows in the countryside and kept his womenfolk busy all the time, for he brought a glass bottle full of really lovely looking, clean butter—that was, alas! already thoroughly rancid. "I had new vessels, and I didn't let them use gourds, and I got it made your way," he boasted. It was really tragic. We had to eat a little for a day or two, not to hurt his feelings; but it nearly made us sick. The pantry stank of it, and the dining-room stank of it, and the stink was steadily creeping into the study! Then I had to break it to him that though his butter was beautifully clean and perfectly lovely, we ate so little at a time that it could not keep in this heat, and so he must please take it away and store it as *maltash* for his family. A few days later he brought just a couple of ounces, made as nearly European-wise as possible, and David was just able to eat it smothered under marmalade for a couple of days. We then pleaded for only an ounce or two now and again, and gave Dádo some salt to blend into it. I renounced my share of this luxury with pleasure (I really could not eat it), but David, who has had longer practice in non-faddiness, could manage a little and even preferred it to eternal dry bread.

Dádo would not hear of payment; but at last I persuaded him, since this exotic butter-making must give trouble to his people and deprive them of *maltash*, to allow me to pay him three rupees a month or so—"for the baby boy." He adored the little boy—a rather ugly mite of about eighteen months whom he brought from time to time to show us—and he ultimately accepted this compromise and solemnly took "Akíl Sháh's butter-money" with his own wages. No payment, however, could repay the goodwill and kind thought that he used to put into procuring butter for us before it had become *maltash*. We had had many native servants of many races and shades of colour in our time—including a French-speaking negro in Kerman long ago—whom we have grown fond of and who, I think, have been fond of us, but never anyone so entirely lovable as Dádo of Hunza.

While the summer lasted we were able to have as much fresh fruit, green vegetables, and potatoes as we could use, so that we were really very well off.

Several other problems that had threatened in advance to be serious solved themselves more easily than we had feared. The Political Agent's office in Gilgit has to send a post bag up to Hunza three times a week and they allowed our letters and parcels to come along in a separate bag to be dropped at Aliábád without payment of any extra postage. This was a great luxury, and we were amazed to find letters and newspapers coming through to us in exactly a calendar month from home. They could also send up in the mail-bag small quantities of white flour, sugar, raisins, rice, salt, matches, and cigarettes from the Gilgit bazaar—all unobtainable locally.

We needed money only to pay the wages and the daily milk, vegetables, etc. We had a strong suspicion that Shafi, for the few days he spent in charge of things, was gravely over-charging on the petty account, as well as making away with tea and sugar—having learnt, as I have said, more than his prayers in India. All the real Hunza men are so scrupulously straight that this distressed us. So we were doubly glad to have exchanged him for honest Zaidu.

At first all sorts of people kept bringing us gifts of fruit—apricots, pears, melons, peaches, apples, tomatoes (introduced like the potato by the British and much appreciated because they can be dried for winter use). This gift-business, however, is expensive for the recipient. If the Mir or any of the princes or any person of importance sent things, we must of course tip the people who brought them—not in proportion to the actual value of the articles, but to the dignity of the sender and ourselves. If a humbler person brought them we obviously must tip him also. As we could in season buy as much fruit and vegetables as we could use for about a half-

Group on roof of No. 1 watching passers-by in street below. Small boy is carrying baby on his back of whom nothing is visible but tiny fists on brother's shoulders.

(*See Chap.* 16)

penny a day (even when Shafi was profiteering!), and as you can't well tip anyone, even the humblest, less than about sixpence (and if there are several big man's retainers it may run into many shillings), the getting of gifts is very costly! We were glad when the flow of gifts presently dried up a bit. There was always great rejoicing in our back quarters when *maltash* was presented, for as we could not possibly use it ourselves (not even for cooking) it was solemnly passed on (as soon as the donor was out of sight) to the servants to divide. I called them all up and handed it over publicly to ensure that all should get a fair share. They never seemed to quarrel about the division, but effected it on some well-understood principle of their own, so perhaps my precaution was unnecessary; but it's unfair to lead such generous-hearted people into temptation, and *maltash* is dearer to their hearts than much fine gold.

The only other major problem was the washing. I had quite expected that we might have to get the things washed in the house, and do with rough-dried sheets and towels, occasionally sending shirts and collars down to Gilgit. I do wish men could wear silk undies that only need a rinse. But we heard that there was in Báltít a "merchant" who had at one time been washerman to some British officer, so we made enquiries and asked him to come and see me. He didn't seem at all keen; he wasn't really a *dhobi*, he said, and he hadn't a "proper iron," and he could not starch or "get up" evening shirts. (I could not myself imagine David wilfully wearing "boiled shirts" in camp.) But we turned Qudrat Ullah on to have a talk with him as knowing all the local conditions and people, and so friend Baráto of Báltít agreed to take a small "wash" and see what he could do with it. To my delight he brought everything back clean and beautifully pressed with whatever "improper" iron he had. We had another chat, and if that was all I wanted done he was more than willing to do all our washing for 15s. a month—less than half my laundry bill at home, where we only send the larger things out! In theory he was going to earn his money. He was to carry the wash to the springs at Murtazábád, by the big river. You will remember it is a good five or six miles away, across the Hasanábád gorge and down some 1,500 feet on the other side. He was to provide his own native Indian soap and heat his own iron somehow. In fact, however, I saw him unashamedly spreading out the things to dry on the grass behind the bungalow, having coaxed hot water out of Zaidu. And as Indian soap is made with ghee or some odious, smelly fat which we had no mind to breathe in off our sheets and pillows at night, I agreed to give him one cake of Sunlight soap per week (one of the few supplies I had prudently brought with me). Presently I found that he would much prefer to iron in the kitchen, "it would be so much better for the clothes than being carried to and fro to Báltít," and that he would take it kindly if I would supply the charcoal for his iron. You will deduce that Baráto, like Shafi, had learnt a thing or two in India besides his *dhobing*. However, from my point of view the bargain was a good one, and I was glad it should be a good one from his side too. I don't doubt that my "merchant" saved one bar of soap in four, or perhaps one in two, to stock his "shop" in Báltít; but our clothes were nicely washed and he had no competitor within sixty-four miles and deserved to profit by his own enterprise.

He was an entertaining fellow, the *dhobi*, with a humorous kink in his face, and a quaint, half-defiant, half-amusing way of talking that made his calls rather pleasant episodes. His air implied: "Of course you can't afford to lose me; there's no one else in Hunza you could get instead. On the other hand, of course, 15s. a month for your little scrap of work is money for jam, and I like coming over for a chat with your people, so it suits us to be friends."

There is something very winning about the complete lack of servility in Hunza. The people are hospitable, courteous, and polite, and too self-respecting to omit the deference due to "The Great," but they own their soil and live their own lives and can look the whole world in the face. They serve you faithfully and ungrudgingly and more than earn what you pay, but they are servants of none. For which reason I wish we had some other word for these lovable peasants who worked for us.

Two other points remained: heat and light. The Hunza

mountains face south, and in contrast to the north-facing Nagir heights where pines are plentiful, are absolutely bare of trees. So fuel is a serious problem; each household has to manage on such wood as they can spare from their own gardens and orchards. If a tree has to be felled or pruned, or an old vine rooted up, they may be in relative luxury for a time, or if they have to cut down poplars for a house the trimmings will keep them going, but normally they must do with an occasional fallen branch or a few twigs. Even in the depth of winter no one can afford a fire merely to warm the house; they cook their bread and vegetables as economically as possible, and just sit round the ashes of the tiny fire till it is time to blow it into life again for the next meal. We feared we might therefore have to import wood from Nagir or even farther off, which would have been serious, for we needed a good deal for cooking, baths, etc., and would need more when it came to trying to heat the large and draughty sitting-room. We consulted our people about it, and presently one day they brought a charming man to see us. He had been dabbling in commerce and had contrived to contract a debt in Gilgit and was going to be forced to cut down some of his fruit trees to pay it. It would suit him far better to sell the lot to one buyer than to peddle it about amongst his fellow countrymen, who rarely had money to spend. So we easily made a bargain with him, and he delivered into one of the outhouses (with a rickety door which could be padlocked) a fine supply which with care lasted out our time for all purposes. What was more he was delighted to take notes in payment. We had brought up some ten and five rupee notes with us before we realized that only small silver would be any use. So that was that. I had no further trouble but the usual routine job of weighing out the day's wood.

In the old days in Gilgit, though oil was expensive, there was never any trouble in getting it. The S. and T. carried an ample supply both of the finer Snowflake and of the everyday kerosene. Remembering this, we had not brought any up with us from Kashmir. But the S. and T. was about to disappear, in consequence of various political developments which are not necessary to explain, and their supplies were almost done. We hastily earmarked all the Snowflake they could possibly spare; for our treasured Aladdin lamps would have been little use to us if we had had nothing to feed them on and they can't digest the coarser oil. Snowflake worked out at 4s. 6d. a gallon plus carriage from Gilgit! But it was one of the absolute essentials to work. We bought also as much of the ordinary kerosene, as we could, so as to have oil for hurricane lanterns for bedrooms and bathrooms. But all through the winter we had to ration ourselves to *one* Aladdin lamp. It was annoying to think that we could have brought as many extra pony-loads as necessary up with us if we had realized the need. It was by July too late to order from down-country; the passes would be closed before a consignment could get through.

Chapter 14

FIRST WALKS ABROAD

THE very day after our arrival we went out for a stroll to take stock of our immediate surroundings. Along the Dála, the little stream which ran in front of our house, there is a tiny foot-path, just wide enough for one. On our right was the channel in its carefully made bed with a stone revetting wall above it holding up the field above; on our left a fine hedge of quick-thorn to keep passing beasts from jumping into the field 4 or 5 feet below. We could hear a merry sound of drums and pipes coming from somewhere downhill, and asked what was on. It seemed that just before we arrived the first barley-cutting had been celebrated with various ceremonies, which we could only hope to see in detail next year, and some of the jollification was still being kept up. Qudrat Ullah was with us, and a "levy." I must explain the levies. In most villages Government chooses, no doubt on the Mir's advice, one or two of the most respected peasant-farmers who are not head-men or officials of the Mir himself, and pays them a small (very small) monthly wage so that they may be ready to do any little Government jobs that are wanted. There are three in Aliábád, which is relatively a large place with about two hundred scattered houses, and the Political Agent had kindly instructed them that one of their jobs was to be useful to us. I may as well at once introduce the two first: Kalbi is a fine upstanding man, rather darker in colour than the average; and Hurmat, a younger, very cheery fellow with dashing mous-taches. They are both intelligent and extremely friendly and eager to help. We didn't see why they should waste time on us for nothing, so David at once agreed with them that he would pay them a small retaining fee if they would take it in turns to be "on duty" with him in their spare time. They would obviously be useful informants.

We had to walk along in single file. There is no "road" in Hunza where two people can walk abreast, or along which you can ride, except the "Great North Road" running through from Kashmir to Kashgar, and even it is never more than 4 to 6 feet wide. The other tracks run mostly beside small water-channels to enable people to get from one sluice to another to juggle the water now off, now on. Even when you have a neat little track fairly horizontal (there are only three of these possible for ordinary walking) it is broken every few yards by a sluice which you must jump or step over carefully so as not to interfere with the water arrangements or, alternatively, break your leg. The sluices are the simplest things imaginable—just a gap in the side wall of the channel which can be closed with a couple of convenient, slab-like stones and plastered up with mud from the watercourse. Occasionally there is a little wooden shutter which can be raised or lowered in wooden slots at the side.

As we went along David asked the names of the various kinds of water-channels, fields, etc., that we saw (the *names* he already knew, but not at first hand which kind was which), and presently we had a train of bright-eyed boys in the fields on each side, full of amusement at this new game. One would cry: "This stone is a flint; this is a stink-stone," whereupon he would crack it and give it to us to notice the faint smell of sulphur it gave out. Another would run up: "Here's a poppy and a poppy-head"—so we were not going to lack for willing teachers.

After a little we turned down a narrow "lane," less like an English lane than anything else on earth. It plunged downhill pretty steeply, sometimes just a rocky slope, sometimes just one boulder below another making a very crude flight of steps varying from 18 inches to 3 feet or so. Beside the "path" ran the inevitable water-gutter in which you could walk, as it happened at the moment to be dry.

On each side, a bare 3 feet apart, were the usual walls of

loose stone. It is amazing how they get these walls to stand up, 6, 7, 10 feet high, without an ounce of mortar or mud. At the bottom they put huge stones like portmanteaux, then smaller ones like bandboxes, then others the size of quartern loaves, till as you get towards the top they have come down to the size of penny buns. Each is carefully chosen to fit as neatly as possible into the space left by the last, and wherever there is a gap left they choose a small stone that will just fit and wedge it in tight. The walls are really a beautiful sight. These side ones they build partly because they want a boundary to their field, but much more, I think, because if you didn't pile the stones somewhere there would be no field at all. There are no gates. Wood is scarce and very precious and, besides, at different seasons and for different purposes you might want the gate now in one place, now in another. So when you want to get in, you just pull down as much of the wall as necessary and build it up again when your work is done.

Presently we came to a large garden with handsome walnut trees, its long wall broken by a wooden door now open. Hurmat told us that this was the semi-royal domain, where the Mir's first wife and what the German royalties would call his morganatic family were settled. Festivities were going on inside, and we were assured that anyone might enter. Fortified by this we went in and were made welcome by two semi-royal grandsons, one a lad of seventeen or eighteen and one a jolly little boy of perhaps ten, who were sitting on a carpet spread on a raised piece of ground below some trees. Our hosts made us immediately at home, and a chair was fetched for me.

There was a little grass under the trees, and just inside the wall an open earthen space like a bit of a school playground. The band was sitting against the wall, while men and boys were dancing and a largish audience was clapping and hurrahing at intervals. Baskets and dishes of ripe apricots were lying about everywhere, and everyone helped himself as inclined. Fruit was brought for us and the merry-making went on as before. It was delightfully gay and informal and our young hosts did not allow us to feel out of things. We took care not to stay too long, for fear we were in any way spoiling the fun. We took another route home, where a tiny 2-foot track at the base of a high wall led us past a fine reservoir of water and out on to the main road.

The whole countryside is dotted with these deep open-air reservoirs, their sides built of stone walls. They are drained from a hole at one side of the floor, and this can be plugged by a skilfully shaped wooden stopper mounted on a long slim poplar pole. It may happen that your turn for water comes at a moment when you don't immediately want to use it. In that case you store it till wanted and draw it off as required. When one of these *pferis* is full in summer time the men and boys use them as swimming pools. In winter everyone fills his *pferi* before the water ceases to flow, and this gives him a reserve of water for his animals and for washing purposes. The drinking water is carefully stored in smaller similar dugout pits which are scrupulously roofed over almost at ground level and approached down several rude steep steps, so that there is no fear of their being polluted by the animals. The Hunzukuts are most fastidious in their habits, and do not allow any of their water to be fouled.

Next evening David and I went out for another walk alone. We had no intention of being dogged by our retainers, however helpful, for we knew we could not hope to get into touch with the people themselves if any third parties were present. We pursued the Dála as before but without turning downhill. In the very first empty field (just reaped) there was a nice little girl about eight, whose name she told us was Kaníza—she will turn up again frequently, for she lives in one of the very nearest houses. She was carrying a small youngster on her back and wasn't in the very least shy. The small child was a girl and was her married sister's and had come over from Báltít to spend the day. The baby was two and would walk and talk, she said, and her house was just along there in front and she was going home. She came along behind us chattering away. These single-file paths are unsociable, and the fact that no one can ever walk beside you does not make it easier to talk Burushaski. Kaníza had evidently heard the boys yesterday telling us the

PLATE VIII

1. Grandfather minding Baby Faqér. (*See p.* 282)

2. Baby worship. Naját standing in field. (*See p.* 117)

names of things, so she took up the good work: "That's our roof; that thing sticking out is a cross rafter," and "That's our ladder." Presently we came to the corner of her square, stone house, the wall of which rose straight from the water-channel, and there we found her father and a couple of small boys. We crossed a tiny two-trunk bridge to talk to them at the door, and papa was evidently much pleased that we had taken notice of the two small girls. Mother and an auntie were sitting a little farther back under some fine mulberry trees splitting apricots, which they were going to spread presently on a big boulder or on the roof to dry. Everywhere we looked boulders and roofs were decorated with glorious golden-pink pools of drying apricots.

I slipped over to the women while David continued to chat to the master of the house. With luck the dried apricots would last them all through the winter, for this had been a good year. The apricot stones they were keeping carefully as they worked. Presently the children would crack them between stones and the kernels would be hoarded. Eaten with dried apricots they make a delicious almond-and-raisin dessert for feast days or offerings to guests, while a good proportion of them must be pounded by the women till the oil is squeezed out that will give their sole indoor light. If by good luck there is any oil to spare, it makes a prized unguent for the hair and most families contrive to have enough to sleek their plaits or fringes for great occasions. This cheery family bade us a friendly good-bye as we moved on, and a little farther along the channel, which was now making a curved sweep round, we saw a man standing in a reaped field below us. This crop had been lucerne, he said; he gets two crops of it off one field each season. David told him how they get seven or eight crops in Persia, but consider the first crop bad for the animals (for some reason which we never discovered). He was much interested, and said they did not notice any difference in the wholesomeness of their first and second crop: Hunza animals are not encouraged to be faddy. Presently we came to a fine, walled-in mulberry orchard on our left and climbed up into a sloping field where a slight crop of grass was growing between boulders. We sat down to admire the view with a fine stretch of terraced fields below us, quaint little stone houses with groups of trees dotted here and there, and behind all, in every direction, the great mountains. On our way back there was a small boy, of perhaps thirteen, in the ex-lucerne field: "Who does this field belong to?" Just in the boastful way of small boys at home, he answered: "Oh, this is my field and that's my mulberry orchard you passed just now, and here's my house with the big mulberry tree over it, and this is my apricot tree and that is my father over there," pointing to our earlier friend who had moved some distance off. "I'm going home now," and he came along with us chattering away. "That's one of our lambs, and that's a kid." He passed his own door and walked all the way back with us. When we came to the bungalow David imitated his way of speaking: "And this is our house, and that's our chair in the verandah, and now we are going in to eat bread." The boy burst out laughing, evidently quite aware that we were chaffing him, waved his hand in farewell, and ran home at the double to tell his family all about it.

We had quite expected that the people would be friendly, but we had no idea they would be so spontaneously forthcoming and so quick to guess what we were driving at. Already by our second day we had made two sets of friends in the two nearest houses, and were sure of a welcome as we passed.

I asked Levy Kalbi next morning whether there was anyone who could make us a wastepaper basket. Within an hour or two he came along with an armful of willow twigs, squatted in the verandah: "If the Sahib will show what shape he would like, I'll make it now." So David made him a rough sketch, and in an hour or two he had finished a capacious basket that only needed to dry for a day or two in the sun. We asked what it should cost. He was almost hurt: "You shall not pay me for it. I am already eating your salt. And a basket is nothing, anyway." The day after he came along with a bunch of goat's hair under his arm which he was going to spin, and he thought we might like to watch. Oddly, the men spin the goat's hair and the women the wool. All these Hunza people are refreshingly competent. There's nothing connected with their every-day life that they cannot all do, and do well.

I saw a couple of pretty young women sitting together in a little orchard spinning, as they watched a few sheep grazing on some odd blades of grass that grew between the trees. I scrambled over the wall and sat beside them to watch. They showed me what they were doing, and as we talked a fine old greybeard passed by driving a few goats and sheep downhill. "What are you doing there, Mother?" "Naját and Zaida are showing me how to spin." "But don't you *know*?" Half shamefaced, wholly amused, I tried to explain that unfortunately in our country most of the spinning was done with "wheels" (a general sort of word for machinery of any kind—a thing which, of course, they have never seen), and quite a lot of women besides myself did not know how to spin. He shook his head sadly as if to say, "What is the world coming to?" and stood a moment to watch us. Then sympathetically but firmly he said: "You'll never learn now, I'm afraid. You should have begun as a child; it takes a lot of practice. Good-bye." And as he went after his animals I saw him still gently shaking his head over my lost youth—which he could not regret more than I.

Wherever she is going, whether to the orchard to gather twigs for firewood, or to the mill with a small sack of grain to be ground, the woman carries under her arm a quaint little kidney-shaped receptacle for her well-washed wool. It is usually made of wild rowan bark. The menfolk when up at the summer pastures cut a strip of bark and bend the two ends towards the centre, forming two circular chambers. They then bury it for a year or two till it has taken the required shape. Then they lash on a thin wooden base and lash the two circular chambers together, and the wife's *pfurúkus* is ready for her. In one side she puts the clean wool which she teases by hand, removing any lumps or bits of straw, which she puts into the odd-shaped cavity between the two circles. She then coaxes bits of the cleaned lump into a neat ribbon of wool about 6 inches long and 1½ inches wide, and beats it well on her knee till it is perfectly flat and even and coheres together, and this little strip is folded and placed in the second chamber. When she has enough of these *dapping* prepared, she takes out her little spindle, also shaped at home, puts the point of it into a little dish like a small ash-tray, which prevents it from wandering about while she rotates it. Then with a *dap* of wool in her left hand and the spindle in her right, she conjures somehow a fine even thread on to the whirring spindle. So many *dapping* make a spindleful, so many spindlefuls make a ball, so many balls suffice for a winter cloak. Undoubtedly you must learn as a child. The shape of the *pfurúkus* makes it most convenient to carry; even if you have a child on your shoulders and a basket on your back, it sits under your arm and stays there of itself, one circular chamber projecting back and front. The little ash-tray is cleverly moulded by the women from the malleable mush left when they have squeezed every drop of oil from their apricot kernels. It dries in a day or two and serves for many a year.

There was a jolly family party who worked the fields just below our house. I used to wish the fields didn't slope down and down and we could then have watched them better from the windows. When we arrived they had just reaped two fields of wheat (which ripens a fortnight later than the barley) and piled the sheaves in two big stacks. Then they made their threshing-floor as earlier described. When the floor was dry they spread the entire circle 2 or 3 feet deep with cut wheat and got a team of five cows, tied their muzzles loosely together with a soft rope round each and then drove them round to tread out the grain. It is usually a woman or girl who drives the team, but sometimes a man or boy will take a hand. The outside beast has, of course, to make the biggest circle, while the centre one just buzzes round as nearly as possible in the same spot. As the driver gently touches them with her switch she keeps shouting "Hai, hai, hai!" to encourage them. When she gets tired one of the others comes on duty and she goes and sits down in the shade of the stack. As you can imagine, it is pretty hot in the noonday sun. I joined the women in the shade where they sat spinning away and keeping an eye on the toddlers. There were two dear little girls, Shamúli and

Banu, about six and four, who played with me and let me tickle them with straws and play "One little pig went to market . . ." with their dusty little toes. This game proved such a success that I roughly translated it into "One little sheep went to drink. . . ." They would never have seen a pig, and if they had they *ought* to think it unclean, so I thought a lamb was safer. My first version gave one little lamb bread to eat, "bread" being a general word for "food." This caused great laughter: "Lambs wouldn't like bread, Mother dear." "Well, what do you think they'd like best?" "Oh, grass or leaves." "One little lamb had grass to eat and one little lamb had none." Thus amended, my little rhyme was approved, and other youngsters turned up to play "little lambs" till the game grew so popular that whenever I sat down on anyone's threshing-floor baby feet would be stretched out towards me: "One little lamb, Mother . . ." till I got quite tired of ". . . baa, baa, baa, all the way home," but it never palled on them. Centuries hence, when we shall have long been sleeping in the Garden of Rest at Golders Green, some anthropologist will come along and wonder what process of "diffusion" took "one little pig" to Hunza, or whether Hunza spontaneously generated the jingle for itself.

My pencil and little notebook were a great source of amusement, and the youngsters would crowd round: "Have you put my name in? I'm Shamúli." "So you are; but whose Shamúli are you? I've got two Shamúlis already. Who's your Daddy? How many brothers have you got; how many sisters, are they bigger or smaller, what are *their* names? And which house is yours?" Thus gradually I got to know most of our immediate neighbours, but it was no easy matter to sort the families out, for groups would gather on each other's threshing-floors, and anyone whose own immediate work was done would join in to help the workers. I finally gave numbers of my own to all the nearest houses, and tried bit by bit to plot out the various relationships.

Meantime the threshing went steadily on, and I noticed that the driver carried always a flat bowl shoulder high in her left hand. "Now what's that for?" asked I. "Why, that's the dung-dish," and right enough the driver quickly anticipated her cows' needs, and when her dish was full went off and emptied it on a little heap of manure. You thus keep your grain uncontaminated and salvage your manure—most priceless of products. If the driver lapses into a daydream a warning yell from the onlookers would call her attention back in time. I don't know whether the dung-dish is in use elsewhere, but it is at any rate one more symbol of Hunza fastidiousness. You *plough* with oxen, but you thresh with *cows*, whose slighter needs can also be forestalled. When all the wheat is thoroughly trampled the men take great wooden five-pronged forks, most gracefully shaped things (made, of course, at home), and towards evening when there comes a little breeze they toss the broken wheat up into the air to winnow it. The broken straw is blown to one side while the heavier grain falls into a heap. Then they take wooden, home-made spades and toss the grain again to get rid of any remaining straw. These processes take many hours' hard work, and will not be completed in one day; but they have no rain to fear and can leave their stacks of straw and heaps of grain from one day till the next. They leave their threshing-floors unguarded when they go home at night; pilfering a neighbour's food is simply "not done."

When the winnowing is over the women take a big sieve, made of thin strips of leather criss-crossed over a round frame. This is coarse enough to let the grain through but to catch any scraps of straw. When this first sieving is over, they take a finer sieve (with, of course, a totally different name) which keeps the grain and lets the dust fall through. But even then they don't consider the job quite finished. The women turn the pile over with their hands, carefully picking out any sliver of straw that may have previously escaped. When at last it is ready, the grain is filled into large skin sacks, which will take up to 160 lb. or so, and the men carry these off to the storeroom while the broken straw is loaded into huge open-ribbed baskets that can also be carried only by a man. The straw is taken up on to the flat roof and poured down through a central hole into the straw shed.

There is no hard and fast rule about what is woman's work

and what is man's except that, for obvious reasons, the extra-heavy loads are handled by the men; but a man will gladly take a turn at driving the threshing team or carrying the baby, and a woman will readily do a spell with the winnowing fork or shovel. No job is taboo for anyone able to tackle it, and the result is the pleasantest possible family co-operation. The great thing is to get this particular work polished off as soon as possible for there are other urgent things waiting to be done.

Chapter 15

ILLNESS CALLS A HALT

WHEN after three days we had got the house habitable, cupboards and bookshelves ordered, lamps burning, water and food routine running smoothly, and the first friendly contacts with our neighbours established, we asked leave to pay our first call on the Mir, the king of the country and our host.

Two horses were found for us—it was a welcome let-off that the nature of the country made it useless to keep our own horses—and we started early, while it was still cool, on the four-mile ride to Báltít, his capital. The Great North Road from Kashmir to Central Asia is here some four to five feet wide; the only rideable road in the country. For the first couple of miles it runs fairly level between high field walls, just dipping 50 feet now and again to cross a stony gully, down which pour at times irresistible floods of mud and boulders; then it staggers almost perpendicularly up some hundreds of feet till it reaches the level of the Dála and runs along with the water channel (which is perhaps 4 feet wide and 2 feet deep) on its left and a steep drop on the right into the first fields below. High above us towered staircases of narrow fields and behind them great serrated snow peaks, the most interesting of which culminates in a 2,000-foot needle of sheer granite too steep ever to hold the snow.

This is Princess Búbuli's Peak, and the story goes that when the hero Kiser (the Gesar of Tibetan myth[1] and an

[1] For original Tibetan versions of his story, see Madame Alexandra David-Neel, *Gesar of Ling*; for the Burushaski version, see D. L. R. L., in *Folklore*, XLII, June 2, 1931.

incarnate deity) conquered Hai Hai Yúl (= Hunza) he took to wife the Princess Búbuli. He had not been long in the country till he saw in a dream Tibet invaded and his earlier queen carried into captivity, so he determined to return and deal with his enemies. Even in the Tibetan versions of the Gesar Saga it is difficult to avoid thinking him an ugly type of hero, a still more unpleasant manifestation of the divine, and the absolute limit in undesirable husbands. Princess Búbuli asked when she might look for his return: "I'll go to-morrow and return yesterday"; he said, "when donkeys grow horns, when millstones grow beards, when the river flows uphill, I shall come back." Lest she should get into trouble during this brief grass-widowhood he seated her on this granite spike with a 200-lb. bag of millet-seed and a cock: "Give him one grain a year, and when the grain is done, I shall return." And there the luckless princess sits, and you can hear her wailing in the winter storm.

The road commands a fine view of the junction of the Nagir with the Hunza River, and the rugged, savage valley which leads to the Nagir capital, tucked away out of sight amongst its sunless mountains near the great Hispar glacier. On our Hunza side the ground falls steeply with fertile bays of terraced fields and groves of apricots, all still in late July laden with their golden fruit. The road winds round various bluffs, following of course the contours of the mountain-side, and you can see several villages below, including Ganesh, clustered on the very edge of the river cliffs. High above the field-terraces on our left we presently espied the white front of the fortress-palace that has looked down over the fields of Hunza for at least six hundred years—surely the most dominating seat of kings in the wide world. It is built on the cliff edge of a projecting promontory that falls perpendicularly—but from the road invisibly—behind it; and behind that again lies the mighty ravine of the Ulter Ber, up which, far out of sight, is the almost inaccessible glacier that supplies all the waters of Hunza, from Áltít (two miles beyond and some hundreds of feet below Báltít) to Aliábád, feeding five or six different aqueducts, including, of course, the Dála.

Some time in the days of our earliest Edwards, a princess of Baltistán married the reigning prince of Hunza. For the last hundred years or so the direct route to Baltistán has been completely blocked by advancing glaciers, but for centuries before, the two countries had been in communication with each other. Hunza consisted then of three small villages only: Áltít and Ganesh on the river cliffs, and Báltít high above. The princess's father sent with the bride an army of Balti masons, carpenters, and craftsmen, who built the two forts of Áltít and Báltít as part of the royal dowry, and to-day they still stand proudly on their cliffs, impregnable to assault, centres of ancient ceremonial. To this day, too, the Hunzukuts modestly attribute all their simple arts to Balti influence.

The original inhabitants of Hunza proper are said to be descended from three soldiers of Alexander the Great, who were left behind sick, presumably plus their womenfolk, and thus while their comrades marched on became the founders of the three first villages in this inhospitable region. Like so many royal houses in Central Asia, the family that has ruled for more than six centuries in Hunza and Nagir likes to claim descent from Alexander himself. But while the Mir of Nagir, Sir Sikander (= Alexander) Khan still upholds this tradition, we noticed that the shrewder Mir of Hunza—who must have seen many a courteously-veiled smile greet this familiar genealogy—shied off the topic.

What seems probable is that the royal family is not in origin of the same stock as the people, and that it may well—as tradition asserts—have come from Persia at some prehistoric date. What is certain is that it can trace its authentic ancestry as far back as can the House of Windsor.

There may well be truth in the legend of the European descent of the Hunza Burusho, for in temperament and looks our Hunza friends have nothing of the "Oriental" about them. Take from them the very lightly bronzed complexion, "the shadow'd livery of the burnished sun," to which at this altitude they are "neighbour and near bred," and you could transplant them without incongruity to the moors of Yorkshire or the Scottish lowlands.

Above and below us as we rode the barley harvest was being speedily gathered in; family groups were reaping, threshing, winnowing, while the more advanced were already hastily reploughing their land for various kinds of millet. Though the Hunza summer is short, the sun at these heights is hot, and with luck each hard-worked field will bear two crops a season. The barley field which is soonest clear will ripen a later crop of millet; the wheat field, ready a fortnight or three weeks later, will still be in time for one or other type of buckwheat. Barley must in olden days have been the standard crop, for all the sowing and harvest festivals centre round it. But the Hunzukuts[1] of to-day vastly prefers wheaten bread and sows as much wheat as he dares. Even the winter-sown wheat, however, ripens later than the spring barley, and since every ingenious device of agriculture only "just gives what life requires, but gives no more," he cannot afford to concentrate on wheat alone. Each year the peasant farmer makes his calculations afresh; experience has taught him much about the rotation of crops, the different varieties of grain that each field —according to soil, water, and aspect—can most profitably bear, and his gamble with nature is a highly intelligent one. In the opener fields of Aliábád we reckoned that the proportion of wheat to barley was roughly two to one, nearer Báltít one to two.

If later in the year you point to a field and ask "What crop is that?" the answer will not be "Such and such a millet, or such and such a buckwheat," but the name of the growing crop with the additional information "On top of wheat" or "On top of barley," which will give you the difference of some weeks in the date of sowing and probably also indicate some subtle difference in the quality of the soil if you have learnt enough basic agriculture to interpret the facts aright.

Our narrow mountain track skirted the face of a magnificent amphitheatre of storeyed cultivation, plunging every now and then into welcome belts of fruit trees, willows and poplars, crossing foaming mountain torrents in cracks of the hillside, none too easy to ford in July, though only rock-strewn gullies

[1] Hunzukuts is both singular and plural.

in winter. Rounding the last bend of the road, we saw before us, below the Fort, the park-like promontory on which the Mir has laid out royal gardens and orchards and built himself roomy summer quarters with two or three European guest-houses. As soon as we were sighted, the band broke out into the hospitable welcome music, and at the gate of the park a young prince stood to greet us, the loveliest boy of thirteen I have ever seen. He was Sháh Khán, one of the Mir's youngest sons, but I christened him forthwith Lord Fauntleroy. Short dark curls framed his homespun cap, and with him were two playmates armed with wooden rifles, whom he calls his "bodyguard." They laughingly presented arms in fine style, and we rode on through the trees to a row of hospitable mangers where we left our ponies and saw Prince Ghazan Khan (the "Prince of Wales"[1]) advancing on foot to meet us.

On our right we left the large open courtyard banked up on to the hillside with verandahs on two sides, where the Mir sits daily in public to dispense justice in the final court of appeal. A steep flight of irregular stone steps is fitted to the contour of the hill; above them on a large granite boulder is picturesquely and ingeniously perched one of the Mir's new guest-houses ornamented outside with ibex horns and stuffed game animals. Then the stairs turned abruptly left through a fine gateway of cut granite with two heraldic monsters couchant on the lintel, where the Mir himself was standing to await us.

Though nearly seventy, he was still a fine figure of a man, every inch a king, as befitted one of the few true, hereditary autocrats left in a topsy-turvy world. He led us through into a lovely English-looking orchard with apple trees bending laden boughs above the grass, to where carpets were spread on the turf beside a miniature playing fountain. A gaily decked tea-table had been set out. Our meeting was one of genuine happiness on both sides. He laughed as he shouted for the tea. "I haven't forgotten, Colonel Sahib," he said, "any hour of the day or night is tea-time, isn't it?" This dear old chestnut-

[1] Now the Mir, 1938.

joke recalled a journey he and David had made in company twelve or thirteen years before to meet the Commander-in-Chief, Lord Rawlinson, on the Thui Pass as he entered Hunza from Chitral. Mir and Political Agent had messed together, and their shared passion for tea at any hour had strengthened the less frivolous bonds between them.

We noticed that our old friend was wearing coloured glasses and heard that his eyes were giving trouble. They looked as keen and shrewd and kindly as ever when he doffed his glasses, but he was awaiting an operation for cataract. It should have been performed in May, but Major Ledger, the Agency Surgeon, had himself gone down with typhus and was now recuperating in Kashmir, so the operation had been postponed until September. The Mir was also having to diet himself carefully to keep diabetes at bay, but despite these trifles he looked extremely well and very cheerful as he talked with expert knowledge of Central Asian politics and the tangled interactions of "Bolsheviki," Chinese, Turkis, and Tungáns, and the mysterious disappearance into Russia of Ma Chung-yin.

We all enjoyed our tea, which was served by Mirza Hasan, a valued old retainer, sometime cook to a British officer, who is summoned to act as chef whenever European guests are expected. In the delightful informality of the Mir's intimate circle, Mirza Hasan stepped forward presently to welcome us and was gratified when I congratulated him on his cakes and biscuits (as I was conscientiously able to do). After a pleasant hour of interchanging news, we took our leave of the royal party, augmented meanwhile by the royal grandsons and a tiny son of two or three, and were seen out of the park with great solemnity by Lord Fauntleroy and bodyguard.

All initial duties were now performed and we could begin our work in Aliábád in all seriousness. The Gods thought otherwise.

The ride home through noonday heat was hot and wearying; towards evening David felt feverish, before morning his temperature was close on 105°. There followed four anxious weeks. Five times his temperature ran up like this; five times after a spell of high fever it plunged down in five or six hours to 95°

or a shade below, leaving him swimming in sweat and weaker than a new-born kitten. As everyone knows who has lived in the East, these acute subnormal spells are almost more alarming than raging fever, and are more exhausting to the patient. Slowly, slowly he would regain strength on Zaidu's "chicken broth," on milk and custard, and creep, decimal by decimal, towards 98·4, and each time as we congratulated ourselves that he was nearly well, and he was sitting out on the verandah, observing the life about him and chatting to the passers-by—whizz bang—he was up to 105° once more.

Nothing like our people's devotion was ever seen. Dádo would carry off soaking sheets and drenched pyjamas, wash them and dry them in the sun. Zaidu would devise and cook such invalid dishes as our scanty resources permitted. Everyone, including Sagi and the levies, wanted to sit up all night, but this I would not allow; they had their fields to till and their harvest to gather in. I had a little Meta stove and could heat milk or soup or Ovaltine during the night myself; but always Dádo slept near the bedroom door, and no admonition would drive him from it.

Again and again those many nights I listened in vain for a sound of breathing, and often I feared my patient would be too exhausted to wake to see another dawn creep up on Rakaposhi.

When the fever fiend had played his last card and lost the trick, there started a fortnight of the most gruesome headache. All his life DL has been liable to an occasional bad headache, but they usually wear out their violence in twenty-four hours. This brute went on day and night for fourteen days so that he could neither read nor write nor sleep. That seems, however, to have been the last frantic struggle of the evil spirit before being exorcised.

It wasn't till nine weeks of illness and convalescence were past that I realized that I had never for a moment felt lonely or given a thought to the absence of a doctor. The servants had been such trumps, the neighbours so sympathetic and kindly, that I was never consciously aware that the nearest white person was not even four days off in Gilgit, but 150 miles off in Rama or 300 in Kashmir (for no one stays in Gilgit in the summer), or that with luck we might see a doctor in a month or two. In our little home-town there are indignation meetings because we have to travel seven miles in a motor ambulance to reach our nearest hospital.

Another pleasant thing had been the presence of the Indian sub-assistant surgeon in charge of the local dispensary. True when you were sick you would echo George the What-ever-it-was: "Give the doctor my compliments and say I am too ill to see him," but he had a store of any simple drugs absent from our own medicine chest and he kindly acted as sanitary inspector and supervised the disposal of the kitchen refuse, etc., and directed the activities of the sweeper. This removed a source of possible anxiety.

Altogether things might have been a lot worse. It was perfectly maddening for David to have missed all these interesting weeks of the harvest; but he had seen something of it from his window, and from the verandah, and if he was pretty fit again by mid-September we still had an entire year's cycle ahead of us. And I had sat about a good deal in the fields (within sight of the house and within earshot of his whistle—though he never blew it), and made lots of friends and taken what notes I could with as much of my mind as was on the spot. It wasn't a lot, for I was often anxious and always rather underslept. But with luck we should fill in the missing bits next year.

The September weather was delightful; the "bitter" heat had gone, and it was like the best days of an early English summer, but with perfect dryness and the security we never have at home that to-morrow and the day after would equally be fine.

Before coming we had been afraid that further knowledge might reveal all sorts of mistakes in the Grammar and the Texts (now finally in print and about to appear). We were immensely relieved to find as we worked that there was *nothing* incorrect. It seemed almost incredible. A few difficult points could be further cleared up, but there was nothing to retract. The Vocabulary proofs were beginning to come—and a hideous fag it was correcting them!—but this gave opportunity to eliminate a few question marks and occasionally to add a new meaning without disturbing the main text. DL did not attempt to incorporate new material. It would be better not to tinker with the existing work but to wait till our work here was done and put new facts into shape for a supplementary volume.

The anthropological material would in any case be an entirely separate business.

One very tiresome task connected with the Vocabulary was to achieve what certainty was possible about aspirates and cerebrals. Neither David nor I had when young any scientific training in phonetics—the modern science of phonetics simply did not then exist—and perhaps our ears are not naturally acute. Anyhow, neither of us can distinguish these finer shades of sound with any certainty. Burushaski has, for instance, four different t's: a dental t and a cerebral t (= t and ṭ) and the same two sounds plus a light aspiration (= th and ṭh). It is practically convenient and scientifically lamentable that the English t holds an intermediate position between them. Our ordinary t does quite beautifully for conversational use. No doubt in all cases it sounds slightly "foreign" to a Hunza ear, but it seems to be perfectly acceptable. This, however, isn't good enough for accurate recording. Fortunately Qudrat Ullah was intelligent enough to detect the difference, and David has taught him to be on the *qui vive*; so they set to work through the whole Vocabulary to check every single spelling authoritatively. The scientist and phonetician will therefore be able to get the accurate spellings there and the more casual spellings of the Grammar and Texts will be good enough for the ordinary student.

If it was only the t's! But there are a dozen other sounds afflicted with cerebral and aspirate doubles. It was a long and weary business to register them all, but one at least which could only have been tackled on the spot. The ordinary speaker is of course unaware of these refinements of his own pronunciation. An odd point is that the aspiration is frequently dropped in Hunza speech in derived forms, whereas Nagir Burushaski is more logical in the matter; with them apparently "once an aspirate, always an aspirate" is the usual rule.

IX

1. Threshing. (*See p.* 100)

2. Winnowing. Foreground, Afiato and Yaman. (*See pp.* 102, 147)

Personally I felt at times impatient of the time that had to be "wasted" on these subtleties; but my better self acknowledges their importance—or potential importance—for comparative philology. I am, I fear, a curious mixture of a shameless philistine and a scholar *manquée*!

Chapter 16

HOME LIFE AT No. 1

WHEN the women are working in the fields through the heat of the day—and it is very, very hot at 7,800 feet with a temperature of 105° in the shade—they usually have a large square of cotton cloth with them, which they sometimes throw over their heads for protection. This cloth turns in for all sorts of purposes; if you are carrying a small quantity of flour home from the mill you can wrap it up and tie it across from one shoulder to the other armpit and so keep both hands free. If the baby is too small to sit safely on your back or shoulders, you treat it in the same way. In fact, if you see a woman with this kind of bundle that appears to have two lumps in it you may safely guess that it's a baby.

I made great friends with the family who worked just below us (I have named them in my notebook Household No. 1), and I felt quite sad when their wheat harvest was over—it was so convenient just to run down and join them in sight of our own windows. They asked me, however: "Won't you come home and sit in our shade?" Of course I accepted with delight. It was just a few steps along the Dála and down one of the little lanes, half path, half watercourse. We came to a slightly taller, mud-plastered wall on the left with a wooden door in it. Through this I stepped in to a tiny courtyard with a shed on each side, one for straw and one for the lambs and kids. The house itself is just a rough cube of stones plastered with mud, and it has a flat roof with a smoke-hole in it above the central hearth. You go up by a ladder, and the roof makes a nice place for sitting out, watching the neighbours go by, spinning, and drying apricots. It has a second store-room built on a part of

PLATE X

1. Dumping manure.

(*See p.* 237)

2. Afiato ploughing.

(*See p.* 147)

3. Aliko sowing. Small boy interrupted in game of "foot-polo."

(*See p.* 184)

4. Party of women weeding.

it, exactly over the main store-room below. There is no parapet, only a tiny raised rim to direct the rain into a small gutter-hole, on the rare occasions when there is rain; but it has a fringe of cut thorn bushes arranged round the edge to prevent an enterprising goat jumping across from the next-door roof not many feet away. I didn't, however, go up on to the roof, but on into a larger courtyard where there was a pool in the corner at which their washing is done. They would not dream of polluting the running water by washing themselves or their clothes in it as it flows by; they draw off what they want for these purposes into a separate pond of their own. Then under a large shady tree there was a raised stone platform which acts as a "sofa" by day and as a double or treble or quadruple bed by night—for, except in the depth of winter, nobody sleeps indoors. There was another raised platform, with a wall at the back and open in front and sides, roofed in for another sleeping place. It had a railing along under the roof, and over this were hung all sorts of padded quilts, homespun blankets, sheepskins, etc.—the family bedding. All the bedding is taken out and hung up every day, which helps to account for the complete lack of vermin—which I confess came to us as a happy surprise. In all our year in Hunza we saw only *one* flea, and that, as David said, was emphatically our own!

Round the corner from these sleeping places I got into a walled-in shady garden full of fruit trees—apples, mulberries, peaches, apricots, and vines. It is incredible how luxurious mere *shade* is at such a temperature. It wasn't remotely like a garden in our sense. The earth was bare without one blade of grass or green, and was all cut up into little beds round each precious tree, with banks between them, so that the water could be directed to each tree as desired, when it was No. 1's turn to have water at all. In the far corner of the garden was a neat little circular "open-air pulpit." We had seen these pulpits dotted about, but—stupidly—did not at once guess what they were for. Coming straight from Kashmir, where the approach to each homestead is ankle deep in filth, or remembering Arab habits in Iráq, we never expected that we should find in Hunza a people as scrupulously decent as ourselves in matters of sanitation. The lower chamber of their little pulpits is closed with one large slab, which makes them easy to clean; the upper is well supplied with nice clean sand, and has a small hole in the floor. The entrance opening to the upper part is narrow, and anyone inside is completely hidden; even so we never saw man, woman, or child disappear into one. The most prudish maiden aunt would never need to blush as she would in the streets of Paris or by the creeks of Basrah; and whatever Islám may recommend, the Hunzukuts does not dream of allowing his running water or his drinking tanks to be fouled by man or beast.

The pulpits must be regularly and frequently cleaned out, for, though they often stand beside the path, you never get a whiff from them to suggest their necessary purpose, yet I have never seen one being emptied; that also is a job they evidently prefer to do in the privacy of darkness.

A red felt carpet was quickly brought and spread for me, and soon the entire family was sitting round, making conversation. I went back another day soon after, also by invitation, and was allowed to watch Bibi Gímo cook the greens and bread for the mid-day meal. In the summer they cook in the open, in the garden or on the roof, which often has a roofed verandah or even a lightly enclosed upper room added on in front of the upper store-room. She had a little hearth of big stones to hold her tiny fire, and over it sat the big stone cooking pot of vegetables. In olden days the bread was cooked on hot stones, but nowadays everyone has a convex iron griddle which can rest either on the stones or on a tiny iron trivet. They have a neat, shallow wooden tray in which they knead their flour, adding a little water till it has become a flaky dough. Then they take the lid and on that roll out small lumps of the dough with the most ridiculous-looking toy rolling-pin hardly half an inch in diameter. They roll the dough into thin, thin pancakes, lift these with a wooden spatula on to the griddle, and turn them with a skilful twitch. Each takes only a second or so to cook, and is then twitched off on to a big flat wicket platter till there is a sufficient pile. When mealtime comes the family gather round, squatting just anywhere that is convenient. Each person has his own wooden bowl and wooden spoon. They roll up their pancakes and dip them in their bowl of thick vegetable soup or take up the soup with the spoon. The head woman of the house apportions a fair share to each, and I fear there is rarely enough to allow of second helpings.

The art of rationing the family all through the year is recognized as a difficult one; each able-bodied man is entitled to double a woman's ration, but the expectant or nursing mother gets a larger share than the other women; each child after weaning gets a certain ration according to its age.

If a *rúli gus* (housewife-in-chief) is over-generous with her rationing during the post-harvest months of plenty the whole family may starve before next year; so a "competent woman" is highly valued, and incompetence is a fair ground for divorce. No ill-will is felt or expressed, but back she goes to the father and mother who bred her.

The No. 1 Household consists of grandfather, a charming old man, who proudly boasts that he built the house they live in and himself laid out the fruit garden; his two sons, who now do all the heavy work and who both are lucky enough to have small jobs connected with the hospital—this accounts for the family's relative well-to-do-ness; the elder son's wife is my friend Bibi Gímo, the *rúli gus*; the younger son's wife is a beautiful girl Naját, who became one of our best friends. In a community where all faces are happy and kindly, she has the happiest face I have ever seen, and a natural grace of bearing and manner that would adorn any station in any country. Naját so far has no children, but Bibi Gímo's married daughter was staying with her at the moment. There is also an adolescent daughter, Shukuru, who is already growing her hair, and will no doubt presently be married; two nice boys of perhaps thirteen and nine, and the two little girls I have mentioned already, Shamúli, say six, and Banu of three or four, and I imagined there would ere long be another child.

On my second visit, since they had all been so kind to me, I took a tiny rubber ball for Banu. It was a great success. Not only she and Shamúli played with it, but the grown-ups "stotted" it far more skilfully than I. They say the women and girls play a lot of ball, and in autumn the women sweep a smooth place under a willow tree, choose teams, and play matches! They *are* a sporting, jolly crowd. It is no use at all merely to bounce the ball and hit it down again as I did; you must spin round on your own axis between each stroke if it is to count. I didn't find this at all easy to learn at my age, and my feeble attempts gave much amusement. They laugh so openly and heartily that there is no offence in their merriment at your expense; even so, they are sensitive lest you might feel hurt, and Naját hastened to console me: "But, you see, you can read and write, and none of us can do that." So they saved my face for me, if it needed saving.

I had also brought a small coloured comb and offered it to Bibi Gímo for the children's fringes. All the youngsters, boys and girls alike, have their heads shaven—which makes for cleanliness—with just a neat fringe showing all round under their little caps. Banu at once appropriated the comb and started on her front hair, to the amusement of the congregation—which by now included many neighbours. She is the dearest little devil, and not a bit more grubby than any English child would be who played barefoot in a garden which is mostly half wet.

Whichever way I turned on my walks everyone was full of friendliness and welcome, and boys and girls ran along with me telling me all about their animals and naming anything I wanted; but I was longing to have David's company again, and felt rather mean to have been stealing marches on him and making friends in advance. I determined, however, that even after he was well enough to come out for walks I should still go back sometimes to sit with my women friends by myself. It would take too long to tell you about the other families I met and the people I made friends with: there were literally dozens. I solemnly entered their names in my little book and tried to memorize them all and assign them as well as I could to the different houses, but for a long time they all looked rather alike to me and all their dresses are much the same so that it was easy to confuse those I saw less often. Happily this

XI

Hunza fields, Background, Raka in cloud. (*See p.* 211)

only made them laugh, and luckily they all kept forgetting my name, so that I could laugh *tu quoque*. "Larimair memsahib," they would say laboriously, but they had forgotten again before the morrow, and from the first day I was just "Mother dear" to everyone, and sometimes "Granny dear" to the kiddies. It was a delight to be quit of the formal "Memsahib" of India.

Meantime David would be seated in his chair in the big study window or out in the verandah, and everyone who passed by would try to catch his eye and wave a salaam, men and women alike. It was a joy to get away from the furtive, veiled women-folk of India and Kashmir. When little batches of kids and lambs or an occasional cow passed by, the children in charge waved and showed off with an occasional hullabaloo as one beast broke away, leapt a wall, and started tucking in to the new green crop or the vegetable patch. The children dashed after it, chucking well-directed stones, and drove it out in double quick time, and the animals seemed to think it as much fun as the youngsters. After one of these asides they would run past David again to see whether he had noticed the little adventure and were greatly pleased if he shouted out "Well done!" or "Was that the 'bad goat' again?"

Chapter 17

LAND AND HOUSES IN HUNZA

By far the majority of the peasant families in Hunza are freeholders. The land passes from generation to generation without tax during life or duty after death. In olden days the Mirs owned a certain amount of land in every settlement, and the custom was to have this farmed by forced labour, spread, in theory, justly over the villagers. The Yerpa, or Steward, in charge of such royal demesnes, was obviously in the pleasant position of being able on the one side to cheat his royal master of a large proportion of the produce, and on the other to oppress and squeeze the luckless peasant-labourers. He extorted bribes in kind from anyone able thus to evade the communal work, and he could impose more than a fair share of the labour on anyone who incurred his dislike. When the present Mir (Sir Muhammad Nazím Khán)[1] was a boy he had seen this system at its ugly work under his father, Mir Ghazan Khan, and his elder brother, Mir Safdar Ali, and as he would tell you with a smile: "I knew just how much peculation and bribery went on—had I not acted as Yerpa myself!"

To secure the throne for himself, Safdar Ali, as may be remembered, murdered his father and several brothers in traditional Karakoram style, and ultimately fell foul of the British Government of India by breaking promises and treaties and trying to play off the Chinese and Russian Governments against the Indian. After the brilliant little frontier campaign of 1891–92 he fled—unregretted—to Central Asia, leaving vacant the throne of his ancestors. The British had no wish to annex the country, but it was highly important for the security

[1] Now, alas! the late Mir.—E. O. L., 1938.

of India that it should not be taken over by Russia. It was decided to put on the throne a younger brother of the fugitive Safdar Ali's—who by good luck had escaped murder. This young man, Muhammad Nazím Khán, had had an unusually wide political education. As a boy of only nine or ten he had been sent down by his father as a hostage to Gilgit, and had there met British officers for the first time and gained many new ideas. Later he had acted as ambassador and negotiator for his father and his brother on missions to Chinese Turkestan and Afghanistan, and he could talk Wakhi, Turki, Khowar, and Hindustani, as well as his own Burushaski. Above all, he was an extremely able youth, and had drawn his own deductions from his varied adventures. In 1892[1] he was therefore made king, with the able Humayun Beg as his Wazir, and since that time he has been our trusty and faithful ally, guarding for us the lofty passes that are the extreme northern gates to India on the west. For four and forty years he has now ruled his people with firmness, sympathy, and kindness, maintaining security, dispensing justice in accordance with local custom and public opinion, keeping up and encouraging the traditional festivals that punctuate the year with joust and dance, music and merriment.

During his reign there have been only two murders on Hunza soil, serious crime is unknown, and even theft and petty pilfering are non-existent, though there are in the country no prisons and no police. On rare occasions when some mischief-maker threatens serious trouble, the Mir, with the concurrence of his subjects, may deport the would-be disturber of the peace to the distant valleys of Shimshál to tend the royal flocks that pasture there or to spend his energy on roads or aqueducts. Food and pasturage are plentiful, and life in some respects more luxurious than in lower Hunza; but the Hunzukuts loves his home, his family, his apricots, and after a couple of years' exile the malcontent returns a wiser man. It is amusing to see a recent book indicting the Mir of Hunza for the "tyranny" that imposes so humane and so useful a punish-

[1] A popular account of these high matters may be found in Algernon Durand's *Making of a Frontier*, and in E. F. Knight's *Where Three Empires Meet*.

ment. A few years' exile in Shimshál is incomparably preferable to three years' penal servitude in Wormwood Scrubs, yet Hunza delinquents do not become recidivists.

Young Muhammad Nazím Khán took up his job determined, in the light of his travels and experience, to alter much that had been traditional under his ancestors, and within three years of his accession he had completely abolished the Yerpa system of cultivating the royal lands. Such as lay immediately under his own eye he retained, but all the rest are leased out on easy terms to tenants. For the first years a tenant pays no rent at all for new ground that he brings under the plough; he has to get his fields carved out, his water-channels made, and the soil worked. After the land begins to bear he pays a small fixed rent in kind, and if at any point he finds the bargain unprofitable he is free to resign his holding. A large part of the "new settlements" of Aliábád, including all the district immediately round our house, was *kutúkal* land (viz. royal land leased out), and there was no question that the system was working to everyone's satisfaction. The extra fields available had been eagerly taken up by families in the older settlements who were finding their freehold land too cramped, and many of our neighbours were sons who had hived off from the family freehold and whose relations were still living in Báltít, Haidarábád, or Dorkhan.

We once enquired, *à propos* of the meaning of the words "rich" and "poor": "Now what would you people consider a rich man?" "One who had, say, a hundred animals." (The ordinary peasant household has twenty or so sheep, goats, and cows.) "And is there any rich man in Aliábád?" "Only one, the Yerpa." This struck us as highly significant; the one rich man still bore by courtesy his grandfather's title of "Steward"! He was no doubt still enjoying his grandfather's ill-gotten gains. Our Yerpa was, in fact, a genial, kindly man, reputed generous. He was not envied: "Poor chap, he has no sons; he has to hire herd-boys to mind his flocks, and labourers to work his fields." In Hunza a man's true wealth is in his sons; they work the farm with him; if there are several, some can go abroad and earn. Not that a woman or a woman's work is under-valued, but a boy will bring a wife to the house and children to the hearth, while a daughter will take her labour and her children to her husband's home.

In pre-British days the Hunza men bore a bad name in Central Asia as daring raiders. They are a hardy, fearless race, and they would strike a track through uninhabited and uninhabitable mountain country, leaving dumps of food at intervals as they went, fall on a rich caravan travelling from Leh to Yarqand, carry off the spoil, and return—via their food dumps—to divide the proceeds, the lion's share of which fell, of course, to their brigand chief. Any prisoners captured were sold as slaves into Afghanistan or Central Asia. Alternatively they would raid across the river into Nagir and come back with slaves and cattle.

Since such a form of life invites reprisals the Hunza people lived walled in in tight-packed villages close under their forts. We had in Aliábád the old fort-village, built on a promontory, with ravines protecting it on both sides, surrounded by a wall whose twelve beacon towers could send warning of a raid up and down the river—"and the red glare on Skiddaw roused the burghers of Carlisle." Only one of these beacon towers now remains and the crowded hovels are falling to decay. Since the *Pax Britannica* has come, the peasant builds his house and stores his crops out amongst his fields and orchards—without even a watchdog. A few conservative families move into their old "town house" in winter time perhaps for warmth and companionship, perhaps merely to make a change.

These famous raids were primarily the sport of chieftains, and the peasants of to-day find adventure enough, and danger enough, in their daily life not to regret them. The profits of such raids, which welcomely supplemented the scanty produce of the fields, are nowadays more than compensated by the money which the British put into circulation. The Mir draws a small and well-earned salary for his services as guardian of the frontier, a grant for keeping up the road through his territory, and a subsidy for his bodyguard of twenty-four men or so. Any sons the peasant can temporarily spare take service with the Gilgit Scouts, in the Public Works or other Government departments, act as postal runners or dispensary assistants, do part-time jobs as "levies," or enter the private employment of British officers. Travel where you will in the Agency, some enterprising Hunza man is there before you, as carpenter or washerman, as touring merchant or in Government employ. You may even meet an old Hunza taxi-driver in Bombay or a Hunza *chaprassi* in Lahore.

At first the Mir rather discouraged these farther-afield adventures, and not unwisely. New ideas, new customs, new dress, imported from abroad might well upset the happy balance of the home civilization; but the increasing pressure of population—a dubious benefit the *Pax Britannica* is wont to bring—makes some outlet necessary for ambitious youth, and some supplement necessary for home support, and the Mir's policy has been modified accordingly. With rare exceptions the travellers' hearts remain in their Hunza highlands; they go for a few years and return with newly acquired skill, with a set of carpenter's tools it may be, with a smoothing-iron or a sewing machine, to resume work on the family farm and earn a little "on the side."

We heard that a new house was being built by a certain Kalbi (not the Levy; one of another clan) and were invited to go down—some hundreds of feet—and see it in its half-finished state. "It must cost a lot to build a new house," we said. "How did you come to have money enough to spare?" "Well, you see, I have two sons away working—thank God." And, in fact, except in the few cases where the Hunza man goes over-far afield to Bombay or the Panjab, and needs his own earnings to support a down-country family, the Hunza son remits home every spare anna, knowing well that it will be spent on the home he himself will presently enjoy and share. When he comes back on leave he brings his mother an aluminium cooking-pot or basin to jostle the stone *balosh* and wooden bowl, or an iron bucket which incongruously companions the local gourd when his sisters go to draw the drinking water.

In theory there are any number of sizes and patterns of house which you can build in Hunza: the cow-pattern, the ant-pattern, and half a dozen more, but in actual fact there are exactly two—the old Hunza pattern and the new so-called Wakhi pattern. Most of the Áltít and Báltít houses are, for obvious reasons, of the older type—that designed no doubt by the three original Greeks!—most of the Aliábád houses are of the second, for Aliábád is a new place. Water was only coaxed on to it three or four generations ago; before which it was just barren mountain side with a light sprinkling of thorn jungle.

Having decided on the pattern and proportions of a new house, every peasant family is capable of tracing the foundations and rearing the walls and roof; neighbours will lend a hand, at this as at any other job, asking no fee but a meal when they are working and some return of help another day. In olden days the family, wielding the invaluable adze (when this succeeded the earlier ibex-horn), was competent to rough-hew its doors and cupboards, its posts and rafters. But in more recent years the "standard of living" has risen, and this shows distinctly in indoor architecture. If he can at all afford it, the house-builder will now call in a carpenter-neighbour to put finishing touches of superior excellence. The rough doors of the byres are still picturesquely home-made of adze-hewn poplar slices, threaded on two wooden cross rods and revolving on a spiked wooden post which turns in two rough sockets, but the house doors and cupboards are sawn and panelled, planed and hinged and fitted, to the increased comfort of the inhabitants—and the sorrow of the antiquarian. When we had reached Kalbi's house a cheery carpenter was hard at work sitting on the floor with shavings and sawdust round him, fashioning the elaborate, quadruple frame that forms the smoke-hole. We stayed a while and David wrote up notes about the various woods preferred, and dimensions of the various parts, and took photographs of the interior.

A little later one Mírbán offered to let us inspect his newly finished house before the family moved in. We rode a mile or so along the Báltít road, then turned up a steep, twisting, boulder-strewn lane till a new-fangled wooden door gave entrance to a short of irregular compound with three or four houses in it. The new one looked exactly like the others, for after a day or two the stone-and-mud walls have dried to the same appearance of timeless indestructibility as those of fifty or one hundred years ago. We passed first, as always, through a small byre, not yet inhabited by its cow; then at right angles through a dark, narrow passage 5 or 6 feet long, and then through the low hall-door into the house itself. Your main object in building a house at all is to be as warm and free from draughts as possible during the "Great Cold," and no one in his senses would let his hall-door open straight on to the wind-swept mountain side. Hence the byre ante-room, which not only defeats the direct outside air, but contributes something of animal warmth to the human warmth within.

When we emerged into the living-room (the *atrium*, as it were), beautifully bright with light from the smoke-hole, we were standing in a shallow trough below the floor level where the newcomer kicks off his muddy boots in winter. Most people at all well-to-do wear soft home-made boots up to their knees in winter-time. But skins are precious and, however cold the weather, they take their boots *off* to save them when they come to an extra rough bit of ground. This entrance place has in it the "musicians' bench," under which are stored the family basin and similar utensils and on which is piled a store of firewood.

The floor of the room is a small square of hard-beaten earth which in this gloriously dry climate remains admirably clean; and roughly in the centre of it is a shallow hole, edged with four stone kerbs, which is the hearth. Behind the hearth is a low bench sacred to the lady of the house, the presiding genius of indoors. Beside it she sits to do or superintend the cooking and behind her is a low wooden door opening into the store-room; the home-made wooden key of which hangs always on her person. The store-room runs the whole width and height of the house. It has need to be a roomy place, for here stand the skin sacks of grain, the heaped baskets of potatoes, apples, dried mulberries and apricots, the kernels, the wool, the stone wine-jars, the jars of apricot oil, the basket of savoury herbs—all the family's supplies for a twelvemonth, which it is her duty to guard and to apportion.

As you enter, you turn your eyes left and with your free right hand salute the master of the house and wish him peace. You will find him seated on a spacious dais raised well above the earthen floor and comfortably carpeted with goats' hair rugs of his own weaving, or it may be with felt carpets from Kashgar. The left-hand wall of the dark passage through which you have entered screens the end of this recessed dais, and is lined with a capacious cupboard reaching to the ceiling. At the head of the dais is a gigantic wooden bin, divided into chambers each with its separate lid, in which the various kinds of flour are stored as they are ground for use: barley, wheat, millets, and buckwheats. The dais itself is 6 or 7 feet wide and 10 or 12 feet long, the men's sitting place by day and the major sleeping bench by night. Each person has his own set of bedding—padded quilts or homespun blankets—in which he rolls himself like a sausage. The sleepers lie crosswise on the bench, which is wide enough to let them stretch full length, and when neatly packed for the night eight or ten can be comfortably accommodated. On the opposite side of the room is the minor bench, equally roomy, but an inch or two less raised, which is the women's sitting place by day, and at night the sleeping bench for women and children. It also has a built-up cupboard at the foot, and at the head, corresponding to the large flour bin, the housewife's spacious "yeast-cupboard" in which she keeps her kneading trough and rolling-pin, her cooking-pots and what not. Its door is at her left hand as she sits on her cross-bench, and the top of it serves as general shelf, table, and "dresser." A more admirable scheme of architecture, better suited to the family's needs, would be difficult to devise. The complete absence of windows gives a sense of security and cosiness; the complete absence of senseless "furniture" gives a delightful feeling of space and peace and leisure, and makes you want to go home and make a bonfire of your tables and chairs. How much more we have lost than gained by learning to sit on chairs and losing the pliability of joint that makes squatting natural. How much unnecessary domestic slavery goes to our "housework." Every morning the Hunza women take the family rugs and bedding and hang them in sun and air. Five minutes with a broom and the whole house is effectively cleaned!

The hospitality and goodwill of these people is beyond belief. We had never met or heard of the proud owner of this new house, yet he had spread his benches with rugs and carpets for us, had raised some glass bottles (incredibly precious things these) and filled them with flowers to do us honour. So we sat in comfort and asked innumerable questions, supplementing all we had learned from Kalbi's house and proudly showing off how much we knew. Qudrat Ullah and I worked the measuring tape and sang out various dimensions which David entered on the rough plan he had sketched. And as we worked we chatted about all sorts of things, and found our host most interesting, as indeed all people are who are close in touch with real life—the bore is a pernicious product of civilization. Before we went away they brought two huge dishes of peaches and lovely grapes and bunches of flowers for us to take home. We said all the nice things we could think of and wished the family happiness and long life in the new house and plenty of children to fill it, though to judge by the dozens of merry little faces crowding in the background and peering round the entrance, there was no shortage of these in the neighbourhood. The Hunza children (as I have said more than once) are delightful: bright-eyed and eager, yet perfectly mannered. They never interrupt, they never bother you, they disappear like magic if bidden to go, but they love to see and hear all that is going on. While the men were purposefully, gravely talking, I would keep one half my mind at leisure, smile and nod across at the womenfolk, wordlessly implying: "Yes, we know what men are, don't we, you and I?" I would wag a finger in greeting to one or another of the small boys and girls, and then find another catching my eye and demanding an equal attention; I would tickle an adjacent toddler, who responded with a judiciously muffled squeal, and the whole group of households were our friends.

When finally we said good-bye, we could not insult our host by offering money in return for his kindness and the fruit. So next day I plundered my store-room and took out a small

1. Street scene. Children carrying new-born lambs and kids in their arms to display them to us on our return from Yasin. (*See p.* 282)

PLATE XII

2. The Dála, typical road-cum-waterchannel, flanked by field wall. (*See pp.* 83, 93)

boulder of rock-salt, filled two empty cigarette tins (very valuable these) with sugar, and then wondered how to get them surely conveyed to our friends of yesterday. For sugar and salt are indescribably precious, and an ordinary messenger might be tempted. I consulted Dádo. He fell on them with delight: "Oh, do let me take them. Mírbán is a clansman of mine, and a relation by marriage." That settled it, for you could trust Dádo with untold gold—or salt. An hour or two later he was back with radiant face and messages of thanks and blessing.

Our next experience with a house was when we found that our dear old neighbour, Ustád Nadíro, was planning one for the marriage of his son. The Ustád (master-craftsman) is a wonderful old man. He spent some years in Gilgit in his youth working in the "barrack-cháp" (= workshop) of the divisional engineer, and came back with a fine set of saws, planes, and chisels, so that he is one of the most famous of the carpenters and is frequently employed by the Mir to embellish his quarters in Báltít. He is, in fact, Carpenter to the King by royal letters patent. But he has not scorned to perfect himself also in the local crafts; he is a famous weaver and bootmaker as well. His wife, a sporting old lady of about my own age, with a game leg and toothless gums, indefatigable energy, a priceless sense of humour and an unfailing smile, is his worthy consort. We made friends with this delightful couple, who lived quite near on the water-channel above us, very early in our stay, and none of our neighbours were so thoughtful as they to call us to their house when anything interesting was going on. They had tragically lost their two elder sons, and the courage with which the two old folk carried on all the work which by now ought to have been shared by two sons and two daughters-in-law, awoke our constant admiration. One married daughter came over sometimes to lend a hand, but otherwise the pair at No. 8 had only Kamber, a lad of perhaps fourteen, and Hérul Nisa, a small girl of ten or so, to help them. With his varied crafts the Ustád must have accumulated some considerable wealth, and he had now betrothed his only surviving son to a girl a shade "above" them in rank, belonging to a family in which Prince Ghazan Khán had been fostered, and who had thus acquired the extra land, etc., which is the recognized recompense for fostering royalty. We supposed that it was a desire to live up to this distinguished new connection (possibly it was a stipulation of the bride's people) that prompted his intention to set the young son, Kamber, up in a house of his own instead of bringing the new wife to share the parents' home.

Whatever lay behind this departure from custom, Nadíro sent his Hérul Nisa one day to tell me that he was setting out to "smite his poplars" if I would care to come. It was a *very* hot morning and I was deep in something else, but of course you'd never see anything if you weren't ready to take chances as they turn up. So I shouldered my camera and tripod, seized my long walking-stick (which is a great aid to climbing walls or leaping down them), on which I had made notches every foot to serve for measuring distances, and set off with Hérul Nisa. "Where is father's poplar garden?" I asked. The Aliábád people have a bewildering way of possessing odd scraps of ground dotted about all over the place, just according as they have taken up one plot or another of the sometime royal land. "Oh, quite near," she said. Everything is "quite near" to these active people, who think less of a 500-foot climb than we think of running a hundred yards to the pillar-box at the corner. It was, in fact, a hot, vertical half-mile over the roughest ground without even a track. Here on a rugged patch of stony, steep-sloping ground, carefully walled in, I found the whole of No. 8 and several neighbours busily setting about the felling job. One man scrambled up and attached a rope near the top of the fated tree. Two or three laid hold of the rope and stood at some distance to pull in the right direction, while the old Ustád himself skilfully hacked a triangular bite out of the trunk near to the ground and then axed away. It was only a few minutes till the slender poplar crashed down. Then Kamber and his friends hacked off the few remaining uppermost branches—the lower ones had been cut long ago—and the womenfolk and young people all clustered along the trunk to peel off the bark, taking care to get it off in strips as long and wide as possible; for bark strips are useful for many things. Some of the flakes were 3 or 4 feet long and 8 or 9 inches wide. They would be kept to make large drum-like containers for storage purposes. While the men proceeded to deal with the next tree, the women and young people filled shoulder baskets with chips and twigs and branches and carried them home to store. "Lots of firewood for a long time to come," smiled Bibi Anjir to me gleefully as she limped away as fast and as surefooted as a girl, despite the stiff leg.

I helped, of course, with gathering up the firewood and the bark, but I was never allowed to shoulder a basket. I would have done it gladly enough many a time, but what with silly shoes (which always provoked my companions' sympathy: "It would be so much easier for you to walk safely barefoot, Mother"; I wondered, seeing that my incompetent, soft feet had been for half a century encased in foolish footgear!) and unpractised muscles a cross-country scramble unladen required all my attention. In any case, however, they would never hear of my carrying anything—"the Great must not do that," they said, and as we were enjoying so many privileges of "the Great," we had to pay the recognized penalties.

When the trees were all prostrate, I measured the effective poles that remained and found they ran from 50 to 60 feet: the original trees must have stood 60 or 70 feet high. The Ustád had put the saplings in himself when he walled and planted the "garden" twenty years or so before. Good timber like this is a sound investment. Sixteen good poplars go to the making of a house; up to twenty may be needed if they are smaller. If people are definitely quitting an old house for a new they will dismantle the former for the sake of rafters and cupboards, and you will occasionally see the shell of an old house standing derelict. But the cases of house-building which we actually came across were the hiving-off of son or brother and required new wood. A man who has no trees of his own to cut must, of course, buy them from some neighbour, and this, with the carpentry, will be the major expense.

The Ustád had already levelled the ground for the new house beside his own, and soon the trenches were dug for the foundations, and the walls erected, every stone for which old Nadíro totted down the mountain side on his own back.

We often said to each other : "These Hunza people are no artists; that's one reason perhaps why they are so sensible and so like ourselves." But when we looked at the millions and myriads of stones that held their fields, each one in its place, and all fitted as neatly as a jigsaw puzzle, when we examined the lovely curves and tapering points of their five-pronged winnowing forks and the lashings of gut or sinew that bound them, we agreed that they were artists after all—in their own medium.

For many months we saw Nadíro spending every spare moment on the site, squaring and planing and trimming the posts and rafters, door-frames and cupboards that will be the pride of his posterity. He was lavishing great care on capitals, and ornamenting them and the lintels with fancy carvings. Except in the house of a special carpenter, carving is not indulged in in Hunza (a great contrast in this respect to Chitral, or even Yasin, where the Chitral tradition has penetrated). The few carved doors and windows that you see in the old forts and mosques at Áltít and Báltít probably date back to the Balti craftsmen who built them. There is a little old mosque in Aliábád attractively carved, but no one could tell us for certain whether some foreign craftsman had done the work or local men. The ordinary peasant house, at any rate, has none—Hunza peasant architecture is essentially "functional."

Chapter 18

SEPTEMBER HARVEST

SUMMER is a breathless time in the Hunza fields. No sooner does the ripening grain show a fine "fox-brown" than a line of five or six men and women attack it in unison. They do not "reap" in our sense of the word. They squat in that inimitably convenient way that the East has preserved for working—no backs bent with stooping, no knees worn out with kneeling—and grasp a full handful of the ripe stalks and pull up roots and all; first right, then left; clap the two together to shake off the all-too-valuable earth; lay the bundle behind them; shuffle on a pace and repeat. The fields are small and in an incredibly short space of time a golden field is prostrate and the ground carpeted with neatly aligned rows of swathes. It is beautiful to see a party at work: father and mother, daughters, sons, and wives; they space themselves and keep their line as exactly as soldiers on parade, yet each works individually, each at his own pace and in his own way—without haste and without pause. They possess rude iron sickles, but when these are used at all they are not used to *cut*, but merely to pull against, if the crop is more than usually deep-rooted.

When the *shandiming* (cut crops) have lain a little and been turned over once or twice they are tied into sheaves and gathered into piles, some as big as a man can carry, others smaller to suit a boy—according to the "man-power" available. A double goat's hair rope is slipped round the waist of the pile and ingeniously knotted so as to leave two shoulder loops. The man or boy flings himself down backwards on to it, slips his arms through the loops and hitches the rope fast. Then some kindly bystander gives a touch to the load from behind, and by a gymnastic miracle the bearer staggers to his feet, almost invisible under his tossing burden, and sets off at a trot up a steep flight of rough stones, or a boulder track, or a rude wooden ladder laid against a high field wall, to the threshing-floor. Beside this, a stack is built by other workers as the loads come in. A core of several upright sheaves forms the centre; layers of other sheaves are laid symmetrically round these, heads to centre, roots out, till the stack is 5 or 6 feet high. The priceless grain is thus beyond the greed of passing goats, and if rain threatens a carpet flung on top suffices to keep the whole erection dry. The moment the *shandiming* are off the ground the children drive their tiny flocks, one minute cow, a couple of sheep and goats, on to the empty field, and the hungry beasts greedily snatch at every green blade of grass or weed they chance to sight. There is cruelly little. In the early days the crop is diligently and systematically weeded, and even after the grain has reached some height the field is invaded every few days by the women and children in the hopes that some further weeds may be detected and carried off for fodder. The two stages of weeding are quite distinct. I was much laughed at one day, when the second stage had set in, for asking a party of crouching women whether they were "weeding." "Oh, no," they said, "weeding time is long since over; we are just fetching some green stuff for the cow." Both weedings are done so thoroughly that the expectant beasts who invade the new-reaped field have quickly cleared the few remaining stalks.

When the fields are temporarily empty a great feeling of freedom pervades the land. The boys rejoice in the rare luxury of flat open spaces for foot polo, tip-cat, races, rounders, and a dozen other games; the weavers seize the chance to lay out their warp and the girls romp and play ball—"the fields are free" is joyfully remarked on every side. DL and I rejoiced no less in being able to walk side by side on the flat—an experience foregone these many months—and take short-cuts from one farmstead to another without the usual boulder-jumping scramble.

But the freedom of the fields is short-lived.

While one party is busy on the threshing floor, the empty field is watered, ploughed, and sown again, and before the barley and wheat are well in store the bare fields are green again with the second crops, which seem to understand that they must grow at the double or be doomed.

There are two major kinds of millet grown: the one (called *bay*) has graceful feathery heads not unlike rice, but that the grain is smaller; the other (*cha*) has a tight-packed ear, also with tiny grains like what we call "canary seed." There are many varieties of each. When we arrived in mid-July the barley had all been reaped, and we just saw the wheat come in, but we were happily in time to see the second crops sprout, ripen, and fall. There are also two kinds of buckwheat sown. The sweet buckwheat is a lovely plant with fine dark leaves (something the shape of lilac leaves) and a glorious head of pink feathery blossom; the bitter is a smaller plant with lighter yellower leaves and a minute, unimpressive yellow flower. Neither of the buckwheats is really *liked* as food, and the bitter is definitely *dis*liked, but *they are food*, and a skilful housewife contrives to mix her flour so as to eke out the wheat and barley with a proportion of the buckwheats that is not too unappetizing and not inflict more "bitter buckwheat scones" on her family than she can help. The only reason that the bitter buckwheat is grown at all is that it can better stand the onset of winter, and, if the first crop is delayed, or if winter sets in untimely soon, it is a safer thing to gamble on.

When the terraced fields of Hunza are full again, with waving *bay* and stately *cha* and seas of pink blossom send their delicate perfume drifting over the mountain side; when the trim field walls are vertical rock-gardens with wild thyme and the like crowding their crevices; when the fruit trees are still in full leaf, each variety of apricot turning a different shade of gold and red and flame; and bunches of green and red grapes are ripening under the pergolas of vines, while over all the barren mountain sides glare down and the snow peaks tower into a sky of burning blue—there are no words to tell the country's loveliness.

By the beginning of October the proud millets are laid low.

They are treated differently from the two first crops. You do not throw the whole stalks with roots and ear on to the threshing-floor. You tie a bundle up with one of its own stalks, then cut the ears off and thresh them by themselves, stacking the straw separately. I would scramble up when the millet was being beheaded, sit down with the workers, take out my penknife and ask leave to help. It was the greatest fun. Of course I could not work nearly as fast as others, but in itself the work is light and it makes opportunity for easy conversation. When I first turned up at one or other of several threshing floors—there were a dozen or so within comparatively easy reach—there would be only a couple of women who always made me enthusiastically welcome, but in a few minutes the mad Englishwomen (as I presume I must have appeared) was spotted from afar and quite a crowd soon gathered round; most would come and join in; a few would just politely stare. I always found it far harder to talk when there were a lot. The youngsters all crowded in behind me, and the elder ones constituted an informal advisory committee, for "Mother" was curiously thick-headed and not always sure whether an odd-looking ear was diseased and ought to be thrown away or was merely a little unripe but quite good. I consulted them in doubtful cases till I got to know; then I found that the young monkeys were beginning to think it a joke to pull my leg by misadvising. Fortunately I had learnt the difference before this bright idea struck them, and so I could turn the tables—"a beautiful farmer you'll make if you don't know a bad ear when you see it," said I; "I'm sorry for your poor wife, but perhaps you'll never get one!" and the joker slunk back a pace amid the titters of his friends. At first all my offers to "help" were met by considerate remonstrances—"You'll spoil your hands; it would be a pity." But I laughed and said "They'll wash!" I have always loathed to see a woman with milk-white hands, massaged and creamed and manicured and obviously useless, and have taken a—probably perverse—pride in my own square, ugly, little-cared-for, useful paws. In what odd ways one's snobbishness will out! But I must confess that even the mildest field work tears your skin most uncommonly.

When the threshing floor is heaped with ears, some people turn cows on to trample them; some people prefer to beat the heap with sticks. It depends, I expect, how many cows you have without borrowing, or how many stout arms to wield the flail. It is rather fun to see a family beating, even the children hammering away with tiny poles. The Hunzukuts are kind to their kiddies and fond of them, but have happily no time to spoil them, and as the children have always something new and interesting to do they are very rarely troublesome. If they are, some grown-up will give them a mild smack on the head (the little cap prevents its hurting much) and all is well again. If a child is sick they carry it out with them to the fields (no one can be spared to stay at home to mind it) and chuck a cloth over it to keep the flies off, and let it lie there in peace till it feels better. The youngsters work just as long as they feel interested, then fade away and play for a bit, and join another group and work a while again. There seems to be no attempt to force them or even overtly to encourage them. Their own instinct is to copy the grown-ups or next-older brother. Yet the sense of responsibility wakes early; a five- or six-year-old is often in charge of the two-year-old toddler, rejoices in steadying him as he tries to walk or in mounting him on the shoulders to cross a water-channel or climb a wall. We used sometimes to feel a little anxious about the baby's fate, but its mother never did. I have never heard a Hunza mother shout "Don't do that, darling," or "Take care, you'll drop the baby," or "Don't go so near the edge, you'll fall." Hunza consists of "edges"—the house-roof, the field, the reservoir, the cliff—and no doubt Nature in the course of centuries has weeded out the stocks that lose their balance. Our occasional solicitude was the cause of much merriment; we could not always suppress a "Take care, you'll slip," and this became a standing joke amongst our smaller friends. If all other conversation failed a jesting cry from someone of "Take care, Mother, you'll fall" would set the ball rolling again. Jolly little scamps they are, and pleasant companions for a walk. I counted seven in front and three behind me one day, all between five and seven, with two or three babies mounted on the others' backs. They all thought it rather a thrill to come along and see me safe home and hang about for a salaam to David before they dashed off to some fresh amusement.

As soon as DL was better I began exploring further afield. At first I used to be a little shy of just barging down any rocky track that seemed to end up in someone's back yard. But these tracks are all public ways, and just when you think you have reached a cul-de-sac and are about to plunge into a house, the path gives a sudden twist and leads you on.

No matter how far I strayed from home and my well-known families, the people came up to their garden walls or out on to their flat roofs—crowds of them sometimes—to shout a welcome and good wishes, and to ask where I was going to and what I was doing. This is the recognized Hunza greeting, not a fatuous, unanswered "How do you do?" countered by another. The answer is : "I'm going to fetch firewood from the orchard," or "I'm getting some green stuff for the cow," or "I've been taking the beasts to water," or "I'm off to get some grain ground at the mill," or "I've been spending the day with mother's people." No one "goes for a walk" to get exercise after a futile day of sitting still. So I was driven to reply that I had come "to see the country." "And a good idea, too," they would respond politely; "and do you like it?" Then I could truthfully say how beautiful it was, and how much I admired their walls, and what lovely air and water and fruit they have, but that most of all I liked the friendly people. Then they grinned with pleasure. When I sometimes risked a short cut and found myself at the top of a huge wall with no visible means of getting further, a kindly man or boy would leave his work to come and point out the almost invisible flight of projecting stones or pull down a side wall to let me out into a tiny lane, and always he would offer his hand to help me. I duly thanked him and perhaps added apologetically: "We haven't walls like yours in our country, and I'm not very good at climbing them." "No, and of course you've got shoes on," he would say sympathetically, "and you're not young."

Twice I found my way down to the very edge of the river bank. The river itself, grey and rock-tossed it looked, dashing capriciously from side to side between its beaches, was 500 or 600 feet sheer below, and the great crumbly earthen cliffs on each side were most ominous-looking precipices. There are no paths down them except where a side gorge comes in at intervals. At the spot where I struck the bank there had been a great fall of cliff not long before which had completely carried away a new aqueduct they were—rather too hopefully—trying to engineer across the face of it. If the aqueduct had been successful it would have coaxed some water from the Hasanábád glacier on to a jutting promontory, potentially fertile, but at the moment as bare as the palm of your hand. Six men went over and two of them were killed. Risks like this are all in the day's work in Hunza. People were still prospecting for a more hopeful alignment, but my amateur eyes could see no earthly possibility of getting anything to cling to the friable face of those terrifying cliffs. Meantime I stood well back from the edge! It was pathetic to see gardens and trees within two inches of the treacherous brink and to realize that the farmer on whose land I stood had lost a fertile field or two and half his orchard. I noted that I must go back some day when the light was right and see whether (without committing suicide) I could get a photograph right down the gorge with Raka, of course, rearing herself up in the background. When the light was good it was still very hot in the sun (88° in the shade on an October afternoon), and rocky scrambles over shadeless boulders with a climb of some hundreds of feet to get home were not exactly restful, and I'm not so young!

One autumn morning when I was on the prowl I found a man just about to turn on a small team of cows to thresh a pile of millet heads. He and his children were busy with this in the centre of the floor, while a neighbour and *his* family were beheading another variety at one side. Two or even three neighbours seem amicably to share one threshing floor so as not to waste valuable ground. So I squatted down as usual with my penknife and joined the beheading family and watched the threshing. Only three cows were in the team this time—the millet-heads make a very small heap in comparison with the wheat—the usual "Ha! Ha! Ha!" encouraging them and the usual dung-dish unostentatiously circulating behind. It was an interesting, very typical scene, and not a hundred yards below our house. I sent a message up to David (there is always a small candidate to act proudly as messenger) to tell him that he might care to bring his camera. In a few minutes he was picking his way cautiously down the breakneck track while a great cheer of welcome rang from the little crowd. They had all been genuinely concerned about his illness, and were delighted to see that he was better and able to come down and watch things himself. It was his first visit to one of the field working parties. He sat on a low wall in a tiny speck of shade, made friendly chat all round, and was a great social success.

While I pottered each morning in the fields, enjoying myself among the people, he was usually hard at work indoors with Qudrat Ullah, taking notes of how the irrigation is managed and the system on which the water is distributed by clans and families, and working out genealogical trees. This latter is a weary affair but most useful, for it gives you insight into all their marriage alliances, how many children each family has, how many boys and how many girls, who is allowed to marry whom, and what the relationship terms are, both in the vocative between the various members of a family group, and in the third person when others are talking of them—a highly complicated but most instructive subject. An elder brother will address the younger by one method, while the younger will use a more respectful term towards the elder; all the younger boys of a family will use to their *eldest* sister the same respectful form of address as to their eldest brother, though to the uninitiated it would seem to imply that she was a male. A man addresses his wife's father and mother in precisely the same terms and with the same respect as his own. A child's "uncle" is a mother's brother only; the father's brother is "Little Father" or "Big Father" according as the speaker's own father (about whom there is no ambiguity) is older or younger than the uncle concerned. The children of brothers who all share the one home speak of each other as brother and sister, unless there is need to be more explicit, in which case they will elaborate the statement: "She is my sister, at least: the daughter of my Little Father."

David sadly bemoaned the hideous "waste" of nine weeks spent in illness and convalescence; but in fact he managed to put in a lot of most valuable spade work. Even in the periods of weakness between the fever attacks he got a good deal done—including the Introduction to his first volume of the Burushaski—and during his convalescence he worked steadily and increasingly long hours every day, though he was not able to move freely about the countryside. Qudrat Ullah proved extremely intelligent. David suggested a subject he would like to go into—the rotation of crops; the clans; marriage or funeral rites, etc., etc.—and Qudrat Ullah went home to ponder and collect fuller information than he himself could give offhand, from his entire family, including the elders. Then he wrote out the facts in Burushaski (using still the inadequate and unsatisfactory Arabic script) and came a day or two later to read his "essay." This David took down verbatim—thus getting at least all the relevant technical vocabulary, asked further details, and suggested further lines of enquiry, drawing by this means on a far larger range of informants than he could hope to get into touch with single-handed. As soon as he was able to get about he was able to discuss matters on the spot with a background of knowledge that made it easier for him to understand the less sophisticated speakers, and from their talk and his own observation to check and supplement the information Qudrat Ullah had supplied. This method worked admirably. Nor was Qudrat Ullah his only sedentary informant: the levies and others took their turn in the study.

It proved immensely valuable to have the carefully dictated manuscripts from Qudrat Ullah, with supplementary notes and comments. As soon as these had been worked through, I took them one by one and typed them out in triplicate, so that even if all our manuscript notebooks were to perish by fire or flood or avalanche—which heaven forfend!—we should still have *some* written record to supplement our memory. The two spare copies were posted home to the Bank in separate batches at longish intervals for safe custody till our return. In some ways the typing seemed waste of time that ought preferably to be spent out among the people themselves, but there is a limit to the amount of "field work" you can usefully put into one day, and it was invaluable for me to have to work carefully through the information David had assembled in the study while I was more frivolously employed outside.

I seem to have wandered from the harvest! There is not much more to mention. When the sweet buckwheat was ripe and the gay, sweet-smelling flowers succeeded in due course by small black seeds, when the plants are "covered with black flies" as they picturesquely put it, they are gathered to the threshing floor and beaten with sticks till the seeds fall off and the straw can be stooked to dry. The less romantic bitter buckwheat follows suit, and last of all the potatoes are dug just as at home. The potato crop is much valued, and due credit is given to the British who introduced it: "We can't imagine how we used to manage without potatoes," they say.

After this the fields were bare again—for good. It almost brought tears to my eyes to see the jolly little threshing-floors, where I had spent so many happy hours, flooded with the rest of the fields and ploughed up for the winter. About half the fields round us were left fallow till the spring, the other half were hastily resown with winter wheat, whose early shoots were the first green to greet our eyes next year.

Chapter 19

HARVEST THANKSGIVING

THERE are a couple of minor items of the autumn harvest I have omitted to mention. In Aliábád, the widest and most gently sloping bay of the Hunza mountain side, there is for one short stretch of perhaps a mile a patch of ground above the level of possible fields before the steep cliff face begins. Through and above this run the third and fourth of our horizontal watercourses, offshoots from the Berber Channel that waters the higher levels of Báltít and derives also from the great glacier of the Ulter Ber, but takes off much higher up than the Dála. Sufficient water can occasionally be spared from these two channels (which in the main are needed to irrigate high-lying "gardens" of trees) to flood these rocky slopes, which then bring forth that rarest of Hunza products, natural grass. These *toqs*, as they are called, are divided into strips by loose stone walls and used as grazing grounds by whoever leases them. Two or even four families often combine to share a *toq*, and on your walks you will find children of various sizes in charge of a few animals; a small girl may be sitting gravely alone practising embroidery stitches on a strip of calico, a boy may be twisting the string of horse-gut for his catapult bow, a group may be romping together or playing a game like rounders with a home-spun cap for ball, or "horses" where half the players are mounted on the others' backs and the pairs charge each other to a fall, and any rider thrown becomes in turn a horse. When these livelier games begin to pall, a couple will withdraw to the edge of the little channel and scratch a draught-board on a level patch of ground and play with pebbles white and grey as men. The board is formed of triangles whose apexes (apices? no, no!) are the "squares" and any man can move and take in any direction. It requires quite as much skill and provides quite as much fun as draughts played in our way. There are half a dozen other games of the sort, roughly variants of "marbles," all played with pebbles and governed by complicated rules which we only partially mastered.

We used to watch Nimo, of No. 7, a jolly, bright-eyed mite of eight or nine, pass our window every morning about half-past six, sturdily carrying an empty shoulder basket as she herded her two or three small cows off to the *toq*; sometimes she was taking charge of a small brother or sister as well. Just before nightfall, after a whole summer day on the mountain side, she would return, driving her animals and stooping slightly under her load. One evening in the very early days I stopped her to ask *whose* Nimo she was (their names duplicate each other like our Joans, Anns, and Dorises), and "What have you got in your basket there?" With courteous surprise at being asked a question to which there could be only one answer: "Why, to-day's cow-dung." Sure enough I soon discovered that every little cowherd conscientiously gathers every scrap of the cow's daily output and brings it home to the manure store in the barn—there are no untidy outdoor middens to spoil the landscape or defile the air.

Another day we met Khano of No. 3, one of our first boy-friends, breathlessly chivvying a cow uphill to a spot where he had safely dumped his baby sister Guláb, in charge of his basket. "Hullo, did she run away from you?" "She did, the villain, but I've got her back, and look, Mother, I've lost nothing," he said, as he proudly displayed the contents of his looped-up cloak. He threw his treasure into the basket and resumed his attentions to Guláb, while the cow resigned herself to orthodox grazing. He was playing with the little girl, patiently coaxing her to totter a step or two and flop into his waiting arms, and throwing up little stones for her to catch.

The tenderness of the bigger children to the babies is a beautiful thing to watch. I never saw boy or girl out of temper with a baby brother, sister, or cousin, or resentful of having one in charge. When the bigger ones are busy in some momen-

PLATE XIII:
Young Friends

1. Nimo and sister with the baby.
(*See p.* 144)

3. Zulfi.

2. Dádo with Akíl Sháh aged two.
(*See p.* 87)

4. Kháno with baby sister Guláb.

tarily empty field, playing team games of tipcat or chucking stones at a mark—they have dozens of admirable games, with rules strictly adhered to—the small ones sit about and look on or amuse themselves dabbling in water if there is any or making mud-pies. A group of youngsters were playing round me one day when a tiny girl unaccountably took fright and set up a terrified howl. A big boy stooped to comfort her: "There, there, don't cry, don't be afraid," he said soothingly, and wrapped his cloak round her to shut out whatever was the disturbing sight (I rather think it was I), and patted her reassuringly. "That will be your little sister?" said I. "No, no," was the answer, "I don't know really whose kid it is."

As autumn approaches and no further growth can be hoped from the grass, these mountain meadows are painstakingly reaped, *cut* this time, with the blunt iron sickles—for the roots must be left for next year—and the tiny bunches of grass tied up. There will be a few longer, tougher stalks in each double handful, and these are doubled back over the shorter ones and the bundle tied twice, once at the base where it is fattest, and once near the top where the bent heads are caught. These bundles are then laid out in the sun—a benevolent accessory to harvest that never faileth—and gathered in to form part of the winter fodder. Then follows an incredible sight: every inch of the mountain side is painstakingly swept by the Nímos and Shamúlis, whose besoms are minute thorn bushes. Every pellet of sheep or goat, every half inch of stubbly grass above the root is garnered into the tiny shoulder baskets and added to the manure. When you have seen one strip of ground thus treated you might think the job was done; not a bit of it. A few days later Nímo and Shamúli are at it again and yet again, till not one speck of animal or vegetable matter remains. You can imagine that there is no need when walking round Hunza to "pick your steps" as in an English meadow.

Every individual leaf, from garden or orchard, from water-course or steep hill-garden, is similarly swept up and stored; these dry leaves are the staple winter food for the stalled beasts —no wonder the milk lacks cream-content and the sheep is bare of fat! No wonder that I shudder now to see our autumn bonfires recklessly consuming grass-cuttings and leaves that would be worth gold in Nímo's home.

Burushaski is an amazingly rich language, but it has evolved no word for "litter-lout." Go where you will in lane or courtyard, over field or bare hillside, you will not see an eggshell or a fleck of wool or a nutshell lying about. Hunza must be, bar none, the cleanest and the tidiest spot on earth. If a child is lucky enough to be given a few apricot stones he will crack them on a rock, eat the kernels with gusto, and gather up the shells for mother's fire. Only in a couple of the narrow lanes of the deserted fort did we stumble on a cast-away rag or two. When a homespun cloak has served father for three years' hard work, it will descend to a son, or be handed on to an orphan relation; when it is torn and tattered past repair it is carefully plucked to pieces, washed, beaten, and re-spun to make a girl's cloak, for her work is less strenuous than the boy's, and the re-spun cloak is stout enough for her and quite as warm.

Whatever the theoretical tenets of the Maulai (Ismaili) dissenters may be—and of these Professor Ivanow can best speak—the simple Hunzukuts has evolved for himself quite the most practical and admirable modification of Islam that I have ever seen or heard of. He does not veil his womenfolk nor banish them to separate quarters, but treats them as equal partners in field and home. His standard of morals is so high that when a young husband goes abroad, he trusts his young wife to the care of his father and brothers without misgiving. We heard no case of such a trust being abused. He retains his own custom of exogamic marriage between the clans and the normal first-cousin marriage of Islam (though recognized as religiously allowable and occasionally practised by the upper families) savours to the ordinary peasant of incest, and is in fact avoided, though not in principle taboo; he also, as we have noted, preserves his own fastidious and wholesome ideas about sanitation, and keeps his running water scrupulously pure. No archbishops or bishops (whom he would term *pirs*), and no professional priests or *mullas* reside in his territories, for which no doubt he has to thank some tacit concordat between his wise ruler and His Highness the Agha Khan, the spiritual head of the Ismailis. A few of the peasant farmers have learned to read—as some have learned to carpenter—and they have copied out such essential passages of their sacred Persian books as enable them to preside with due solemnity at a name-giving, a burial, or a betrothal. The Mir appoints a sufficient number of these modestly literate men to be khalifas, and lend a dignity to such ceremonies. When you need their services you send for one—as we send for the plumber when our pipes have burst. He performs his duty, shares with honour in the ensuing family feasting, accepts some small gift in kind according to the family's resources, and goes his way to resume his normal work in his own fields.

We knew Afiato of No. 6, for three months or more, as an obliging neighbour and father of a large batch of our child friends; we admired his skill in ploughing and threshing, and the hard work he had put into levelling an intractable patch of hill within a stone's throw of our house and converting it into a vegetable garden before we realized that he was a khalifa or lay-priest. There was nothing in dress or manner to distinguish him from his fellows; he offered no unsought advice and censored no one's morals but his own. If Hunza is, as I believe, the tidiest corner of God's earth, it is also the least priest-ridden, and the absence of fanaticism and superstition is as remarkable and refreshing as the absence of litter. There is an atmosphere of mental independence that makes the air of Hunza spiritually bracing.

What the pre-Islamic cults of Hunza were—and traces of them are slight though DL may have some conjectures to offer about them later—the Hunzukuts of to-day are extraordinarily enlightened.[1] Their folk-lore (very probably borrowed) may tell of apparitions and miracles, but they look for no marvels in their life of everyday, they see no ghosts and fear no Evil Eye. They indulge in no gymnastic prayers, they keep no Fast of Ramazan, they travel on no Hajj. I saw only one man turn Mecca-wards to pray, and that was our Kashmiri

[1] In astounding contrast to their magic- and witch-ridden Shin neighbours in Gilgit (V. *J.R.A.S.*, July, 1929, *The Supernatural in the Folklore of the Gilgit Region*).

sweeper; I heard only one muezzin sound the Call to Prayer—and saw no one pay heed to it. He was chanting from a cliff in the Mir's garden, and the Mir gathers round him craftsmen of every sort. There are a few shrines in the country reputed holy—including two burial places of Moses within a few hundred yards of each other on one mountain side—where a few rags on sticks flutter unconvincingly in the wind; and one, the shrine of Baba Ghundi in Chupursan, some seven days' march above Báltít, is the object of an occasional pilgrimage. On Tuesdays and Fridays there are said to be services in the House of Assembly, which has supplanted the older Shiah mosque, but I never observed one of our servants or neighbours absent himself from work to go to them.

Yet the people are by no means without faith. It is difficult to know exactly what even church-going Christians of our own country effectively believe—it is impossible to be sure what one effectively believes oneself—so I can offer only a tentative guess as to the average person's simple credo. The Hunzukuts hold, I think, a comforting, unquestioning faith in a good and kindly God, whose ways they cannot profess to understand. They meet bereavement with a murmur that "there is no remedy against the will of God"; they bury their loved ones with genuine sorrow, but without anxiety. They feel that "it is well with the child," and vaguely trust that some day, somewhere, somehow, they will meet again. They assume as axiomatic that God asks of them diligence and truth, fair-dealing and goodwill. They are hard-working and thrifty, tolerant to others; kind and affectionate in the home, gentle to children and the aged; generous beyond their means to the orphan; truthful and just; and they go about their daily work in the happy confidence that God is well pleased. If they din no perfunctory prayers into His ears, there are occasions when they heartily and humbly pray, as will presently be seen.

The Hunzukuts is no mystic, no poet, no artist. This life claims his full attention if he is to live at all; philosophic speculation about "fixed fate, freewill, fore-knowledge absolute" does not line his brow or disturb his rest, nor does he "keep in duty through the toilsome day, because of praise or blame that comes at night." I may be misinterpreting his attitude of mind. These are not subjects you can thresh out as easily as the wheat, and neither his vocabulary nor mine would have sufficed to tackle them. But this I can vouch for, that every face you see looks restfully content, breaks readily into a happy smile; that there are in Hunza no nervous gestures and no haunted eyes, and in normal life no irritable words. There is little amiss with a faith which spells happiness and high-principled living without debasing fear of Hell or over-conscious hope of Heaven.

When the final crops of every kind are safely in, the first duty of the paterfamilias is to take stock of the year's yield. So much is set aside for seed-grain, and not the direst shortage will tempt him to violate the sanctity of this; so much is set aside for rent (if he is a tenant) or for the tax due on any craft he pursues—the miller pays a very small tax on his mill, the weaver on his loom-pit, the khalifa on his learning; and all pay (alas!) a sum as "Peter's pence" to their spiritual head, the Agha Khan. Next he calculates the "emergency reserve" that may be needed for hospitality or charity during the coming year; this also is scrupulously put aside unground. On the rest he and his family must live till next harvest, under the careful rationing of the senior housewife, the importance of whose rôle I have already stressed.

The period of comparative—well-earned and welcome—rest that ensues, is inaugurated by a solemn watch-night service of prayer and thanksgiving in the House of Assembly. One of our main difficulties in the early days was to get due notice of such events beforehand. Our people were slow to realize that the normal routine of their affairs could really interest us. The first news we had of this Harvest Thanksgiving Service was one late evening in October when Dádo casually said as he bade us good-night: "I'm off now to the all-night prayer." In answer to our questions he told us that the Assembly Hall and the women's annex would be packed with the entire population, and that the khalifas in rotation would keep up all night a reading of the sacred Persian books and of the Qur'an. "And shall you be able to understand all that they read?" "Oh no, of course not; but we shall hear the names of God and the Imams, and we shall pray."

Further, it appeared that while the non-stop worship went on inside the Hall, a great communal feast would be prepared outside to be enjoyed at daybreak. We sent Dádo off with our good wishes; when he was gone I raided his pantry, assembled materials for early morning tea, and set the alarm-clock. Up we hopped before dawn and made our way, rather sleepy and unwashed, down to the open space "At the Gate" of the old fort, to see whether we could without offence look on at the morning feast. As we drew near I wondered whether it was altogether wise. If you think of the fanaticism of Pathans or Arabs towards Unbelievers . . . we were still new to the country and had not sounded the depths of Hunza tolerance. Already, however, we had considerable trust in it, and this trust was not misplaced. As we were seen coming round the corner, two headmen of the clans came out to greet us, and a chorus of spontaneous, evidently gratified greeting went up from the crowd. Every inch of the open space was packed with boys and men, while women and girls crowded in the background and round every corner, but the most of them had already hurried home to get their houses ready.

In the centre on a large carpet was a pile of cooked beasts presented by the more well-to-do—two oxen, fifteen sheep, and goats. Round this six men were crouching with a log in front of each, disjointing limbs and chopping off chunks of meat and bone with an adze. Beside the carpet were ranged ten or a dozen immense iron cauldrons, quite 3 feet 6 inches across and 2 feet deep or more. Each of these was full to the very brim of a rich porridge that looked like soft dripping. There were two kinds: one called *sherbet* (but not remotely like the sherbet of Persia) was made of flour and butter well cooked and stirred; the other, of unground wheat similarly blent with butter, was called *harísa*. The humbler families according to their means had contributed these ingredients. Some of the great cooking-pots were still standing on large iron tripods over the ashes of the night's fire. Most of the audience had wooden basins in their hands, a few had aluminium ones, a few had even iron buckets. Several people were busy serving, while the headmen acted as masters of the ceremonies. Every household—there are two hundred all told in Aliábád—was entitled to carry off one chunk of meat and one ladleful each of *sherbet* and *harisa* for each mouth at home.

As always in this happy place, the company was full of jokes, laughter, and good temper. There was no hustling, no jostling, no attempt by anyone to secure more than his due share. Any person who had lent one of the big cauldrons (they are costly vessels brought up from down country) was granted an extra "mouthful" as hire, and anyone who had lent a penknife for cutting up was given an extra chunk of meat impaled on it. The people who had lent the tripods were not entitled to anything extra; this apparent injustice was thus explained: "You are fond of your cooking-cauldron; you are fond of your penknife; but no one could possibly be fond of a tripod."

We moved about for some time among the crowd, greeting old acquaintances and making new ones, then the people insisted that we must sit down, cleared one of the stone sofas, dashed into the Assembly Hall and brought out a carpet and spread it for us, while one of the headmen came and sat by explaining the procedure of the festival and naming the various utensils. As the light grew David took a few photographs, but by that time most of the carcases had been hacked to bits and a large number of households, having got their share, had gone home to celebrate a sort of family Christmas dinner with it. Nor for the first time, still less for the last, I regretted my lack of enterprise in sticking to my old familiar quarter-plate camera with its lens working only to F.6.3. David with his 3.5's could get photographs in much weaker light than I.

They insisted on pressing on us a "share" for each of our servants. How can you assess, how hope to repay, the generosity of these hospitable people? Remember that hardly any house has more than *just enough* to eat for the year; yet they must share their feast with our relatively pampered retainers! We could only gratefully accept and as a poor return offer the headman some money for distribution as they thought best "to the orphans and the poor." Hunza has, of course, no charitable societies, but everyone is related distantly or immediately to other families, and no one, however poor or orphaned, is allowed to starve.

It was sad to think that when this harvest thanksgiving came round again next year we should no longer be in Hunza. If we had been we should, I am certain, have been allowed to attend the all-night prayer. But, so soon after our arrival, to have suggested this might have been bad policy or doubtful taste even if we had had sufficient notice to sound the feeling of headmen and khalifas. We were in every detail most scrupulously careful to give rise to no anxieties by prematurely taking liberties, even such as would be gladly accorded. The slightest breath of resentment or suspicion roused in even one household might have spoiled all our future relations with our neighbours or given trouble to the Mir. It was wiser to forgo an occasional experience, however interesting and unique, than to take risks.

Chapter 20

HUNZA BABIES

EARLY one October morning I saw Naját going off to the mill with a little sheepskin bag on her shoulder. She looked even more radiant than usual as she stopped to talk. After the usual interchanges: "Have you heard our news? Bibi Gímo's baby boy has been born!" This was splendid. No. 1 already possessed four girls, one married, Shukuru almost marriageable and already growing her hair as a preliminary, and our two special friends, Shamúli and Bano, and two boys, Derwish and Man Ali Shah; a third son was the wanted thing. Mother and baby were doing well, and the household was overjoyed.

I took pains to ascertain how soon I might call to offer my congratulations—the eighth day was best. So I set Zaidu to bake biscuits with butter and treacle, which he was sure would be acceptable, and I borrowed Qudrat Ullah for half an hour to coach me in the correct phraseology. When the great day came I threaded my rough way down the lane and turned in at the hospitable door in the wall, through which I had several times entered their garden but never yet their house. Here I was greeted by the four youngest, all looking as pleased as if they had by themselves conjured the baby into being. They led me through the byre, past the cow, who also had a festive air on her bed of nice clean straw, and into the living-room. It was beautifully bright with sunshine pouring through the smokehole, and as neat and clean as a new pin. The chief sleeping bench had a red felt carpet on it and had been left empty for me. On the other dais, also gaily carpeted, Bibi Gímo sat in state beside the cradle. She was looking so fresh and young and tidy that I hardly knew her. Hitherto I had seen her a little dusty as she worked in the fields and somewhat tired perhaps as her time drew on. To-day she had on a gay, green cap, new cotton dress and trousers of bright chintz, and her hair was beautifully brushed and braided. I gave her hearty greetings before accepting the seat of honour left for me. On the cross-bench sat old grandfather, looking very handsome with his grey beard neatly trimmed, and by him stood the proud father and uncle (all ousted by my presence from their normal sitting bench), while an old woman—Bibi Gímo's mother—crouched with the proprietary air of the *accoucheuse* on the ground beside the mother's dais. Derwish and Man Ali Shah joined the menfolk, the two small girls sat round the fireplace with Naját and Shukuru, while the married sister and other women formed a group behind. Dádo came in with me as a matter of course and sat at my feet, though neither a neighbour nor a relative. (I had fully expected him to fade out at the threshold.)

I took a long breath, summoned all my wits and—a little self-consciously because of so large an audience—started carefully firing off one by one the fine phrases with which Qudrat Ullah had furnished me: "God grant your son long life and happiness! May he live to be a comfort to you! May he take your beasts in summer to the mountain pastures! May he bring you gifts when he comes home from his travels! May he give you a good daughter-in-law and children to brighten your age! May he prove a worthy son of worthy parents!" and so forth till I stopped from sheer exhaustion. These admirable sentiments, couched in the best traditional form, sounded so absurdly different from my usual, halting, extempore speech that they provoked giggles of delight from Naját and her companions. They fully realized that these pretty speeches must have been carefully prepared, and they told me afterwards that everyone had been much gratified at my having taken the trouble to learn the right things to say. But, after all, you may as well say the right things as the wrong, and even amid the simplicities of Hunza, ceremonial phrases are valued on ceremonial occasions.

Then, having recovered breath, I consulted Dádo in a whisper as to whether it would be in order to ask to see the baby, who was entirely hidden by a doubled homespun blanket flung over the ridge-pole of his cradle. "Quite the right thing." I made my request and approached the cradle. They turned back the cloth for me, and there was a very handsome baby (for seven days old) in beautifully clean kit, very carefully bolstered in, his eyes painted black all round, which gave his face a comical look of maturest wisdom. This black stuff is supposed to be "cooling" to the eyes, and is quite probably a disinfectant of some kind. I said what a fine baby he was, and how big for his age, and so forth, then wished them all the best of luck, repeated my congratulations, and turned to come away. But they called me back to receive two heaped dishes of grapes and apples. I protested as well as I could against robbing their store-room, especially at such a moment when hordes of hungry guests would come well-wishing—it is for similar occasions that the "emergency reserve" is set apart—but I protested in vain. Derwish and Man Ali Shah followed us up the hill bearing the fruit, and I could only resort to the contemptible expedient of small silver.

Anyone who knows life in the East will realize how incredible it seems that a woman should sit in state to receive visitors of both sexes while her menfolk look proudly on. No wonder the Hunza women have this happy fearlessness, this dignified gait, these courtly manners.

I was typing text next morning when I heard piping voices in the verandah outside my window: "Mother, Mother, Mother, *dear*, do come at once; we are threshing buckwheat on our floor." I went out to find seven of my smallest friends, boys and girls from the Middle Channel above, led by Nímo, dancing with excitement and impatience: "Do come and take photographs! Father and mother say you are *please* to come." I wasn't very keen to go, for we were expecting some Swedish missionaries to lunch. They were passing through on their way to Kashgar—another month's march—and they might arrive at any moment. Still . . . I had asked all our neighbours to send for me when anything was going on, and if I showed reluctance such summonses might stop. I scrambled up to the floor of No. 7 and found a large group of neighbours flailing buckwheat. They made me welcome, and I tried some photographs. "It was very kind of you to send Nímo for me," said I. "But we never sent for you." Then I repeated what the children had said, and we all laughed heartily—the young monkeys had fetched me out on their own account! A few moments later riders were seen approaching. I sped down to welcome them.

Nice folk they proved. The Swedes used to reach Kashgar through Russia in twenty-four days, but Russian travel being uncertain they had been forced to make the long detour via India and our Gilgit road—a matter of at least three months.

Some weeks after my last call on Bibi Gímo I was passing by her home again and was hailed by the children from the roof: "Do come in and see the baby!" I was always chary of too readily accepting such impulsive invitations. "Run down and ask mother if she would like to see me." In a moment Naját came out bearing an authorized welcome. It proved that I had come at a fortunate time, for Baby Faqér had just been lifted for a meal and was kicking and crowing in his mother's arms with wonderful vigour for so small an infant. She took off the kerchief that bound his head—it was a large linen handkerchief I had purloined from David's store for him, and I gathered that its size and quality were prized—and ran her hand lovingly through his fine crop of dark hair, keeping a watchful eye for possible inhabitants which she gladly failed to find. I was laughed at for admiring his head of hair so much. The kerchief had a funny little needlebook affair attached by bright-coloured threads which had a verse from the Qur'an stitched into it to serve as amulet. Most small children's caps are decorated with several of these gaily coloured, dangling charms, but I should guess that they are merely "the thing," and are not taken more seriously than a charm on a girl's bracelet at home or the mascot on her father's car. Grown-ups rarely display them, but Dádo used to sport a string of them underneath his waistcoat when we travelled.

I sat down for a chat while the ceremony proceeded, and I observed that baby-worship is as thorough in Hunza as amongst ourselves. Naját and Shukuru and all the children were gathered round, but the men were out at work and the house was (relatively) empty. So while the mother fed the child I learned all I could about orthodox baby management. Until the baby cuts his first tooth his mother will not take him to any house where there is another infant. Possibly it is felt that with one tooth he will be armed for self-defence against his contemporary; possibly the rival mothers might be tempted into tactless comparisons. Up till this point, too, no male of the house may handle him. An amusing little ceremony heralds the cutting of this all-important tooth. Some elderly man—usually the grandfather—"well skilled with children," takes the baby in his arms and out into the open. After that his father and brothers are free to play with him and carry him about.

Until the child is two or thereabouts he lives the life of a recluse, strapped into his cradle night and day except at meal-times, or when taken out for an airing in grown-up arms.

When the moment came for replacing Faqér in his cradle, Naját and Shukuru bestirred themselves and fetched some dry, finely powdered earth which they gently warmed over the ashes of the fire. Bibo Gímo produced a large square of strong cloth, sweet and clean but dark with use, and spread it on the dais, lying the baby down on it with a tiny cushion under his head. Then plenty of the earth—it proved to be pounded sun-dried cow-dung, as clean and inoffensive to handle as the fibre in which we plant our bulbs—was packed round him above and below, and he was carefully parcelled up, arms, legs, and feet, into the stout cloth, bandaged into it with a long binder, and laid in the cradle. When he is "changed" the last lot of packing is thrown on to the fields for their enrichment—and that's that. Very cleanly and ingenious it all is and vastly preferable to the eternal washing of "nappies," which, indeed, would be a grim task with insufficiency of cloths, cold water, and no soap.

The bottom of the cradle was full of nice clean straw with a padded mattress on top, and by the time baby's cushion was adjusted and a red quilt laid up to his chin and well tucked in round him, he looked extremely comfortable and well-protected. Next, a piece of wide cloth was threaded by its hem on a rod fastened along the side of the cradle, and passed several times over his tummy and under the wooden cot, being finally lashed to the ridge pole. If the cradle had then been knocked over or rolled down hill baby could neither fall out nor get bumped. Finally a thick blanket was thrown over like a tent, and he was safe from dust or smoke or flies—or fresh air. Mother gave a few gentle rocks and he settled into sleep.

The use of the cradle in Hunza is said to be relatively recent, and the pattern of it, wherever it was introduced from, includes the prescription that it shall be made from a special sort of hard wood that grows wild on certain mountain spots and is supposed to possess magical properties. The ridge-pole forms a convenient carrying handle, and wherever you see a group of women working and chatting together, spinning in the shade or on the roof, beating out new-washed wool on a sandy patch beside a stream, pounding kernels, washing clothes, or busy on the threshing floor, you will usually see a cradle or two beside them. Truby King might disapprove of so much infant seclusion; but the flat roof offers a drop of 12 or 14 feet on to boulders, and even the living-room a gentle roll into the open hearth, so that Hunza is no place for crawlers. By the time baby is ripe for toddling, he is old enough to be entrusted to the next-older children, who take him pick-a-back or on their shoulders, scaling walls and leaping streams with him as sure-footed as young goats, and as fearless. They carry him to some flat spot and guard him with the most scrupulous care and proudly watch over his first steps.

Babies in Hunza are spaced at intervals of three and four years, so no mother is worn out with child-bearing or embarrassed in her daily work by ex-babies clinging to her skirts and jealous of the infant in her arms. Banu, for instance, was four, sturdy and ripe for independence, before Faqér came to claim the family's attention. Soon after his arrival we used to see her stalking about, proudly taking her first walks alone, and obviously savouring the new freedom from older supervision. One day she had passed twice or three times up and down on the far side of our Dála. It had gently sloping banks where it passed our door, and was both narrow and shallow, having been divided a mile or so away to give Aliábád the "Middle Channel" that ran 30 or 40 feet above our level and watered the fields between. She looked long at it and pondered. She wanted to come over, but had always before leaped the little stream on Naját's or Derwish's back. Presently she made her decision and her first jump and fell spread-eagled into 18 inches or so of water. She gave a cry, wholly of vexation, not at all of fright, and scrambled safely out. Someone ran up laughing, took off her little shift and spread it for her in the sun to dry. She played about cheerfully on a sunny patch of sand till it was ready, and later we saw her jumping triumphantly to and fro, again and yet again, as if she could never jump enough. By the time Faqér emerges from his cradle she will be leaping the Dála with him astride her back.

Our very first girl friend, Kaníza of No. 3, has a younger sister, Gúlo, a sporting little imp, who had just cut her second teeth. One day she had a difference of opinion with her family, and we met her striding away from home. "Where are you off to?" "I'm annoyed," she said. "I'm going to mother's folk in Báltít," and off she set on a solitary four-mile mountain walk and a climb of hundreds of feet to her grandparents' home. No one tried to call her back or reason with her. She was wisely left to work off her waywardness her own way. She must have tramped home again the same day, for on the morrow we saw her happily busy with her own people again. After that our usual greeting to her was: "Hullo, Gúlo, off to Báltít?" "Not to-day!" she would say with a mischievous twinkle in her eye. Thus the Hunza youngsters learn independence.

The only drawback—from my point of view—about the sheltered life of the Hunza infants, was that when they were out for a walk in someone's arms, they were distinctly world-shy and were apt to set up a howl if I approached too near. The three-year olds were seldom frightened—though you must remember that a pale-faced woman with horrible blue eyes ("cat's eyes" they call them amongst themselves), and an outrageous hat, must be a terrifying sight when it advances on you for the first time—but I learned cautiously to admire the babies from afar, though the father or mother always wanted to show them off. Only little Faqér, initiated so young, was always unafraid, and would stretch out his little hands and gurgle at me and let me take him in my arms or tickle him.

Soni, of the next house to Bibi Gímo's (I had to call it No. 1A, because in my first notes I had confused the two households) had a little girl Afrots—quite the ugliest and brightest atom of three years old in Hunza. She had cried the first day on seeing me but immediately made friends, and ever after if I were sighted would run up to me and put out an abnormally grubby little paw and say "How do you do?" in imitation English fashion. On general principles we resisted all temptation to teach the children English ways or words or tales. This was almost my one lapse from grace, but Afrots was by general consent a special case, and her old grandfather, Aliko, was extraordinarily proud when he was witness to our meetings.

In the very first days of romping with the children of No. 1 and 1A on the threshing floor I had—stupidly—thought it might be fun to teach Shamúli, Bano, and Afrots to dance. So I stood up and started on a Highland schottische, and endeavoured, with little success, to coax them to join in. I was puzzled by something a little frigid in the air and soon gave up the attempt. When I climbed home for breakfast Dádo gravely and kindly said: "Excuse me, Mother, but Hunza women do not dance. It is thought unseemly." I thanked him for the warning; I wasn't sure whether the fear was that I should corrupt the girls or merely make an unseemly exhibition of myself. Either danger was to be avoided, so that began and ended my dancing lessons. Later Qudrat Ullah explained that in the olden days, when the Hunzukuts distilled a powerful *araq* from their mulberries, men and women used to dance together in drunken orgies that had untoward consequences. The Mir had long since forbidden the spirit, which provoked quarrels as well as dances, and "mixed dancing" fell under the same ban. This was the only man-made restriction on woman's freedom that I encountered in Hunza, and it did not seem to worry anyone.

1. Bibi Anjír (left) and a neighbour.

2. Hérul Nisa with baby niece (the first grandchild).

PLATE XIV: Household of No. 8 (See p. 129)

3. Ustád Nadíro and Hérul Nísa.

A couple of months after Bibi Gímo's, Soni's baby son was born—the first grandson of No. 1A—and his arrival was the cause of great rejoicing. I had heard nothing of it till I commented one day to Aliko, whose handsome white beard had suddenly turned orange, on the fact that I had not lately seen Afrots. "She's been staying over with her mother's people in Haiderabad," he said, "but she's coming back to-day." When I next saw her she raced up to me breathless: "How do you do (in English), I've got a baby brother, I've got a baby brother, I've got a BABY BROTHER!" The opportunity of an eighth-day formal visit had passed, so I clambered over a boulder or two into their orchard-garden and called up the blank, unresponsive-looking wall of the house. Soni was busy in the store-room, and put her head out of the one tiny wooden window—the only "window" of a Hunza house is a square, shuttered, ventilation hole in the store-room—inviting me to join her on the roof. I climbed the primitive ladder with caution—a camera and other impedimenta always made me even less agile than need have been—and there she was spinning away and occasionally giving a rock to the cradle beside her. I utilized as many suitable phrases as I could remember without rehearsal, and was rewarded with a peep at a fine little fellow of a fortnight whom any mother might have been proud to own. Soni was gaily dressed, and had dotted her face all over with unsightly brown spots which I learned were supposed to be "good for the complexion" after childbirth. The custom used, it seems, to be universal, but it must be dying out, for I saw only a few young mothers so decorated. Anywhere else one might suppose it a charm against the Evil Eye, but the Burusho of Hunza are so free from any taint of this baleful superstition—so hard-lived where it has once had root—that I think there must be some other explanation. We later found that among the Burushaski speakers of Yasin, all the younger women lived under a permanent coating of similar brown cosmetic, washed off only for feast days, in the belief that it protected their skin against the cold winds of their harsher climate.

Afrots, joining devoutly in the admiration of her baby

brother, volunteered: "And now I put on my tunic right side out!" I looked up at Soni, mystified. She laughed and explained that the last-born of a family always wore its little shift inside out until the next baby came. She could not tell me *why*. It just was "done." If no further child is born, the youngest on reaching seven, is promoted to the right side of its clothes.

Up till six or seven the young children of both sexes wear no garment but the one cotton shift and cap (with a homespun cloak for the cold); after that they are outfitted with baggy trousers of but slightly different cut, the boys' held in at the ankle by a plain, straight band, the girls' by a more elaborate "cuff," something like our spats. There is no rigid rule about the kind of cotton cloth used—it depends, no doubt, primarily on what happens to be available when the family is able to buy—but the men and boys mainly affect plain striped shirtings and the women bright-patterned chintz. Since a whole "piece" will be bought at a time, if often happens that all the women and girls of one household will be dressed at the same time in the same stuff. You often see women in plain stripes, however, and more rarely some boy-Benjamin in an amazing chintz shirt.

Chapter 21

HUNZA CRAFTS

ONE of the most refreshing things about Hunza is the absence of machinery. Every essential tool and utensil can be made and mended at home, and every individual enjoys the self-respect that comes from the exercise of necessary craftsmanship. The picturesquely asymmetrical stone cooking-pots, oil-jars, and crusie-lamps have each been fashioned by father or grandfather, or it may be great-grandfather. Each has its own individuality and its own history. The ladles and wooden spoons of delightful and often fantastic shape have been cut out from suitable branched bough or root—handle and bowl in one piece, no two alike. Your own carefully planted and tended willows supply the flexible withies for a dozen kinds of basket, and the man or woman who could not construct the one required would be hard to find. Reels and spindles for spinning, bobbins and shuttles for weaving, wooden hoes and shovels, two-prong forks cut in one piece from the tree or the graceful five-pronged winnowing forks with neat and skilful lashings of gut holding their curved teeth in place, the plough, the frame and heddles of the loom, the treadles and framework of the lathe that turns the wooden bowl, are all home-made. You cure the skins of your own beasts for sacks and bags and boots. When the women want more wool for spinning, any man at any moment will shear another sheep while the women and children hold its legs.

The only work that the home cannot itself tackle is the ironwork—a very recent substitute for stone and bone and horn. An occasional iron pick or shovel, fork or crowbar is brought up "from below" (India or Kashmir) by a returning son, and is accounted a rare treasure; but for the most part local Béricho make such simple iron goods as are wanted: the slightly convex baking-griddle, the tripod, the simple shears, the sickle blade, the iron tip which shoes the wooden ploughshare, the unpretentious iron razor, the rough tongs, the horseshoe, the spatula for turning bread. The Béricho form the only "caste" in Hunza in anything like the Indian sense.

The story goes that long ago—two hundred years or so, perhaps—some prince of Hunza rendered a service to the ruler of Baltistan, and was duly asked to name his recompense. He coveted neither gold nor horses, but begged for a few families of artisans. These were presented to him and allotted land in Hunza where they settled and multiplied, supplying the Burusho with blacksmiths for such rare iron as they could obtain, and with musicians to enliven their feasts and games of polo. These strangers in the midst are treated with courtesy and kindness, but remain "foreigners" and social inferiors. The Burusho will not intermarry with them. A threat to a troublesome daughter is said to be: "If you don't behave, I'll marry you to a Bérits"; but we never heard the threat employed, still less a case of its being carried out. Each Burusho household pays a small yearly tax to the Béricho community, and in return the blacksmiths tour the villages once or twice a year and make or mend whatever is required. You will see a little crowd gathered in the corner of someone's garden and in the centre the blacksmith crouching beside his simple forge—a few stones ingeniously built up to contain his charcoal fire, with a neat, hollow tube of soapstone below it, into which the bellows play; a stone anvil sunk in the ground; these accessories are provided on the spot and the blacksmith's outfit consists of his hammer and his skill. The bellows is a double one; two goatskin bags are fitted with a nozzle at one end; at the other, two wooden lips that open as you raise your hand and meet tightly in your fist as you press down. They are worked with the right and left hand alternately, and the peasant whose job is in hand is expected to do the blowing.

The Béricho preserve their own customs, and though the menfolk all talk Burushaski, Dumáki is the language of their homes, and the women know no other. The existence of this interesting language-island, within the language-island of Burushaski, had been unsuspected by European scholars till DL set about investigating it. He could not devote much time to it, but gleaned enough to establish the fact—inherently probable—that it is of Indian origin, and that it has (less predictably) interesting affinities with the Gypsy of Europe, which survives even in South Wales. It is a curious fact that the Doms of Gilgit (who conjecturally are of the same stock as the Doms of India and the Béricho of Hunza) have abandoned their own language in favour of Shina. This may well be because Shina has a close relationship to Sanskrit and the modern Indian vernaculars, which Burushaski lacks, and is incomparably easier to learn.

While every Hunza family plies its own essential crafts, there are a few specially expert folk—like the master-carpenters of whom I have spoken—who undertake the weaving, turning, and milling for their neighbours. Amongst the two hundred families of Aliábád there were perhaps seven or eight recognized weavers, twice as many millers, and at least one lathe-master.

We were fortunate in having, on the Middle Channel above us within a few minutes' climb, two master-weavers, old Dádo of No. 7 and Ustád Nadíro of No. 8. The narrow road-plus-water-channel that passed their houses was barely 3 feet wide, and was one of the main internal thoroughfares; but this had not prevented them from digging themselves a loom-pit under the shelter of the house wall, leaving an effective track of scarcely a foot for passers-by to squeeze along, cows, sheep, goats, or people. No one seemed to resent the encroachment. At a pinch you could always step down into the water-channel, full or empty as it might chance. During the pressure of harvest these pits had stood untenanted, and I wondered when the weaving was going to begin.

One day I had been sitting with one of Afiato's daughters-in-law, who was embroidering a festive cap for herself, asking the names of the various stitches and patterns and studying her style of sewing. There is a huge vocabulary connected with embroidering, and I had filled several pages of my notebook when her attention was diverted by the cow she was minding. It had plunged down a 6-foot wall and was enjoying itself in a neighbour's ripening crop. "Excuse me," said Gohir Nimo, "having smitten the cow I shall come back." She did, and we resumed the lesson. I took the needle and ventured on a few stitches. "Oh, you can sew like us!" she exclaimed with surprise. There were so many everyday things I could not do just like them that her surprise was justified. Soon I noticed her growing restive: "I haven't yet had my morning bread; I expect you had yours before you came out. Good-bye." As she left me, chivvying her cow homewards, I looked round for new occupation, and saw old grandfather of No. 7 climbing cautiously down a field wall with a shapeless bundle under his arm. I worked my way across country to the empty field he had made for, to see what was toward and found to my delight that he was getting his loom into order. Moth had played some havoc with his heddle threads and a finicky job he had to replace them. When this was done he called a son or two to help him to lay out the warp. They set up and steadied the loom with stones, then drove a peg into the ground so many cubits off. One of the assistants made fast one end and then paid out the wool from a fat ball of doubled thread, slung it round the peg, and brought it back to grandfather, who attached it with an ingenious knot that defied my analysis, and off went another loop round the distant peg. When these preliminaries were over, for which the flat space of the open field was necessary, the old man assembled his loom again and climbed up the wall to set it up in his pit and get to work. Hunza homespun is of a most beautiful thick quality, as unlike as possible to the loose, semi-transparent cloth that hand-weavers at home achieve, a stuff that would not withstand the hard wear of Hunza fields for an instant. Two hundred and forty warp threads go to the width of 9 or 10 inches of cloth.

The tiny pit is almost square—2 feet by 2 feet 9 inches—and just 2 feet deep; the sides of it are revetted inside with small stones on the model of the field walls and edged at the top with a wooden kerb, fitted with holes into which pegs can be inserted as required. Outside, at the corners, stand four small stone piers, sometimes monoliths, sometimes just cairns of stones, and on these rest the two poles on which two pairs of heddles ride. Four treadles, threaded on a rod, are connected with the heddles by leather thongs. A stone shelf at the back of the pit accommodates the weaver, who hugs to his tummy the wooden bar on which the *pattoo* is rolled up as completed. There is no room in the cramped space of the twisting road to fling out the warp at length as had been done in the field. It is passed round a peg in the front of the pit and then carried in a loosely twisted rope to a second peg at the side within easy reach of the weaver's right hand, who can thus pay it out to himself as wanted.

As the weaver works, some of his family sit by and wind his bobbins, neat little hollow rods which revolve on the pin of his boat-like shuttle. There is an extraordinary fascination about the extreme simplicity and extreme efficiency of all the home-made gadgets of pegs and pins and thongs on which the working of the loom depends. Like lightning the old man works his feet and flings his shuttle to and fro, while with the heavy sliding comb he bangs each new cross thread into its place, as the thick cloth grows under his fingers in the characteristic herring-bone pattern. As the roll grows fatter, the bar is moved out to the next pair of pegs. Grandfather was delighted to hold forth about the details of his craft and explain the uses of his various contraptions, showing the ingenious loops in the vertical heddle-threads that lifted the warp threads in two's to produce the pattern. By his side stood a little rod fitted with a tiny hook. "What on earth is this for?" "Well, you see, sometimes the shuttle falls down into the pit. I have bored a hole in each side of it, and I can hook it up with this."

He would have welcomed photographs, but unfortunately his pitch was heavily and unevenly shaded by a tree in Afiato's garden opposite.

A few days later we were lucky enough to find Ustád Nadíro at work a few hundred yards farther along the road in full sunshine. Even then, in the narrow gangway it was difficult to get room to work a camera at a convenient distance. The

Ustád was wisely initiating two disciples into his art: one his son-in-law and one his next-door neighbour of No. 9. As he stood by, superintending and advising, he was busily twiddling a special spindle for doubling the single woollen thread ready for a new warp. Passers-by halted for a chat, children squatted round watching and taking in all that was said. We learnt that nine yards of *pattoo* go to the making of a man's cloak and seven to a woman's, and that a skilled weaver can complete a nine-yard piece in two full days' work; a real master in a day and a half. If neighbours enlist his services they supply the wool and also the attendant men, women, or children to wind his bobbins. They may likely have a loom-pit near their house, even if none of them weave themselves; in that case he will go and weave in theirs, otherwise they bring their wool to his. His chief fee for weaving is three ample meals a day while he works, and a gift in kind (or cash if they have any) equal to about tenpence of our money.

The autumn is a favourite time for weaving; the harvest work is nearly over, and the weather is still warm enough for sitting out of doors. On our afternoon walks at this season we saw many other weavers dotted about not only in Aliábád, but in the neighbouring hamlets between us and Báltít, and we found looms and pits in all cases substantially identical. In only one house was there an innovator who had set up his loom on the roof, and was seated on a raised bench instead of a sunk one. Nadíro kindly promised that when his season's work was over he would bring his whole apparatus down, let us measure it in detail, and take a studio portrait of it. David devoted every Sunday forenoon to taking quarter-plate photographs in an improvised studio with a proper stand camera, thus obtaining exact records of the various vessels and implements that were most characteristic of the country.

One day Levy Kalbi called us out to see him preparing goats'-hair warp. This was a most entertaining performance. He had a large ball of single goats'-hair thread, ingeniously wound so that one end could be drawn out from the centre of the ball (many knitters at home are familiar with this device). He then took the two ends, one from the centre and one from the circumference, twisted them with his fingers till he had a small nucleus of double thread. With a wooden peg he fastened this tiny ball so that it could not unroll, and started swinging it round his head, letting it touch the ground now and again to increase the spin. It travelled in wider and wider circles till the connecting thread became of unmanageable length and began to kink. Then he hauled it in and wound the beautifully twisted length of doubled thread on to the little ball and again pegged it down. Thus he continued till the original ball was exhausted.

Not long after, the Ustád's Hérul Nisa came to say that they were setting up a goats'-hair loom at their house if we would care to see it. We found that this time a large vertical frame standing on the roof of No. 8, lashed to the rafter of the balcony, and in course of being strung with just such a warp thread as Kalbi had shown us in the making. While Hunza sheep are uniformly white, three kinds of goat are kept: white, brown, and black. Black hair is used for the warp, while the bobbins are wound with white and brown. The bobbins in this case are long, needle-like rods the full width of the cloth, 2 feet or so, with the hair wound round notches in each end. There are only two heddles, thrown backwards and forwards by a forked peg like a boy's catapult. Goats'-hair weaving is a slower job and heavier than wool-weaving, but the Ustád is master of it, too, and was again initiating two younger men. The different coloured hair allows of pattern-weaving, and they enjoy devising new stripes and squares of brown and white. A very heavy comb is needed to beat down the intractable material, and in order to prevent the cloth being drawn too tight by the cross threads, two "bows" of flexible wood were spiked across it to keep it flat and taut. These are inserted as near as possible to the working edge and moved up as work progresses. The goats'-hair strips are used as rugs, or doubled and sewn together to form sacks and saddle-bags.

One day we were exploring the half-ruined village of the old fort, threading the narrow switchback alleys between deserted houses—so narrow that in places you could only edge along sideways—looking for points of vantage from which to take photographs of the picturesque, abandoned Shiah mosque. It has been superseded by the New Assembly Hall in cut granite with pointed roof—an amazing achievement for local architects and masons, and one of which they are justly proud, but a dreadful eyesore in these surroundings and as uninspiring to an artistic eye as a Methodist chapel in a London suburb. Unfortunately it jostles the picturesque old mosque (whose entrance flight of steps is a delightful notched tree-trunk and whose flat roof bristles with a parapet of ibex horns), so that you can only see the older building squint-eye up or down a 3-foot lane. We pushed on and found ourselves emerging on a bluff covered with handsome graves. The Hunzukuts are too necessarily frugal to bury their dead on any ground that can be cultivated, so their graves usually stand on some barren hump that rises above the reach of irrigation water. Ordinary graves are just covered by flat slabs of concrete-like beaten earth, but more important folk have picturesque erections of varied shape to mark their last resting place. In theory all should no doubt be oriented in relation to Mecca, but in fact the graves face in whichever direction the site makes most convenient. We skirted round God's acre, re-entering the unappetizing labyrinth of desolate lanes, and presently came on a debris-strewn patch of ground whose houses had been dismantled (probably for their timber), and had fallen in. Here old Ferrájo had made a lathe-pit outside a rather handsome wooden door with a carved lintel. This had once led to his family's "town house," but now they lived out in Jamu, a suburb, as it were, of Aliábád. In its day, the warren of buildings to which he proudly pointed had boasted fifty-two "smokes." (A smoke represents a hearth-fire, and a hearth represents a household. In enquiring of a hamlet how many families it shelters, the correct phrase is: "How many smokes have you here?")

We begged Ferrájo to let us see him at work. He had, however, no wood in hand at the moment; chunks of root or cross-sections of willow trunks are the raw material of his bowls. But he let us inspect his pit—very similar in size and shape to a loom-pit—with the treadles and a leather belt passing three times round a circular bar. The bar fits at one side into an iron socket, and at the other rests on the edge of the pit, held in place by one of the invaluable forked pegs that serve so many purposes in Hunza. The projecting end of the bar is furnished with three fierce iron spikes, which are driven into the lump of wood that is the future bowl. An ingenious wooden tripod stands beside the turner as he squats to work. It has one very long leg with deep notches, in one of which he rests his rude curved chisel to steady his hand. He had another pit at his country home in Jamu, and he promised he would let us know when he was working. We photographed him and his apparatus at the door of his ex-town house.

In due course we were invited to Jamu and welcomed with a broad grin that lit up his tanned and weather-beaten face. A large crowd was already gathered, some merely to watch, and some bringing lumps of wood and waiting their turn for his attention. He had a small bowl on the lathe, nearly finished. Its owner was seated in the pit, pedalling away for all he was worth, while Ferrájo gave a few final touches to his handiwork. The bowl was hollowed out as thin as fine cardboard, a few lines were added on the outside for ornament, and the bowl was gently levered off the three pegs on which it was impaled. Then with his adze—while we needlessly held our breath—Ferrájo boldly hacked off the rough base in which the pegs had held. A fraction of an inch miscalculated would have shattered the fragile thing. But eye and hand were as true as fearless, and in a moment he held it up for us to handle and admire. A rub with sand and a polish with oil would make it ready for use. While he had been at wòrk an assistant or apprentice had been busy with an adze rough-hewing the next block into a solid hemisphere. It was then rudely but skilfully pounded on to the pegs with a big stone—Hunza has little need of hammers with so many stones of every size to hand—and we saw the new bowl carved out from first to last. When this was finished and we had taken as many photographs as we wished, the old man, with courteous hospitality, left his work to show us his house and fields and bring us out into the nearest lane—paved wholly with broken, wobbling boulders—that would lead us home. A happy man he looked, though he told us that his back ached nowadays at work with lathe or plough, as it never used to do, and perhaps we had English medicines that would meet the case. We could only offer the sad tidings that we too, when we walked or rode or worked, were subject to fatigue and aches undreamt of in younger days, and that even in England the doctors knew no medicines to defeat on-coming age. This, oddly, seemed to comfort him a lot: "We're all ageing together then," he said, and we all three laughed a vain defiance at the years, "and we old ones have more skill and experience than the others, haven't we?"

Apart from their never-ending spinning the women have many valuable crafts, though they are less spectacular than the men's. They all bake a large variety of bread and scones from their blent flour—not only grains being pressed into the service, but pounded mulberries, walnuts, peas and beans, and semi-wild berries—and when *maltash* is available they make cakes and pastries of a dozen kinds. The vegetable patches are in their care, and amongst their many greens, their gourds, cucumbers and marrows, they tend a lot of plants whose seeds or leaves or flowers are valued as flavourings, and grow a little flax and mustard to supplement their apricot oil. In spring their plots are lit with the large blossoms of many-coloured poppies, whose seeds are not wasted on opium but scattered into the vegetable pot. They also grow small quantities of maize as a vegetable, but they do not consider it profitable as a major crop. The kinder-hearted find a corner for tobacco for the men's pipes, which circulate of an evening in the shade when the day's work is done and someone tinkles a zither or tootles on a flute. These instruments are home-made like everything else, and are often very beautifully finished; we were neither of us qualified to judge of the music the players conjured up. To our unskilled ears it sounded amateurish, but eminently cheerful and pleasing. Serious music of drum and pipe and kettledrum is the monopoly of the Béricho. When the women weed their crops they sort out the dandelion, stitchwort, and sorrel for their own brews before throwing the residue to the cow. And they have a varied repertoire of berries, roots, and herbs from which they prepare simple medicines for their needs. Nowadays they are able to attend the Government dispensary in Aliábád, but its nostrums have not yet undermined their faith in their own home-made remedies. We very much wished that we had possessed some knowledge of medical botany and could have brought home records of their medicine; but like so many other branches of knowledge which we regretfully ignored, it would have been a specialist's job, and we had out hands full enough with our own work and all too little time at our disposal.

During the imprisonment of winter the women cut and stitch the winter cloaks, adorning each long seam with a double row of backstitching, which is not only seemly to the eye but serves to hold the raw edges in place. The stiff, shaped collar is decorated with varied designs, diamonds, triangles, and straight lines in the same backstitch. Happily few of them can yet afford to let Dirzi Nazir replace their time-honoured skill with the soulless, cotton stitchery of his sewing machine. We noted with grief that the beautifully hand-embroidered *chogas* with which the Mir presented us this time all had their seams Singer-sewn, and had thus lost (for us) much of their charm.

With prudent foresight the woman makes the *choga* six good inches too long for its destined wearer, and introduces a deep tuck above its lower edge. It will last at least three years and will shrink in successive washings. You can tell at a glance whether a man is wearing his best, or medium, or oldest *choga* by the depth—or absence—of the tuck. In former days embroidery was the monopoly of the few royal ladies who beguiled the tedium of their too-sheltered life by decorating *chogas* with bold designs in bright-coloured silks, or working raised patterns of gold and silver on velvet saddle-cloths, and above all in elaborating delicate designs in cross-stitch for the crown and border of their lovely little caps. Where we clumsily work cross-stitch with wool on canvas, they painstakingly cross-stitch the individual threads of calico with bright, gay silks. The patterns are infinitely varied—we possess dozens of specimens of this fine work, no two are alike—but all appeared to us to suggest Persian inspiration. I heard one lady say with regret for a golden past: "What is the world coming to? Why nowadays the very peasant girls embroider silken caps for themselves!"

True enough; now that a little money filters into almost every home the women can get hold of coloured silk from India or Kashgar, and it was a common sight to see girls and women open a tiny home-made bag that hung on their tunic, and take out a strip or circle of calico, a needle, and a bunch of silk, and continue work on a dainty cap. The threads of the cloth were carefully counted and the design traced out in black thread. The silks they used were unspun, clinging masses that I found impossible to handle, and how they manipulated them so skilfully with fingers roughened, you would have thought, by field work, I could not divine. For about 1s. 6d. they can buy enough silk to cover one cap with minute embroidery, and they blend their colours, red, blue, green, orange, purple, yellow, and black, with unerring taste. We laid in a store of their favourite shades so that on occasion we could make an acceptable gift to a bride preparing her trousseau.

After a first experience of trifling gifts of balls and combs we had decided that it would be a crime to spoil the simple, spontaneous kindness of the children or their parents by indiscriminate giving. So we restrained a longing to distribute even sweets and pins, and only made an occasional present on very special occasions or for very definite services rendered. On the other hand, we made a note of such things as would be useful and acceptable, and gathered a hoard of them for our ultimate visits of farewell.

Amongst the women's crafts I have already mentioned the neat little "ashtrays" they conjure from the residual mush of apricot kernels after they have extracted the oil. Washing is amongst them a simple matter. Having no fat, they can make no soap, but there is a plant, called *híman*, which they grow amongst their vegetables, the seeds of which when pounded yield a delightful soapy lather. This is used for special washings only. Every-day cotton clothes are simply rinsed in cold water, flung on a flat stone and beaten with a wooden mallet. When a *choga* is being washed, a man's greater strength is called into play—nine yards of wet homespun is no joke. He dips it likewise into cold water, lays it on a stone, and tramples it with his full weight. There is, of course, no fuel to spare for washing clothes or persons in hot water.

From our very first days in Hunza the mills had been a source of interest, and we constantly passed them and peeped in as we traced out all the water-channels on our walks. When the water was in flow (no stream, not even the Dála, was continuously in action in any one stretch) the mills were the centre of social gatherings. The miller and his family would be inside superintending operations, while the women with their babies and their work quietly awaited their turn. They had brought small sacks or bags of grain to be ground and would squat in and round the doorway happily gossiping. Occasionally a man would come along, bent double under a huge sack of 80 lb. or so.

We struck a particularly interesting group one day, where the water was plunging steeply down the hillside and turning three mills in succession, one below the other. David was photographing the busy crowd at the door, and I climbed up a little to join two old women busily spinning among the rocks above. "Father won't want to take pictures of us," they said, in a matter-of-fact tone quite free from bitterness, "we are old and wrinkled." As well as my halting speech permitted, I assured them that older people were our best friends, that we liked faces wrinkled like our own, and that if they would allow it, "Father" would much like their photographs. So I scrambled down the hill again to explain to DL where his next duty lay. He came and engaged the old dames in chat, but it was no easy matter to get a photograph for they were shy and self-conscious beyond the ordinary. The picture turned out at least recognizable, but when it came to delivering their copies we found that their houses were "quite near" of course, but down 500 or 600 feet of highly precipitous gorge, rather more of a rock-climbing feat than we were prepared to tackle in the course of an afternoon's walk. Enquiry revealed, however, that old Pfírúz's son was married to Ustád Nadíro's daughter, so we were able to leave the photo for her at No. 8. It was a constantly renewed pleasure to find how our photographs were welcomed and a constantly renewed surprise that these illiterate people, who had never seen a picture in their lives, were able at once to recognize and name the tiny reproductions of themselves. This was the one point in favour of my quarter-plate camera that it yielded larger prints than David's smaller ones. Only one woman in all our experience refused to take any interest in photographs, and that was, oddly enough, my special friend Bibi Gímo, of No. 1. "Take it away; I can't understand it," she would say to the others eagerly crowding round to see the latest of grandfather or baby Faqér. Quite possibly, unsuspected by herself, her eyesight was below par. But for the most part quite old people like the various grandfathers seemed as sharp-sighted as ever. On one occasion a man was studying a group of field-builders, the figures in which were very small, and he mis-identified himself: "Hullo, that's me all right, but *where* is my moustache?" He looked again more carefully, and found himself, moustache and all.

It was no negligible tax on our time to make spare prints for everyone, but we felt it was one small return we could make—without corrupting our friends—for the unstinted kindness we met on every hand.

We visited all the mills within range, studying them critically with future photographs in mind, for they were dark little hovels without smoke-holes, and lit only by the door and a small gap, representing one missing stone in the wall opposite, and we had to make elaborate calculations as to the aspect of doors and light-holes and sun and times of day to decide which offered the best hope of an interior photograph (we had unfortunately brought no flashlight apparatus with us).

When the water was not "on" we made an effort to master their complicatedly simple mechanism. The water is led from some height by a wooden shoot consisting of a hollowed-out log and falls on to the wings of a rude "wheel" below the floor. The central hub is a rough sphere or cylinder hacked out of a root or tree trunk in which the "wings," eight or ten of them, are obliquely set. The axis of this wheel passes up

1. Little girl barely five taking baby brother of two for a ride. Madat, the elder boy, watches the experiment with some anxiety. (See p. 137)

2. Fetching firewood in a shoulder basket. (See p. 131)

PLATE XV

3. Gúlo and friends working mud into "cakes like those Mother makes." A wish-fulfilment of Starvation Springtime. (See p. 290)

through a central hole in the lower mill-stone and engages in an iron socket in the centre of the upper stone which it turns. The other end of the axis is shod with a pointed stone which revolves in a horizontal log. The lower mill-stone is firmly embedded in the floor of the mill, but an ingenious lever arrangement, which can be adjusted by wedges of convenient stones, enables you slightly to raise or lower the log below and thus to graduate the fineness of the flour. From side to side of the little hut runs a horizontal pole, whose ends are built into the walls, and from this the hopper is slung by two of the usual forked pegs. The hopper itself is most frequently a length of solid tree trunk shaped and hollowed out. Levy Kalbi's mill, in other respects highly suitable because better lit than most,was struck off our list of desirables because it had a horrible, carpentered hopper of planed planks—incongruously modern for our taste, though a source of natural pride to its owner. The narrow opening at the base of the hopper lets the grain trickle into a little sloping tray to which a wooden clapper is attached, ingeniously balanced by a thong so as to tap-tap on the revolving stone and gently shake the grain down to its fate. Another hollowed log acts as trough to receive the flour as it whirls out from between the stones. When the trough is full the flour is scooped up in double handfuls into its owner's bag. Beside the hopper lies a small wooden trowel of standard size, and the miller's fee for grinding the contents of an 80-lb. sack is one trowelful of flour. Another indispensable adjunct of the mill is a doubled piece of woolly sheepskin, which serves to sweep up any straying grain or flour.

Having calculated as best we might the most propitious lighting and a day when the Dála was not flowing we betook ourselves to our chosen Double Mill a mile or two away on the boundary between Aliábád and Dorkhan, where the Dála divides to give us our Middle Channel. There is a picturesque Mesopotamia here, with the mill-race and the mill-escape on one side and the divided stream on the other, and a fine grouping of trees above and below the Double Mill. We were armed with tripods and DL with his bigger camera, for at best exposures would have to run into several minutes. For an hour and a half we crawled about the interior of the amusing little mill—the roof was not high enough for us to stand upright—trying points of view and focuses to suit, and then propping our tripods steady with stones for each lengthy exposure. Our faithful escort was immensely amused by our clumsy antics, recking nothing of our aching legs and backs, and we could overhear them answering questions of this sort from the occasional passers-by: "What are you hanging about here for? The mill's not working. There's no water to-day!" "Of course not; we're waiting for Father and Mother." "Where are they?" "Inside here." "What on earth are they doing?" "Taking photographs." "What *of*?" "Oh, the hoppers and the mill-stones." Shouts of laughter! Our eccentricities were a never-failing delight to the populace, and our retainers loved acting as showmen. When at last we crawled out, half crippled with stooping and covered with dust and flour, we were greeted by a large crowd, friendly and mystified, to whom we had to explain how much better we liked their mills than our own at home. This of course pleased them, and they perhaps had visions of our attaining fame—perchance even riches—by erecting Hunza water-mills on the Isis or the Cam.

Chapter 22

MARRIAGE IN HUNZA

THE Burusho population of Hunza is divided into four major clans, centred in Báltít, and several minor clans scattered over other villages. Aliábád, being a "new settlement," contained amongst its two hundred houses representatives of almost all the clans. Marriage outside the race is rare, but (as I have already said) exogamous marriage between the clans is the rule.

On the whole the Burusho cling to their settlements along the eight or nine-mile stretch of river below Áltít (two or three miles up-river of Báltít), at a height of 6,000 to 8,000 feet above sea-level. They are not eager to colonize higher-lying districts, for they say their womenfolk refuse to live where the apricot will not ripen. If this is so the women show sound sense, for the dried apricot is one of their staple foods and almost their only source of sugar. The favourite winter breakfast is a hot porridge of these *batéring*. It thus happens that the higher river-stretches above Báltít are mainly settled (if at all) by Wakhi immigrants from Afghanistan. These are a quiet, peaceable folk, markedly less intelligent than the Burusho, loyal subjects of the Mir, well content with their good pasturages and crops of barley and not missing the wheat and the apricot to which they are unaccustomed. A few Burusho colonies are scattered among the Wakhi ones, but, though friendly relations exist, the two learn little of each other's language; and intermarriage, though it would not be taboo, is very rare.

Similarly a couple of the lower Hunza villages are inhabited by Shins, of the same stock as the Gilgit people, but again intermarriage is the exception. We had fully expected to find much more of it, and David had hoped to get some interesting notes on the bi-lingualism of children whose parents were of different stocks, but we came across no household among the Burusho we met where the wife was a foreigner.

Social intercourse with Nagir is virtually non-existent. The Hunza menfolk occasionally cross the river to barter Hunza wool for Nagir grain, for the former is much valued, though why, with far more extensive pasturage, the Nagir sheep should yield inferior wool was a mystery we never solved. But though a common language might appear to unite the two people, a difference of religion sunders them, and profoundly different social customs. Centuries of rivalry have left strong, latent feelings of hostility and distrust, probably reinforced—though this is a point on which possibly neither side has consciously reflected—by a difference of race. The Nagir women enjoy no such freedom and equality as the Hunza women do. They still wear unbecoming, dark homespun bonnets concealing all their hair while in Aliábád only one such bonnet had survived the comparatively recent coming of the merry cotton cap. Nagir sheep are predominantly dark brown, and in consequence Nagir caps and *chogas* are of a sombre hue that fittingly symbolizes the less genial temperament. Their Shi'ah mosques are called "Houses of Mourning" (*ma'tim sera*), and their interpretation of Islam seems to be as cheerless as would be a form of Christianity that concentrated all its devotion on the sorrows of Good Friday, and spared no thought for the rejoicings of Easter and Christmas. Now it happens that the Arabic word for mourning (*ma'tim*) sounds very similar to the Burushaski *matum* (black). As we rode through Nagir and noted the dour looks of the Nagirkuts, the crouching, face-averted women, the absence of spontaneous "good days" which brighten every Hunza chance encounter, the fact that when a Nagir prince was riding with us his passage was unmarked by any welcome or salute, our Hunza men would murmur with a grim satisfaction: "Their caps are black, and their cloaks are black, and their mosques are black, and by Allah their hearts are black!" All travellers who have passed through the two adjacent states have noted the relative gloom of Nagir, and some have attributed it to the north-facing mountains which though richer in grass and timber are sorely stinted of the sun.

Whatever the difference is—racial, temperamental, religious, political, or climatic—it is too deep-seated to favour intermarriage. Only the royal houses, sprung from a common ancester—Alexander or another—frequently exchange princesses across the water.

Within Hunza the clans are all reckoned of equal status, but the clan of the Diramiting enjoys a considerable measure of prestige, and at communal ceremonies a Diramiting sets the pace or leads the dance. The story of their origin is interesting. There was once a clan of Tapkients who grew so bold and arrogant that their offences cried to heaven. They were reported to put bread to ignoble uses, they were known to address their mothers by the term *zizi*, which is the exclusive privilege of royal or saiyyid families, and they were haughty and stiff-necked towards their Mir. In vain the eldest royal son implored his father to "do something about it," and when the Mir refused to take suitable measures, the young prince impatiently laid his own schemes. A great gathering of all the clans was to be held on a nameless space of open desert where Aliábád now stands, and the Tapkients attended in full force. The prince plied them with strong *'araq*, and when they had well drunk fell upon them with his retainers and slew every man, boy, and male infant. He did not know that one of the Tapkients had allowed his wife to return to her own people for the birth of her first child. The posthumous infant was called Diram, and from him are sprung the Diramiting of to-day, who carry themselves without arrogance and do not call their mothers *zizi*.

Child marriages do not take place in Hunza, but a girl will rarely pass sixteen or a boy eighteen unwed. The parents seek out a house among some other clan—frequently a house with which marriage relationships already exist—where there is a potential mate of suitable age and standing, and negotiations proceed between the families. In theory the young folk are not consulted; but in practice, where children have romped and played and worked together there is no doubt that personal preferences carry weight. The business preliminaries include a small payment from the bridegroom's people in recognition of the fact that the bride's family have had the expense of rearing her and are about to lose her services, an interchange of gifts between the houses, and the provision by the bride's father of an outfit for his daughter. In average peasant families a girl will bring to her new home three sets of every-day cotton clothes and caps, a winter cloak, a set of bedding, and for feast days an embroidered cap or two and a coloured scarf; possibly in addition an aluminium pot or iron bucket; details will vary in every individual case.

The laws of inheritance in Hunza show the same equitable common sense as distinguishes the Burusho's other customs. A woman cannot inherit land, since only a man can tackle irrigation work, field making, and so forth. But if a girl is still unmarried when her father dies, it is her brothers' duty to see her adequately outfitted, dowried, and settled. Among the gifts that may accompany a girl are apricot trees; her father or brothers may settle on her the right to the fruit of one or more of the family trees. Our friends of No. 3, who were very straitened and possessed only mulberry trees, had fortunately the right to an apricot tree in Zénába's home garden. We saw Kaníza and her sisters coming home one day, all carrying shoulder-baskets piled high with golden apricots: "We've been to Báltít to gather the fruit of mother's tree," they told us, "and this isn't nearly all. There's shaking-down for two or three days more." When the father dies the family property is fairly divided between the sons, who either work it in common or if they prefer divide it up. Questions then arise as to how many poplars equal an apricot tree, or how many willow trees a wheat field, but the distribution rarely gives rise to quarrels, for the people are just-minded and at need will call in neighbours to adjudicate over knotty points.

One of their customs is particularly sane: if a father of grown sons elects to marry again, he is free to do so, but in that case he must share the property as if he were himself a son; and a son by the second wife will only inherit a grandson's share. If a woman is widowed young, she will in the natural course marry again, taking with her to her new home any unweaned child, but leaving older children with her first husband's parents. If, however, she has grown sons, it is considered not obligatory but more honourable of her "to guard her husband's grave" as they phrase it; the sons will either retain her at home as still the *rúli gus* of the joint house, or they may give her an adjacent home of her own with her still unmarried girls. In either case they will maintain her with all deference and respect.

When a woman marries she by no means loses her identity. She becomes a "wife of the Diramiting" without ceasing to be "a daughter of the Buróng," and when in due course she dies, her own tribal brothers will assist her husband's in performing the last rites. She pays frequent visits to her parents' house, joining when she comes in whatever work is going on; if her family can afford to receive her, she may even go to stay for a lengthy period; it is not unusual for her to take her first baby home and stay for a year after its birth. This does not mean neglect of her husband, for he will still have his mother and sisters-in-law to fend for him. We used to chaff Bibo Gímo's married daughter, whose husband lived in Dorkhan, and ask what he would say to her long absence; but she had, in fact, come to help her mother before and after baby Faqér's birth.

Marriage-related families continually exchange small gifts of fruit or vegetables in season, for at different levels fruit will ripen earlier or later by several weeks; we would see Kaniza, for instance, carrying a small basket of early mulberries to her mother's people or to her married sister in Báltít, who would no doubt send in return some late fruit from Báltít when ours in Aliábád was over. In rush times of harvest, too, relations-in-law are quick to help each other, and a man owes the same courtesies of speech to his wife's parents as to his own.

Except for the physical difficulties of moving about it, Hunza is distinctly a place for the old. No detestable scientific innovations have come to create a gulf between the generations; long after he is unable to help with the heavy work the old man's experience is of value to his great-grandchildren. Levy

Hurmat was telling me about his home affairs one day: "Our father and mother are fortunately still with us; they can't *do* very much nowadays, of course; but they are still able to give us orders, thank God." And he meant the "thank God." In the same way the uncanny skill of the old *rúli gus* in husbanding the year's supplies is fully appreciated, and her skill with wool and spindle still puts her daughters-in-law to shame.

Old Aliko of No. 1A was past all serious work, though he kept up a plucky effort to preserve his youth by the constant dyeing of his fine white beard; but he was a renowned sower and could spread the seed more advantageously on the prepared field than younger men. There is no reckless wastage of precious seed-grain in Hunza; it is never flung where thorns could spring up and choke it, nor by the wayside to be trodden by the feet of men. And the neighbours would call Aliko in to sow for them. A real centenarian is a family treasure. Old Aliko's father was still living at the old homestead in Dorkhan with the other brothers (Aliko had hived off to Aliábád), and we made a special journey by request to see him and take his photograph. He was seated on a roof commanding a magnificent view of a steep hillside on which the farmstead straggled downhill in several storeys, as Hunza houses often do where the ground is steep. He had put on his best silk robe to receive us, and as we climbed the ladder and popped up over the roof brink, he apologized that he could not rise to greet us. Mentally he was as bright as ever and not even slightly deaf, and while David was busy with the portraiture I sat beside him and heard how he had lived through the reigns of four Mirs and four Maharajahs of Kashmir (the Mir, it should not be forgotten, had already reigned forty-five years); how proud he was that his son, Sangi Khan, was one of the headmen of Dorkhan, and how he had three sons and twelve grandsons still living at home (not to mention daughters and their children elsewhere). Before we reached the tale of his great-grandchildren, the photography and our visit were drawing to a close. He counted himself at least a hundred, and was certainly well on in the nineties, but still seemed full of the joy of life.

1. "The Merry Widow" just about to be remarried: "And I'm in great demand, I can tell you," she said.

2. Washing a homespun cloak.

(*See p.* 175)

3. Brother and sister.

4. The "Cheshire Cat" of No. 4 with small sister.

PLATE XVI

One day when we were visiting a wine-press, far below the old fort and its graveyards, I made friends with a dear little boy of five who seemed exceptionally active and intelligent, even in a country where all children are peculiarly alive and bright. A beautiful old woman joined us, her handsome face framed by two becoming silver plaits. "Tawálut must be your grandson," I ventured. "'Deed then and he's not," she retorted, "he's my great-grandson. His father was my favourite grandson, and when the poor wife died at this baby's birth, I took and suckled him myself"—a feat with which not many of our great-grandmothers could compete. But of course if you marry at sixteen, you may with luck be a great-grandmother by fifty. Still, it was a good effort, and the boy was an excellent witness to her vitality.

The Burusho population is not large, ten thousand or so at most, and the ramification of well-remembered pedigrees—the humblest can record his genealogy for an astounding number of generations back—brings it about that all families seem ultimately related to one another. It may be this racial purity, judiciously combined with avoidance of close in-breeding, that has produced a stock so markedly fit and healthy. Travelling up through Astor, Gilgit, and Nagir to Hunza, the strong contrast in physical fitness and general intelligence is apparent to the most casual observer; and anyone who knows the races of the Agency will engage a Hunza servant in preference to any other.

Marriages normally take place in winter when the people have leisure to give thought to new alliances. The solemn betrothal, presided over by a khalifa, is the effective part of the ceremony. It is usually performed in the bride's house in a semi-private gathering attended only by the members of the families concerned. We were most anxious to be allowed to see one, but by no means hopeful of securing the privilege, to which of course we had not the slightest claim. The servants promised to negotiate matters if possible, and at last Dádo brought us word one day that a girl-relation of Sagi's was about to be betrothed and her people were willing to invite us, but said: "We are poor folk, and our house is humble and we feel ashamed." We sent Sagi off with all the reassuring messages we could devise and a couple of bottles of our hoarded kerosene to help to light the feasting. The house lay near our own, down one steep lane and across some now open fields. We were met some yards outside the door and escorted in. The kind people had vacated one entire dais for us, which drove some of the younger folk on to the roof, and we could see bright eyes peeping in through the smoke-hole. The whole house was clean and swept and gay with rugs and carpets; the fire was bright, and over it capacious cooking-pots were simmering. On the major dais, opposite us, four people only were in evidence: the khalifa, whose badge of office was a huge pair of spectacles; the bridegroom in a bright silk overdress, a new *choga*, and cap of spotless white homespun (his eyes were blackened and a row of tiny dots of black becomingly distributed on his cheek bones); the "best man" and an equivalent representative of the bride, probably a maternal uncle. Every available inch of other space was gradually filled with members of the two families who, as they arrived at the door, were ceremonially sprinkled on cap and left shoulder with flour. The bride's father was standing near the store-room door, the mother modestly just inside it. Probably but for our space-consuming presence—which filled us with some compunction—they would have been seated on the second dais.

After we had taken our places and had exchanged greetings and congratulations all round, the simple but impressive ceremony began. The khalifa, with his open manuscript, sat at the outer edge of the dais, the bridegroom squatting beside him on his left, while the two best men stood gravely facing them. A railing, hung with a silk curtain, screened the further section of the dais, where the bride was temporarily concealed, supported by her brothers and maternal uncles. The service was in Persian, with a strong admixture of Arabic, and was read—or repeated from memory—clearly and reverently in a pleasant sing-song recitative, which rose to a beautiful intoning when rehearsing the names of God, the Merciful, the Compassionate, the Forgiver of Sins.

When the religious exercise was over, the khalifa reverted

to the Burushaski of everyday, and enquired of the father whether the milk-money had been duly agreed on. "Yes," he replied, "500 rupees (about £35)." This left us fairly gasping till the colloquy went on: "And are you willing to remit 20 rupees in the name of Allah?" "Assuredly." "And 20 rupees in the name of the Prophet, on whom be peace?" "Agreed." "And 40 rupees in the name of the Imáms?"—and so on. The khalifa eventually thus worked the sum down to 40 rupees (£3). We afterwards heard criticisms of what was otherwise acknowledged to have been a fine performance of the khalifa's: he should have persevered till he got the milk-money down to 5 rupees (= 7s. 6d.); "but it doesn't matter, they won't in any case pay more; seven and sixpence is the current rate."

Then the embers of the fire were blown upon and some Syrian Rue thrown in, which filled the house with a delightful smell of incense. The khalifa now turned to the bridegroom: "I now ask of you, So and So, the son of So and So, Barataling, are you willing to take this girl, Rahil, daughter of So and So, Khurukuts, to be your wedded wife?" The question was put three times, and three times the bridegroom answered clearly: "Yes, willing." Then the girl's uncle, acting as her best man, stepped to the screen and looking over proposed to her the complementary question, and her voice answered: "Yes, willing, willing, willing."

The bridegroom's best man now lifted a silken handkerchief off a small wooden cup of water which the uncle had been holding all the while and passed the cup to the priest, who breathed over it in blessing, and gave it to the bridegroom, who solemnly—and audibly—sipped three times. The uncle now took the cup and passed it under the silken curtain to the bride, who did likewise. The two were now man and wife; the silk curtain was withdrawn and the bride tenderly led out. This courtesy might have been performed by the officiating uncle, but it seemed that he had been twice married, so another male relative, "the husband of one wife," gave her his arm. Bride and groom then seated themselves with linked arms side by side in the centre of the dais while a flat platter of very thin wheaten pancakes was brought and presented to them. The bridegroom broke a piece of bread and, before eating, ceremonially touched with it his lips and forehead. The gesture was not unlike that with which a devout Roman Catholic crosses himself before meat. The bride followed suit, and then retired again to her corner now unscreened. She was dressed in red silk and wore a pair of red-dyed soft leather boots; a tinsel scarf shot with gold and orange had been flung over her cap.

The ceremony was now complete, so we said good-bye to our host and hostess, thanking them most warmly for having allowed strangers to come, and pressing into their hands a modest gift of silver for the young husband and a bundle of embroidery silks wrapped in silver paper for the bride. With all-round greetings and best wishes we then withdrew, winning a special smile from the bride, leaving the two families to get down unembarrassed to their feast.

The silken handkerchief which covers the ceremonial drinking-cup is one of the perquisites of the khalifa, and we heard that—having no use for it himself—he usually trades it off to the next clients who summon him for a betrothal, and so it goes the rounds.

It had for a time looked as if we should altogether fail to witness a betrothal, but the ice having now been broken, we were honoured by several further invitations. We accepted one other in which the bridegroom was a relative of Qudrat Ullah's. It more or less duplicated the first; the khalifa recited somewhat less well, and the whole proceedings seemed to us a trifle less well organized. When the milk-money discussion was proceeding Qudrat Ullah suddenly broke in: "Oh, cut the cackle, and get down to five rupees at once!" The suggestion was duly acted on amid much laughter. The fictitious figure first quoted is a compliment to the bride, and in Nagir it is the custom, we were told, to start at thousands of imaginary rupees. This second bride was unusually plain, poor girl—scarcely worth 7s. 6d. at prevailing rates, we thought.

David was pressed to take photographs, which he duly tried to do. It was no easy task in a smoke-darkened, crowded room, with a shaft of bright sunlight striking obliquely through the smoke-hole, and innumerable youngsters in continuous movement. Still, he got some records, if not exhibition photographs, of the event.

In many ways Hunza marriage customs are more enlightened than our own. The newly wedded pair are permitted the privacy of some barn or outhouse for their early days, but the two are not abandoned to their own inexperience to make or mar their future physical relations; no terrified bride is forcibly raped on her wedding night by the clumsy impetuosity of her mate, no diffident and chivalrous boy left agape in ignorance of acceptable advances. The bridegroom's mother stays with them, and teaches him to woo and win in such fashion that both may have the maximum joy of their new experience. In cases where the bride is over-fearful or over-young, the boy's mother will sleep between them to protect her till the couple are ripe for mating, and should the bride conceive an unconquerable aversion for her husband the marriage is tolerantly annulled by consent. Her own mother will reason with her and endeavour to persuade her, but the girl will not be coerced against her will.

When the instructional honeymoon is over the young people take their place with the other married pairs in the common living-room, where kindly darkness gives privacy at night to all.

As soon as a woman is aware that she has conceived, she quits her husband's side and joins the other women on their sleeping bench, while he rejoins the group of bachelors, and not until their child is weaned will the couple mate again. A husband who babbled of marital rights as overriding the rights of wife and child would be an outcast amongst his kin. If a father by impatience robs his child of the full period of its mother's nursing—usually three years for a boy and two for a girl—the pirate baby that ensues is stigmatized by a name more opprobrious than "bastard." This enforced continence appears to inflict no hardship on the husband; he is not asked to exercise it in a *solitude à deux* or the provocative proximity of a barbaric double bed. Moreover, he has known from babyhood that such a forbearance forms an integral part of the scheme of married life; he has been married early and has no arrears of sex-starvation to make up, and he lives a healthy, active, outdoor life with no unwholesomely suggestive literature or cinema shows to stir his blood to rebellion. This admirable convention automatically spaces Hunza infants at decent intervals without artificial birth-control.

Unfaithfulness on either side is extremely rare, and I venture to assert without fear of contradiction that in Hunza morals are higher than in any other country in the world. There is no prostitute in the country, and no venereal disease. We may, I think, fairly ascribe this to high principle and a strongly developed tradition of fine practice, but we need not overlook the fact that circumstances conspire to reinforce principle. DL and I used sometimes to amuse ourselves speculating on the possible ways in which a pair of errant lovers, if such existed, could gratify their guilty passion, and we decided that the way of transgressors would be exceptionally hard.

No man or woman could be absent from the usual sleeping place without immediate comment, and by day each person's duties and destinations and occupations are common knowledge. The countryside lies sloping and open to view, and every corner and cranny of it, even the desolate rocky mountain sides where large boulders or ravines or semi-caves might seem to offer privacy, is subject to invasion at any moment by a herd-child with his goats. One tale was told us of an intriguing pair. The woman lover went to the edge of the river cliff, left some identifiable articles on the brink, and staged an accident. She then hid herself with the mother's connivance in the locked store-room of her lover's house. No search was made for the body, for these mountain rivers reveal no secrets, but it was, of course, not long before her presence in her lover's house was discovered. The unusual case came up before the Mir, whose sane judgment was that the guilty pair had better be divorced from their lawful partners and married to each other. Public opinion would have none of it, and while discussion was proceeding the disgraced woman drowned herself in earnest. I don't remember what the man's fate was, but general odium would certainly compel him to seek voluntary exile.

Where a couple are definitely ill-matched, or the daughter-in-law fails to fit into the family scheme, the regrettable fact is faced, the two families meet to arrange a divorce, and each party is free to remarry and hope for better luck. Nothing, however, in our Hunza observations amazed us more than the amicable relations that normally prevailed among the women of a household. There would be a mother-in-law with three or four sons' wives, all perhaps with growing families about them, an adolescent girl or two, and the herd of youngsters. They work together from dawn to dusk without argument or recrimination, and apparently without anyone's attempting to shirk her fair share of the common tasks.

An expectant mother works on in house and field till the very last, but by common consent the heavier tasks are divided amongst the others, and an extra-nourishing ration is assigned to her both before and after the baby's birth. There is no sentimental pampering of the mother, but her immediate job is the baby, and she is expected naturally to concentrate on that. When a woman's monthly affliction overtakes her, she dresses in her oldest clothes and lies immobile by the fire till she is well again. The others make *daudo* for her, a porridge of flour well boiled in water, which is reputed very sustaining, and bring it to her, saying, "Sister, eat." After two days she is herself again, takes a bath, washes her clothes, and sweeps the house; but she is not banished as a pariah nor subject to any degrading superstitions nor to any taboo not imposed by nature.

Shyly one day my friend Zénába asked me was it true that white women were immune from monthly trouble. "We notice that English ladies seem to ride and camp at all times; we have never heard of one of you having to lie up." I explained our habits and conventions, and that we made it our pride to carry on outwardly unruffled. "But surely it can't be good for you?" "I don't believe it is; but there you are; it is our custom, and we should think it shame if the household noticed any difference in our behaviour. It sometimes makes us cross and fretful perhaps, and then our menfolk just think how unreasonable women are." She laughed heartily: "So that's how it is; we've always wondered; but I think our way is better."

"I'm sure it is," said I, "and you are well again in two days, whereas our discomfort lasts twice as long."

So I betrayed to them some of our minor secrets, but I could not bear to reveal to these innocent, clean-minded people the cankers of our vaunted civilization: the dark, unanswered questions that cloud our childhood (in this matter there is nowadays, thank God, much more, though still only sporadic enlightenment); the too-long postponed marriage; the widespread sex-starvation; the so-called wild oats of so many young men; prostitution, unmarried motherhood, or the unwanted celibacy of so many young women; the secret, second establishments of so many respectable fathers of families; the sordid adulteries that lead to the divorce court—all the tangled maladjustments of our modern life in the West, where insane economics have trampled the humanities in the dust.

One of my gravest disappointments in Hunza was that for all my free and easy intercourse with the womenfolk I was not able to glean much of the more intimate detail of their married life: of their pregnancies and child-bearing and the like, from the woman's point of view. I had hoped to be able in such matters to offer a useful complement to David's masculine researches, but in fact he learned far more than I did. I rarely or never got a chance to speak to an older woman alone, or quietly, for any length of time; friends, relations, children, and babies were always buzzing round. There is no false prudery in Hunza, and children know the basic facts of life from infancy and hear grown-up discussion on any topic under heaven; but there is great fastidiousness and decency in speech, and it would have required far more subtle knowledge of their conventions than I possessed to have framed my questions inoffensively, even if I had mustered the nerve to frame them at all.

This mattered the less that DL in his quiet *tête-à-tête* in the study, with his various informants, was able to go into all such matters with unembarrassed freedom. I had also hoped to be perhaps allowed to be present at the birth of a child, and to this end had taken a superficial course of study at Queen Charlotte's Hospital, which, as things turned out, I had no opportunity of utilizing. I should not, of course, have dreamt of offering advice or help—the reckless courage with which some travellers ply their medical ignorance has always horrified me—but I thought that some knowledge of birth-rites at home might enable me to follow Hunza procedure with more intelligence. But if an Englishman's house is his castle, the fortress-like home of the Hunzukuts is no less inviolable, and in the event I could no more have proposed to a Hunza woman to let me attend her confinement for mere scientific curiosity than I could make the same proposal to an English friend.

Like women in many other parts of the East, the Hunza woman bears her child in a crouching posture, which gives full play to her muscles—admirably developed by varied exercise and unatrophied by chair-sitting—and speeds up the period of labour. An experienced woman, usually her own mother, acts as midwife, while her husband guards the threshold and her brother the smoke-hole to prevent the instrusion of evil man or evil spirit. Within a week, as has been related, she is ready to receive visitors, and within a fortnight she is out of doors again doing light work in the fields.

There are, of course, no vital statistics available for infant or maternal mortality, but as far as my enquiries and observations extended, casualties are rare. This is not to be wondered at, since for countless generations Nature has here been at her beneficent work of weeding out inferior stocks, uninterrupted by soppy sentiment or misguided philanthropy. No C3 girl baby can be reared in an incubator to die in childbirth or burden the community with D4 offspring.

Chapter 23

WINTER AND THE "GREAT COLD"

No climate could be more delightful than the autumn and early winter of Hunza, from October till far on in December, and the Burusho make the most of these bracing, genial days, hurrying to get through every sort of outdoor job before the six or eight weeks of the "Great Cold."

Not by any means every household can spare water, manure, or space for a vineyard, but those who can value not only the fresh grapes which ripen later than all other fruits, but also the home-made wine which helps to brighten the cheerless winter days. Unfortunately, by the time the grapes are ripe, the sun has already lost its heat and raisin-drying is impossible. At least this was the only plausible explanation we could get for the fact that the Hunzukuts who dry their mulberries and apricots do not make raisins.

The vines are trained over low pergolas only 3 or 4 feet high, less frequently allowed to climb up living trees. Since the Hunzukuts greatly value shady sitting places we wondered why they did not go in for loftier pergolas like those the Persians love. The explanation is cruelly simple—they cannot spare the extra length of poles.

There were not many vineyards in Aliábád, but we located two favourably situated ones and paid several visits to each. One was many hundred feet down, at Gulkhan, below the old fort. Though the vine leaves were still green, every bunch of fruit had been already cut when we came down to see the wine-making. Under the roof of an open-faced shed were three "mangers," as it were, set side by side, the two end ones stacked high with ripe grapes. There must have been 3 or 4 cwt. at least in each. The centre one was only partially full.

The central compartment—not unlike a kitchen sink—had a stone floor slightly sloping towards a hole in front which was fitted with a neat little spout of birchbark, below which a great iron cauldron stood. One of the young men of the family (having doubtless washed his feet) leapt into the sink, rested his hands on the sides of it, and tramped, tramped, tramped, with all his weight. It looked very like hard work. Another man crouched alongside the spout, holding a large-meshed basket which filtered the juice as it ran out into the cauldron. The skins thus trapped were thrown back for another trampling. As required, further supplies of grapes were taken from the side compartments and thrown into the wine-press. After seeing our fill of this process and taking what photographs were possible in the patchwork of light and shade, we climbed steeply uphill to a flattish spot where other even more interesting activities were afoot.

Under a big boulder a flat stone had been converted into a trough by little "concrete" walls made of sand mixed with fat. The slimy mush of skins, stalks, and stones left after yesterday's pressing had been brought up here. In the trough they laid a wicker ring 9 or 10 inches across and a couple of inches thick. Into this they dumped as much of the green stuff as it would hold; then they laid another ring on the top of the first and filled it till they had a pile a foot high or so. On top they now placed a flat slab of stone, and across it a stout pole for lever, which they wedged firmly under the boulder as a fulcrum. The pole projected like one half of a see-saw. On to it a man leapt, thus pressing down the stone slab on to the articulated basket, and out gushed the juice into a vessel below. Then the stone was lifted, the top ring of the ingenious basket thrown aside, and the squeezing process repeated till nothing was left but a wet round cake of skins, seeds, and stalks. This is then put in the sun to dry, and is much valued as a cattle food. Our wine-friends told us that the wine made from this second pressing is counted superior to the first.

When the receiving vessels are full, the juice is transferred through a wooden funnel into a skin sack and set aside to ferment. It is not allowed to stand overlong, for October's brew will all be finished by the end of December, but a man is looked on as over-impetuous who does not keep it for at least a month. Old vintages are luxuries for wealthier lands. The Hunzukuts do not profess to be expert vintners or connoisseurs of wine. They consider it rather a gamble how the wine turns out: "Sometimes it is sweet and sometimes sour. Either is good to drink. But if we have enough manure and if the season has been hot enough fully to ripen the grapes, then the wine is sweet."

The wine and weaving having been disposed of and the winter-wheat sown, the year's serious work is over, and little remains but to fumigate the empty manure shed. We had come in from our walk one evening and were settling down to work after tea when I heard a modest little "Mother dear!" outside the window, and found Hérul Nisa had been sent down to tell us that Ustád Nadíro and Bibi Anjír were going to fumigate their byre in the good old style, if we would care to come. So we flung on our coats, seized a lantern, and scrambled up the particularly rocky track that led to No. 8. Bibi Anjír and her married daughter were watching proceedings from the roof of the byre which also forms the landing at the top of the ladder that leads to their verandah and summer living-room. The couple at No. 8 are old-fashioned and scrupulously keep up the ancient fumigating ceremony which many of their younger neighbours neglect.

The wall of their manure byre sticks out at right angles into the lane, and the door of it is sideways on. In the angle formed between it and the house, Nadíro had a little fire of dry sticks already burning. He took an iron ladle with a long handle and filled it full of precious apricot-kernel oil and heated it over the fire. There was a cold circular wind whizzing round which delayed the oil's getting warm and catching fire. We and a lot of interested neighbours pressed in round him as closely as we could to shelter the flame, which at last blazed up like the brandy in our tablespoons to light the Christmas pudding. Then the old man went into the byre and Hérul Nisa followed him with a bowl of cold water. He took a little of the water and flung it into the ladle four times, causing a lovely flare addressed to each of the four corners of the shed. To our amazement we saw by the light of the flames that the shed was chock full of goats (we had imagined that they would have been cleared out for the ceremony) who seemed not in the least perturbed. Nadíro then came out again and lit a torch of juniper twigs at the fire and went in to wave it similarly into each of the four corners. Bibi Anjír then handed down a big wooden basin of *múl* which looked like a rather slushy brown pudding with pinkish trimming on top. This festive dish is made only on special occasions, such as a child's birth or the like. Before starting in to eat the *múl* or hand it round, the old man took his stand in the door of the byre and with great dignity and reverence lifted his eyes to heaven and recited the fumigating prayer. Bits of it ran something like this: "O Moses, Holy Prophet, grant that one hundred milking vessels may be required, and that our shears may be used on a hundred sheep! May kid follow after kid and lamb after lamb! May there be rams with curly horns and he-goats with short horns turned in! May milk flow in floods and may the butter pit be filled with butter!"

Happily DL had already got the prayer written down so we were able to follow it better than if we had been hearing it for the first time, and were even able to note that the Ustád got it a bit mixed in parts. We ascertained what was the point of the "short horns turned in." It is simply a question of packing. The byres are small and the beasts have all got to live crowded together in them throughout the winter, so that a princely he-goat with spreading horns is a disaster to his owner and a danger to his fellows.

Now came the moment when the family and friends would tuck into the *múl*, and we thanked our kind hosts most warmly for letting us see the little ceremony, and fled to the warmth of our own fire and our butterless tea. I was in terror lest we should be pressed to partake of the *múl* which is so special a dish that it was sure to be reeking of priceless *maltash*—of which we had no wish to rob them.

The next item on the Hunza communal programme is the Great Wedding Day, which falls about mid-December on some

Thursday fixed by the Mir in consultation with the diviners. The sensible plan prevails of having all weddings celebrated on the same day throughout the country. This avoids all cross-entertaining and much reduces expense. The hungriest guest cannot attend more than one big feed at a time. All betrothals have taken place quietly a few weeks earlier at each family's own convenience. The Wedding Day is only the jollification which sets the seal of publicity on the existing private contract.

All the morning feasting is in progress at the bridegroom's house, attended by the menfolk of both families and by twelve of the bridegroom's tribal brothers who act as his "best men." In the early afternoon the bridegrooms and their guests all repair to "The Gate" of their village where every spare space is already packed with spectators. The women and children are collected roughly at one side, the men and boys at the other, but there is no taboo about this, and no offence is given if one or another happens to stray into or wishes to pass through a crowd of the other sex, nor was it thought odd or unseemly that I usually sat beside DL amongst the men.

Before we arrived, the tops of walls, the branches of the nearest trees, and all the adjacent roofs were packed (till we feared the slight rafters were bound to give). Everybody had turned out in their best and brightest clothes, our little boy and girl friends almost unrecognizable, their jolly little fringes soaked in oil and plastered down into most unwonted and unbecoming tidiness. The women and girls were very gay with bright-coloured scarves flung over their prettiest caps; poor ones might have only a piece of chintz or muslin, but by far the greater number sported lengths of Bukhara silk in daring blendings of bright green, yellow, red, blue, or purple. The general effect was delightful, and the bunches of womenfolk on the roofs would have needed colour photography to do them justice. Not to be wholly outdone, the men had coloured cotton shirts of marvellous hues and gay silken embroidery trimming their woollen *chogas*.

The Béricho band, with big drum, pipe, and kettledrums,

squatted at the base of a big tree, and the tribal brothers of each bridegroom led him to the dance. The Diramiting led off and the other clans followed in their recognized order of precedence. Each unhappy bridegroom was amazingly got up. Instead of his ordinary homespun cap he was coiffed with an exotic white or coloured turban with a tuft of feathers at one side held in place by a fancy brooch and a dangling string of beads looped on to it. A brightly coloured silk shirt floated out over a startlingly white pair of baggy cotton trousers and (if he could afford it) a loose silk robe replaced his normal homespun *choga*. He carried in his right hand an old-fashioned battle-axe tied with silken ribbons, and in this gaudy attire he looked as ill at ease as bridegrooms the world over.

The picturesqueness of the Hunza dancing, which is the mainstay of every form of merry-making, is nowadays much impaired by dancers who have acquired short-sleeved, would-be European shooting-jackets or tight trousers, or—worse still—have adopted tennis shoes or ammunition boots or some other form of horrible non-local footgear instead of the orthodox bare feet or soft leather boot. When carried out in the correct dress of the country Hunza dancing is amusing and interesting. Most of the footwork is merely a variant of a sort of polka-step—now short, now long, now in great leaps, now in fierce stamps, now on the toe, now on the flat foot. There is one characteristic step which would require a lot of practice: with one knee bent very deep, you rotate on that foot giving regular little taps on the ground with the other till the circle is complete; then you reverse and repeat in the opposite direction.

Each dancer dances independently, but the five or ten in the ring at any one moment all try to synchronize their steps in time to the music. The footwork, however, is but a small part of the dance; what is most admired is the action of the body and of the arms; these are waved and flung about and bent in a hundred different patterns. The long *choga* sleeves which dangle 6 or 8 inches below the hand give a most fantastic effect to these gestures.

When the second bridegroom's group came to dance they

were joined by a young princeling (a morganatic grandson of the Mir's) and a small friend of his, both in lovely silken gowns. They were a picturesque wee pair. The younger was about six, and his fond mother had got him up as a bridegroom, complete to the blackened eyes and fantastic dots on the cheek bones. The two boys polkaed round, stamping their bare feet and waving their tiny arms in perfect imitation of the grown-ups, and whenever they were in danger of being danced down, some kind hand would gently shove them to a safer place in the centre, where they went on gyrating. It was a jolly scene. Whenever there was room other small boys would join in, each normally venturing to do so only when his own clansmen were dancing. Once or twice some little dare-devil would intrude into the wrong group, and another small boy would try to punch his head. At once good-humoured bystanders would collar the pair and dump them out of mischief at some distance from each other.

All the spectators were very merry in their orderly way, and there were bursts of applause at frequent intervals. No small share of the fun was contributed by the bandsmen, who varied the time and pace and worked the dancers up to a fine climax. The big drummer of Aliábád is an old humorist called Húko. He waves his body and his arms about as he lustily attacks his drum and chaffs the dancers: "Go it, man! Leap, can't you, leap! Do you call that *dancing*? What are your legs for? Let your body swing, man! Get a move on there! Wave your arms, can't you? Oh, come alive!" etc., etc. The kettle-drummer flaunts his two sticks and wags his head, but being a younger and less privileged person than Húko does not venture on any verbal chaff. The poor piper who has mouth and hands glued to his funny-looking instrument that is half flute half trumpet just flings his body about and looks volumes. All three are so very much alive and on the spot that they imply that nothing else in life is quite such fun as playing while other men dance and marry. Their special efforts on such occasions are rewarded by extra gifts of bread, flour, and butter.

After about an hour and a half we came away, but for long

after we could still hear the dance-music going on. When dusk begins to fall the bridegroom betakes himself with his train of tribal brothers to his bride's house, where feasting is resumed. When the guests can eat no more or the food is finished—which ever happens first—the bridegroom's party carry off the bride to her new home. In theory they carry her all the way, but as that may be for some miles across rough country they frankly admit that they soon set her down and let her walk herself, but carry her again when near their goal. On arrival the bridegroom's family welcome her at the door with incense and thin bread. Then the pair take hands and step over the threshold together putting their feet down simultaneously. The bride then advances to the hearth which is henceforth to be her own. She touches the hearth-stones with her fingers which she then kisses. She is then led to the seat of honour by the main pillar of the house and food is brought for her party, who presently return home. A brother or maternal uncle and a bridesmaid remain with her that first night.

Next morning the mother-in-law leads the bride to the flour bin and sets her to bake thin wheaten bread. She kneads the flour, rolls out the thin pancake, and flings it on the griddle for the waiting bridegroom to turn. If she spoils the bread he is entitled to tap her with the bread-turner; if, on the other hand, he botches the baking she is entitled to smack him with the rolling-pin.

The last public episode before the Great Cold is the Tumushelling, the Midnight Bonfire of the Winter Solstice, a ceremony which, so far as anyone could tell us, had never before been witnessed in Hunza by a European, and small wonder, for late December is no time for a Political Agent to be on tour nor for globe-trotters to trot. We owed our chance of seeing it to our temerity in wintering on the spot. The Hunzukuts have long since adopted the Muslim Nauroz (the vernal equinox) as their official New Year, but not improbably their earlier custom was to reckon the turn of the year from mid-winter.

We had been told that we should be awakened in the small

hours by the loud drumming of a warning drum; then after an interval we should hear two outbursts and soon after, three, at which point we should set out. We could not ascertain how long the intervals would be between the summonses, but Dádo promised to waken us at the sound of the first. He was so fearful of oversleeping that he lay awake all night, and with characteristic zeal brought us morning tea two hours too soon. The third drumming was not, in fact, heard till about 5 a.m. It called us out into the inkiest night I ever saw, but it was windless and not unduly cold. Thick snow clouds over the whole sky hid every suspicion of a star, so that though the great mountains all round were white with snow to within a few feet of our level there was not even a glimmer from them.

All over the hillsides we could see tiny points of light converging on the rendezvous and hear the lively chatter of men and boys from every homestead. Their torches were faggots of juniper held high on a long pole. From the polo-ground came the sound of music punctuated by unison cheers of Ha-Ha-Ha that echoed up the hill to hurry stragglers. By the time we got down there was already a goodly group of men thronging three deep round a princely bonfire, and each new party as it came flung in its torch over the heads of the crowd sending a shower of rocket sparks into the darkness of the night. Our arrival was greeted by a cheer and a lane was made for us to a stone sofa, where we speedily obliterated ourselves not to interfere with the progress of events, regretting only that our people had not thought to provide us with torches instead of the prosaic hurricane lamps which they doubtless thought more dignified.

The bonfire leapt, the band played, the jolly Ha-Ha-Ha sounded at intervals, and still the velvet darkness was starred by points of oncoming light. As soon as a sufficient congregation had assembled, the band struck up in earnest and dancing began. In the flickering firelight the scene looked extraordinarily romantic. Prominent among the dancers were the bridegrooms of a few days ago, who thus made their re-entry into public life, clad happily once more in caps and woollen *chogas*. The dancers sprang and capered, their long sleeves dangling fantastically as they waved their arms; now you saw them in inky silhouette, now full-lit by the flames; and behind the serried rows of eager laughing faces was nothing but the impenetrable blackness of the starless night.

After a short spell of ordinary dancing, more spirited and vigorous in the darkness than by day, swords and shields were brought and two men stepped into the ring. They threw their arms up into the air with sword and shield, leaped several times as high as they could with both feet together, and then staged a splendid duel: the one pursuing, the other fleeing, now this way, now that, and all the time the great curved swords flashed in the firelight and cut the air. When one fighter overtook the other, sometimes by a daring leap across the fire, they slashed and hacked till you felt sure that at any moment an ear or nose would go. When one pair was exhausted, they would suddenly fling up their weaponed arms again, turn sharply about, and bang their backs together in the oddest gesture imaginable, then lay down sword and shield and merge into the crowd as another pair stepped forward. Now and again the crowd would call by name on some favourite champions, who came forth with modest reluctance to take the challenge.

The variety of their poses and feints and gestures was astonishing; each couple improvised at will but kept in perfect time to the music. It was the best display of sword dancing I have ever seen, and the duels were more real than any I have witnessed on a stage at home: just as safe and incomparably more convincing. All the while the crowd shouted and cheered and bandied jests about, the band banged indefatigably, and every now and then in would whizz yet another blazing torch with its attendant shower of sparks.

We watched the ever-changing pageant for a couple of hours without the slightest boredom. Still there was not the faintest streak of dawn, and the pessimists were whispering anxiously: "Great Scott, we must have started too soon, the wood will never last out!" And in truth the apparently inexhaustible mound of firewood was waning fast. At last the eastern sky above the mighty mountain rampart of the Nagir side showed faintly pale. With a cry of delight willing hands flung on all the remaining wood for a final flare up; there was one last uproarious scamper of many dancers: and all was still. Then up stood a pair of men, reverent, solemn, sword in hand, and recited a moving litany:

> May the New Year be blessed!
> May the seed bring forth an hundredfold!
> May every ear be filled with golden grain!
> May the mountain side be piebald with goats!
> May the pastures be piebald with sheep!
> May kid follow after kid and lamb after lamb!
> May our houses be filled with children and empty of sickness!

and to each clause the congregation fervently shouted "Yá! Yá!" as an earnest Amen.

After some time the older man who was leading began to repeat himself somewhat, and a good-humoured protest went up: "Enough, Uncle, enough!" which brought the litany to a speedy conclusion. (What a useful innovation this would be in Church and Parliament!)

Then half a dozen grey-bearded men formed a semi-circle to face the rising but still long invisible sun, and struck up a delightful solemn chant that sounded not unlike a Te Deum. In contrast to the litany which was in wholesome, rhythmic Burushaski prose, the chant was in so-called Shina, mangled by generations of Burusho singers into an almost unintelligible, though impressive anthem. David later took it down verbatim, but could only very partially reconstruct or divine the Shina original, and so far he has not been able to trace the ungarbled Shina text, which is quite possibly no longer known in its country of origin.

Then, while drum and kettledrum and pipe still played and the old men still chanted, we all moved slowly downhill in the growing daylight to "The Gate," where dancing was resumed by those who wished it, and a faint lamp burning in the Assembly Hall silently summoned the pious to morning prayer, and the ice-bound pond invited them less cordially to the preliminary ablutions. Few seemed to accept the chilly invitation.

Except myself, no woman had attended the Midnight Bonfire, but the usual gaily dressed crowd were at "The Gate," just as on the recent Wedding Day. I slipped across to join the women and got a warm reception from many whom I knew and more whom I did not. Then an old crone came along, bearing a huge dish of flour and sprinkled a pinch on every woman's cap and left shoulder, saying as she did so: "Ya Ali!" All seemed pleased when I said: "Nay, mother, would you forget me?" and as she duly sprinkled me too I slipped a few pence into her hand. Then I extricated myself from the women's throng, scattering good wishes as I went, to rejoin David, whom I found similarly be-floured.

We thankfully toiled uphill home, too hot now in our midnight wrappings, and very shortly faithful Zaidu and Dádo produced a hot breakfast, after which we turned in and slept. There must be some magic in the Hunza air. You would hardly contemplate sitting out of doors to watch an open-air show at home at 7,600 feet from 5 to 8 a.m. on December 21st (or even on December 16th, for the Hunza calendar has got its Solstice slightly "fast") with the thermometer reading 22° Fahrenheit.

There was to be more dancing that p.m., but we felt we had seen enough for one day, and the headmen seemed relieved when we said we would not come. They confessed that after the bonfire people went home and made merry with their wine, and that there might be some mild rowdyism—and since they have no other drink but water, who shall blame them? Not we, dissolute bibbers of hot tea! We did not want to spoil our impression of the astounding orderliness of the night's merry-making. Though everyone was in the highest spirits and the youngsters full of excitement, the crowd's behaviour was perfect. Even when one torch flew right across the circle into the faces of half a dozen spectators, there was only a laughing stampede, and when the circle drew in too close and threatened to impede the dancing, some responsible grown-up simply snatched a brand from the fire and swept it round the front ranks, driving the children back amidst fun and laughter. Considering that there are no police in the country, and that the headmen have no authority except their personal influence, we found the lack of even minor misdemeanours among the Hunzukuts perennially astonishing.

The Tumushelling Bonfire would seem to have originated amongst the Shins, but the Hunza Burusho, with their delight in pageantry, have lifted it and made it the central item in whatever were their own original Solstice rites. The oft-told story of the Bonfire is this: Once upon a time there lived a tyrant King of Gilgit, Shíri Badat by name, who exacted the tribute of one lamb or kid daily from his people. The custom was that each house in turn should pay the tribute. One day the turn fell to a poor old woman who possessed nothing in the world but one well-beloved pet lamb. Shíri Badat ate the lamb as usual, but remarked that it had a peculiarly delicate flavour, and asked its history. The old woman was summoned to the presence and cross-questioned. Yes, it was rather a special lamb. The ewe, its mother, had died when it was born, and the old woman had given it to her daughter-in-law to suckle; so the lamb had been reared on human milk.

This proved an unfortunate revelation, for from that day forward Shíri Badat demanded a human infant per day, and would not be gainsaid. The country groaned in misery, but the people were helpless, for Shíri Badat was no mortal man to be easily murdered; he was of Peri stock, and bore a charmed life.

Now it happened that a young prince from a neighbouring country had fled in disguise to Gilgit to escape intriguers seeking his life at home. He had taken sanctuary in the Wazir's house, and there he met Princess Nur Bakht, who was a foster-child of the Wazir's. The two young people fell in love, and when the Princess found she was with child she was filled with fear lest her baby should fall a victim to her father's unnatural appetite. So the Wazir, the Prince, and she hatched out a plot in which Nur Bakht was to play the rôle of Delilah to the cannibal Samson, Shíri Badat.

"Father," she said one day, "your subjects are full of wrath and hate because of the baby-tax you levy on them; I fear me they will find some means to slay you. Now if I knew the secret of your life I could the better protect you against harm."

The old simpleton thereupon revealed to her that while he was invulnerable to spear or arrow, axe or sword, his heart was made of butter and he could be destroyed by fire.

The conspirators thereupon, working privily by night, dug a trench close under the walls of the King's fort and filled it with dry wood, and on a given night at a given signal every Gilgit household poured forth its menfolk armed with blazing torches which they flung into the trench with a great cry: "The enemy is upon you!" The butter-hearted tyrant ran forth and perished miserably in the circle of fierce heat, and the Prince and Princess reigned in his stead.

While Gilgit itself has long since ceased to celebrate its deliverance, the Tumushelling Bonfire in Hunza keeps aflame the memory of Shíri Badat and his heart of butter. In olden days it seems that every Hunza household let its fire die out and rekindled the hearth by a brand from the Tumushelling Fire, but this practice had lapsed before any of our informants could remember.

One winter day, after a gruelling forenoon of solid hard note-taking, DL said: "I'm just about half dead. We must take a quiet walk this afternoon. We'll go up to the Mir's Stables; we can't meet anyone up there. I positively could not talk or listen any more."

The "Mir's Stables" bear no relation to a stable as we understand it. Above the line of terraced fields that sweep round the bay of Aliábád there are 200 or 300 feet of sloping mountain side, forming rude pasture grounds: the *toqs*. Above them rise the steep sand and rock slopes that flow down from the towering crags above. A little farther down the valley from us there is a kind of shelf above the *toqs*, a small roughly level plateau, scattered thick with huge boulders, which is called the "Mir's Stables." It isn't irrigated from any channel; it lies above the highest one, which in any case has petered completely out before it gets so far; but as it is fairly flat it catches any rain or snow there is, and it gets a certain amount of snow and rain drainage from the rocks above, and so in between the boulders and rocks there are patches of coarse, natural grass and thorn bushes. This bit of ground belongs to the Mir, and once or twice a year he sends people to cut the grass, such as it is, and bring it in for his horses. It was rather a favourite walk of ours when we felt inclined for an upward scramble, for there is a fine view from it over the whole of the Aliábád Bay and the smaller Bay of Jamu, before the ground falls sheer away into the great Hasanabad gorge with the glacier at the top that waters the village of Hasanabad, our next neighbour downstream. Moreover, it is one of the rare places where, once you have got there, you can walk a little on the level, dodging about between the boulders. We were about halfway up to the Stables when Khano overtook us, desperately out of breath: "I've parked my animals in that garden over there, and I'm coming with you," he said. The "garden" was a desert of stones and rocks, with a rough, loose-stone wall about it and a few miserable stunted trees. "But we know the way quite well, thanks." "Oh no, you don't, not half so well as I do," he retorted. (This, of course, was true enough.) "I'll come with you."

So along he came, chattering away nineteen to the dozen, and most entertaining he was. "Do you see the Red Rock?" "There are heaps of red rocks." "Yes, but there's only the one big red boulder; that's the Red Rock. There's a cave under it where we boys shelter when it rains, and on top there are cracks in the rock that hold rain water where we can drink." Right enough, the great boulder—50 or 60 feet high, I suppose—overhung a hollow (you could hardly call it a cave) and the youngsters had built themselves a rude wall and made a very cosy nest that would hold several dozen animals. We scrambled up on to the top and found as he had said that there were several deep cracks which would evidently make neat little drinking troughs when they weren't dry. Then Khano took us round in and out of the boulders and showed us all the boys' pet places. In one they had improved a natural stone sofa and built a sheltering wall and rigged up a fireplace with a few stones, and there they cook potatoes for themselves (when they can get any). They have a very merry life out all day on the hillside in every sort of weather instead of crouching indoors over lessons. The goats climb for miles and miles, up and up amongst the stones till they look like mites in a cheese. What they find to eat is a mystery, for there is not one visible blade of grass and not one inch of thorn. But they "feed" there all day with the boys in the offing to see that they do not stray too far.

The Hunza sheep have prudently established the tradition that they cannot climb so high without breaking their legs, so they stay farther down where there is a small amount of very scanty grass (a home sheep would not recognize it as such) and an occasional dead leaf to gorge on.

Khano pointed out the "lizards' apricots"; patches of yellow, green, grey, and white lichen, which he says the lizards live on. He showed us the spoor of a fox and the tracks of his friends and a host of other interesting things. He's an amusing little play-actor. "Oh, I've got a thorn in my foot!" and he pretended to cry and limp helplessly about. Then with a laugh he clutched his foot, stooped to meet it, and whisked the thorn out with his teeth—a huge thing it was. Next he pulled a *mindak* out of some unexpected recess in his clothing and tried to teach us to play shuttlecock. The *mindak* is a most attractive toy. You get a small flat central button of lead and somehow contrive to attach to it a horizontal frill of kids' hair, black or white preferred. You then throw it in the air and try to kick it up with your foot, counting how often you succeed before letting it fall to the ground. You may kick it with your instep in an amateurish way, but the stylish thing is to strike it with the sole of your bare foot. The boys are extraordinarily adept, but the art is one not easily acquired in leather-shod middle age. Our indifferent attempts reduced us all three to helpless laughter. We were much amused to note that just as with the girls stotting their balls, the reckoning started at three and your first successful stroke was counted "four." In return for this demonstration lesson I tried to teach Khano to do handstands and cart-wheels, but my attempts to demonstrate these arts were somewhat unconvincing.

On the way home we met Kamber (Ustád Nadíro's boy) driving his herd of goats helter-skelter downhill. DL had recently burnt a hole in one of his pockets and a cigarette mouthpiece was sticking out (this was the first I had heard of the catastrophe). "Shame, shame! Mother dear!" the boys shrieked with delight. "Why won't you mend it for him?" and the imp Khano officiously produced a needle from his woollen cap and offered it me with a bow worthy of Sir Walter Raleigh.

It was one of the most amusing of many delightful afternoons I remember with our boy companions, if not the entirely quiet and restful one we had set out to seek. Khano asked me to take a photograph of him. "But, my dear boy, I took a beauty of you the other day with your shoulder basket on your back." (His mother had been delighted with this.) "Yes, I know, but a basket is disgusting. I'd like one of just me." I could not resist the plea, and took a snapshot of him seated on a boulder, his merry, handsome face a-grin and a magnificent background of mighty mountains and eternal snow. Alas and alas! amidst our merriment I was careless and slightly shook the camera, and that photographic masterpiece was one of my most bitterly regretted duds. I took him many times again, but never hit off the "just him" that I missed that afternoon.

I have mentioned more than once the utter pricelessness of manure in Hunza. Every child out in charge of even only one cow or calf carries a shoulder basket on its back and scrupulously collects every ounce as it emerges. This keeps fields and lanes, courtyards and mountain sides as clean as a drawing-room floor (if only people would do this sort of thing at home!). As we were making our way home Khano spotted a few scraps that some careless herd had left behind, and hastily gathered them into the skirt of his *choga*. "Ah, ha," said I, "if you'd had your 'disgusting' basket with you, you would not have had to soil your *choga*." "That's no matter," he grinned as he carried his treasure trove along. Presently he saw a nice little hidey-hole under a rock and threw his find in there: "I'll come back and fetch it to-morrow."

If you have a decent cow she will yield you a basketful in two days, and it takes sixty baskets to manure a fair-sized field properly for the winter wheat. Very few people have more than two cows. . . . You can work it out yourself. I'd like to give our litter louts a few years' training in Hunza.

Salt is a crying need in Hunza, and while down-country rock-salt can be obtained on payment from Gilgit, few families can afford to buy. Hence in the relatively idle days of early winter you will see parties of women and girls and boys scouring the mountain side high up, and tasting as they go, till they find a patch of ground that seems to have a trace of saltiness in it. They scoop up the full of their baskets and carry this earth home. When salt is wanted they mount a conical basket filled with the saline earth over some receiving vessel. By pouring water through, they get a discoloured fluid, containing heaven alone knows what (probably a minimum of sodium chloride), which they pour straight into the vegetable pot.

Another job which is kept for winter days is the making of new fields. It is all too true that the Hunzukuts have not enough water to serve their existing fields. But there are optimists who cannot resist the attraction of making a new field wherever they see a patch of ground that might with luck be irrigated in a good year. It's a serious business tackling a rocky bit of mountain side. You roughly plan your field and then start hacking out a great triangular gash at the upper side. It is full of stones and boulders which have to be removed; the smaller ones are set aside for the revetting walls; the larger ones are laboriously broken up with sledge-hammers (or blasted if you can get hold of a little gunpowder); the stony earth is carefully sifted into separate piles of varying degrees of fineness. Then the lower supporting wall is built to the level required, stones are thrown in for a foundation, next the coarser earth, and the surface is dressed with the finer. Field-making is the only occasion on which a barrow of any kind is of use. These barrows, of which in our whole time we only saw four, are the only wheeled vehicles known in Hunza. Whether the Hunzukuts invented them themselves or whether someone once saw a wheelbarrow in use elsewhere and imported the idea, who shall say? Anyhow, the Hunza wheelbarrow is a delightful affair. A sort of rude ladder with four or five rungs is made. A thick section of a tree trunk about

9 to 12 inches in diameter is impaled on one of the rungs to form the wheel. Axis and wheel rotate together in the two side holes of the frame, and to reduce the friction a tough ring of wicker work is placed between the wheel and the side of the ladder-frame. One of the usual shoulder baskets is then lashed between a pair of the rungs, and *voilà* . . . your apparatus is complete.

There were several batches of field-making enthusiasts whom we used to visit on our afternoon excursions—cold work it must have been with the snow lying to within a few feet of where they were working, but they did not seem to feel it, or perhaps the vision of future crops helped to keep them warm.

When once the Great Cold lays its icy hand on the country all outdoor human activity ceases as suddenly and completely as the sound of flowing water, and no one voluntarily stirs abroad. Occasionally you may see a woman, wrapped in the warmest *choga* available, dash with a gourd or bucket to the nearest drinking tank, break the thick crust of ice re-formed since yesterday and bring home the needed water. The steep, irregular stone steps were glassy with frozen water; it would have been easy to fall in and difficult to scramble out, but we heard of no casualties. Once again we noted that families prone to accident are weeded out by beneficent Mother Nature when her ways are not interfered with.

Once a day some man or boy drives out the beasts to the nearest open reservoir to drink, breaking the ice anew for them. As the water level sinks the ice crust cracks like pastry, the centre falls in, leaving stratum after stratum 6 or 8 inches thick adhering shelf-wise to the stone walls of the reservoir.

The winter was in many ways a disappointment to us. We had hoped for bright days and clear air and magnificent photographs. In fact, all the great mountains round were wrapped day after day in swathes of dark, snow-depositing cloud, and the floor of heaven, impenetrably grey, seemed suspended menacingly just a few inches above our heads. The immediate visible landscape was the dreariest it is possible to conceive; not an evergreen tree or bush, not a square inch of green grass to break the grim monotony of sepia-grey-khaki rocks, cliffs, boulders, and gaunt tree-skeletons amidst which the cubes of stone-and-mud houses were indistinguishable save for the thin spiral of blue smoke that rose from their flat roofs at feeding time.

We were able to work on indoors, for informants were glad enough to come and sit by our fire and tell all they knew about any question asked, but we sorely missed the cheering chance encounters, the casual wayside chats that normally brightened our walks.

Indoors during the Great Cold the family is merry and happy enough. The recurrent tiny fire, whose ashes never quite grow cold and which is stirred into life at baking time, reinforced by human heat and not squandered by wanton draughts, keeps sufficient warmth alive for comfort, and the weeks of enforced leisure from outdoor work are thoroughly enjoyed. The women spin and sew and bake and tend the babies; the men mend and make their various implements; the children eagerly demand the right to help in every job for which they are ripe, while the old people come into their own and entertain the company by telling tales of every kind; not only nor even mainly tales of heroes and of kings, of raiding chiefs and bandit exploits from the good old days before the Serkár brought peace and security at the cost of adventure, nor folklore yarns borrowed from other times and climes—though they have good store of these; but the history of their country and its clans and anecdotes of every day. In this homely school the Hunza child learns all that it needs to know, the elements of ethics, morals, and religion, the accepted codes of decent behaviour, and all the accumulated wisdom of the land.

The Hunzukuts have no artistic gift of story-telling, and no professional story-tellers; they have no oral literature to match the Sagas of the North or the Persian wealth of the Thousand and One Nights, but they can tell a straightforward story simply and well and with considerable humour, and the phrases in which their yarns are couched have become sanctified and semi-stereotyped by frequent repetition. Some of these DL had recorded in 1923–24, and they were already in print when we returned to Hunza ten years later. We were surprised and delighted to find that if he read a paragraph aloud from his massive Volume II, it was not only understood by the hearer but would be continued verbatim to the end.

Many of the anecdotes of daily life are amusing and delightful; a few are tragic. DL has made a large and representative collection of them. I shall only summarize a couple here which particularly took my fancy. A certain Alipo (let us call him) had married Nuri, whose home was several miles away. As wives not seldom do, she had gone home to spend the day at her parents' house, and her mother baked a rich cake with butter, walnuts, and what not for the girl to take back with her to her husband's home. Now though she had undoubtedly been hospitably fed by her own people, Nuri on the homeward way could not resist taking the cake out from under her arm and eyeing it covetously, and from looking she advanced to tasting, and from tasting to eating, till quite half of the cake was gone. On arriving, she presented what was left of it to her mother-in-law with suitable expressions of goodwill. Her husband, jealous of his wife's reputation, looked at it in dismay. "What hungry person did you meet on the way?" he tactfully enquired. "I met no one." "Who, then, has been eating at the cake?" "Nobody. My Mother baked only half a cake." Next morning Alipo restored Nuri to her family for keeps, saying: "She is not only a greedy-guts but a liar; and not only a liar but a fool as well."

There is a sadder story of a young wife: Nimo's job was to shut the kids and lambs into a byre at some distance from the house before coming home at night. One evening she had left the task over long and was afraid of reproof if she were late returning. "They will come to no harm," she thought, "if I leave them out for once." By bad luck, however, there was a fox or wolf about, and when she returned to round up her charges next morning she found only their torn and scattered corpses. In grief and remorse she fled home to her own people. No undue reproach was levelled at her, but there was no disguising the gravity of the catastrophe. She brooded over the calamity her carelessness had caused, and one day her father found her dead in the byre, where she had hanged herself.

I had expressed a wish to see what winter life "By the Lamp" was like, and one day Levy Kalbi brought an invitation from his womenfolk to join them some evening in their house. I was warmly welcomed into the living-room, where twenty people were at home and many guests besides myself had been invited. The guests included all our own household except the Kashmiri sweeper. I made my way over to the women's side of the house and murmured such compliments as I could improvise, on the skill and diligence with which they stitched and teazed and span. It was amazing. I could only hope that their zeal was perhaps a little extra on my account. Presently, when all had settled down after my incursion, a princely dish of potatoes cooked in *maltash* (producing a sort of Irish stew effect) was set on the floor in the centre and a wicker platter heaped with bread and another piled with grapes. Kalbi had most thoughtfully asked me to have my own dinner before coming, for he feared that I might not be able to enjoy their food (as *maltash* is an inevitable ingredient in any food set before a guest, this was both tactful and humane). Another large dish of grapes was set near me, and the children who clustered round shared them with me without reluctance.

Again I marvelled at the spaciousness and freedom gained by an absence of furniture. We must have been thirty or forty in that tiny-seeming room, yet there was no sense of crowding, and there was perfect ease of movement. And again I marvelled at the natural graciousness and instinctive good manners of these unsophisticated folk. My hosts and hostesses, who had never had a European in their house before, made me feel welcome and at home, and were evidently not conscious of the slightest embarrassment themselves. In a few minutes two or three prostrate sausage-rolls of bedding came to life, bright eyes peeped out and the respective mothers' exhortations, "Go to sleep again, darling!" were just as successful as their equivalents in similar circumstances at home.

Only a couple of the very senior men of the family shared the extra feast, but the guests were warmly pressed to fall to. Each folded a flap of bread round his potato and ate it neatly as from an egg-cup. Then Kalbi's old father, the patriarch of the twenty, whose great-grandchildren were present in the room, a fine old greybeard, active and handsome still despite his years, set out to tell us his memories of the siege of Chitral and Kelly's famous march to its relief, in which he himself had taken part. That was only four or five years after "the downfall of Hunza," as he phrased it, but numbers of Hunza men enlisted in the British relieving force. (Another neighbour of ours in No. 6 was also one of Kelly's volunteers.) He showed me the sword he had carried and the handsome muzzle-loader with its forked rest, both carefully greased and kept in good condition as befits heirlooms of the kind. He discoursed with a tinge of unconcealed regret on the olden days when men were men and fighting was toward, "though of course peace is best," he added with incomplete conviction in his voice. The others broke in with questions, and led him on to talk of this episode and that, rehearsed no doubt many a time before, and to cap the tale he proudly put his finger through his jaw and out under his ear tracing the path of a Chitrali bullet. This honourable wound he wore more proudly than his medal, though this also was displayed with pride.

While he talked away with ease and modesty even the little children listened with intelligent attention, and you could easily picture them in years to come telling their great-grandchildren: "My great-grandfather used to say . . ." Their tastes uncorrupted by the sensational gossip of the daily press and the melodramatic improbabilities of the screen, their memories not undermined by second-hand book learning, these humble Hunza folk are immensely better educated than the products of our costly schools; not one of them but can tell you all the details of his own lineage for eight or nine generations back on either side. Outside Debrettites, how many of us British folk can do as much?

A youngster who has a taste that way or who covets the position of a priest in the future, can easily learn to read and write a little Persian and Urdu at the feet of one of the local khalifas. Burushaski has no script and is never written; nor would it carry anywhere outside the Hunza and Yasin valleys if it were. If he is more ambitious of letters, he can foot the four miles daily to Báltít, as Yaman and a couple of our other young friends did, and attend the Government-supported school with the sons and grandsons of the Mir and the Wazir. Promising children of the more well-to-do can attend a more advanced school at Gilgit, and the really studious may even make their way down to Srinagar.

Ninety-nine per cent of the population, however, happily still remain illiterate, and have not fallen victims to compulsory education. When the people would question me about conditions in England, they were horrified to learn of such things as rates and income-tax, but even more aghast at the tyranny that compels both boys and girls to spend the years from five to fourteen at school. "But that's the time when they ought to be *learning things*," they said.

When my pleasant evening "By the Lamp" was ended and I had said good-bye, cautiously descended the ladder and mounted my waiting horse, I was shocked to see my host accompanying us carrying a tray of food. I had expressly stipulated that I would only accept his kind invitation on condition of not being laden with food gifts to take home. To my protests Kalbi said: "Yes, yes, Mother dear, it's all right. I'm not forgetting. I'm only taking up his supper to the sweeper."

With honourable simplicity the Hunzukuts abide by the fundamentals of Islam as they understand them. They may not be strong on ostentatious prayer and fasting, they rack their brains over no theological subtleties, but a Believer is a man and a brother, be he a Kashmiri, be he twenty times a sweeper. Here was a man of substance, a Levy, a grandfather, a much respected citizen in his small community, climbing a mile uphill to carry with his own hands a share of the evening's feast to his absentee guest. That the man was absent was no doubt a tactful concession to any caste-prejudice with which India might have infected me.

The boys lighten the monotony of the indoor weeks of the Great Cold by occasionally dashing out for a hasty game of foot polo or tipcat with their friends or keeping themselves warm with *mindak* matches. Such young men as are real dance enthusiasts may dance every afternoon at The Gate, but they do not draw a large circle of spectators.

On one of the rare bright days that we were blessed with, word was sent us that a special show was being got up for that evening if we would care to come. We reached "The Gate" just before dusk and found a stone sofa duly carpeted for us. As the evening grew darker, the crowd became larger and the general feeling of infectious excitement increased, till at last the organizers of the show went round the crowd using their long sleeves as conductors' batons to mark time for the magnificent Ha-Ha-Ha and the unison clapping they so much enjoy which now announced the arrival of the performers. A lot of young men had got themselves up in various disguises, pairs of them stooping under a blanket with a horse's head fixed in front, pranced about most realistically under two boy-riders. Two other pairs were got up as markhor with real horns in front, while a fantastic huntsman with an aged muzzle-loading matchlock stalked them with exaggerated caution. Five or six were dressed up as women with silken veils to hide their moustaches. The best of all were two bent old men with flowing white beards; they were dressed in sheepskins with huge humps on their backs, and tottered very effectively on stout sticks. They contrived to look very aged and very frail. Then they got up a sham quarrel about the wife of one whom the other was supposed to have stolen. Thereupon they laid about each other with their cudgels—very carefully smiting only each other's well-padded humps—and did amazing leaps with their staves as jumping poles, the one lighting on the other's back and rolling him in the dust. This excellent horseplay was wildly applauded.

There were two absurd little boys with tiny besoms who made admirable clowns. They fussed about, sweeping the ground just in front of the dancers and choking everyone with dust, getting kicked out of the way and looking innocently pained at being so misunderstood. When anyone was knocked down in the rough and tumble they would officiously dash up to brush him down and get cuffed for their pains.

Altogether it was an extremely clever rag, mostly nonsense

and horseplay, of course, but with both humour and first-class mimicry. A lot of the witticisms were lost on us, being in the nature of "family jokes" only to be understood by the initiate, but they must have hit the mark, for they brought down the house. At one point one of the humped old men produced a mysterious black box from under his sheepskin and flung himself into a skilful caricature of DL taking photographs, pacing distances, peeping through view-finders, jotting things in notebooks, etc., etc. This was the star turn, and had been kept for the end. It was greeted with roars and howls of laughter, in which we joined till our sides ached.

After about half an hour, when everybody had been beaten and banged and rolled about enough to be tired out, we scattered home, surprised afresh at the magic in the air that made a show like this possible at 19° F. on a winter evening.

As we climbed home the great mountains of Nagir across the river were looking their best in the evening light with massed patches of fresh-fallen snow and Raka resplendent in a new silver satin coat. But in many ways the winter snows—on the rare occasions when you can see them at all—are disappointing. We had pictured the whole land above, say, 10,000 feet one mass of snow; but in fact most of the cliffs and slopes are far too steep to *hold* snow, however much may fall, and while you do get magnificent stretches of pure white these are spoiled artistically by intervening scars of black and brown, khaki or dull grey. The topmost peak of Raka herself is a sheer rock-face of some thousands of feet whose grey austerity renders it almost invisible above the eternal snows beneath.

We had now reached the month which the people call "Crazy January," with its sudden and erratic storms of wind, and when the wind chooses to roar down these gorges from the glaciers then, by Jove! you do feel a temperature of 19°. We personally were lucky, for our bunaglow was in a kind of sheltered pocket—a fact we regretted during the hot weather—and even when a wild wind was hurtling round it seemed just to miss our windows.

Our sponges had been frozen solid for weeks and our bathrooms were not places to linger in, but it was cosy near the fire—less cosy at our working-tables near the light—and when mealtimes came we would carry in a couple of blazing logs from the study to thaw the air of the dining-room. Lucky as we were about fuel, we could not afford a continuous fire in a second room. But wood is gracious stuff, and a quick blaze just for meals was better than nothing.

Chapter 24

BARLEY SOWING AND "STARVATION SPRINGTIME"

AFTER weeks and weeks of dismal weather, which except for absence of rain or damp was about as cheerful as Fleet Street in December, we woke on February 1st to a white world, a glorious clear sky and SUNSHINE, so we downed tools and went out with our cameras to enjoy life again. When it snows here —a very rare phenomenon at this level, 7,600 to 8,000 feet— it is a disappointing sight. There are no "flakes" at all. It is as if Someone were very half-heartedly shaking the finest castor sugar out of one of those inefficient sugar-casters that people exchange as wedding presents. Even when it had snowed all night there was only a tiny sprinkling on the ground, and long before it was light enough to take a photograph with a Christmas-card foreground the stuff had evaporated, leaving you with the dark, empty fields.

It was delightful to see the whole place full of people again as if by magic. The old folk out on their roofs "taking the sun," and the whole place a-twitter with kiddies of every size. The little ones had been invisible for three months, and even the bigger ones rarely seen and in small numbers: partly because they really haven't enough clothes. They wear no under-things at all, and in the bitterest weather, though they may be huddled in a tattered *choga* or two, you see their bare chests peeping through their cotton shirts. Oddly, though they cuddle their *chogas* over their heads, they never dream of crossing them in front. If Papa happens to possess a padded coat from Yarqand or a skin coat with its own wool inside, the family is well off, and anyone who has to go out will take the loan of it. In Kanízah's house (No. 3), though they are very, very poor, they are lucky enough to possess a woman's cloak of feather-wool. It looks extremely cosy and furry—though very old and greasy—with feathers sticking out all over it. When you can get enough down you spin the feathers in with the wool before you weave it. You can only use the breast feathers of the wild duck for the purpose, and it must take a lot of wild duck, which are seasonal and rare, to yield enough for seven yards of feather cloth. This cloak of No. 3 is the only one we have seen. So we watch "the cloak" go out for walks—now on Zenába, the cheery old mother, who is one of the few really ugly women here but who always wears a happy grin that would redeem any face, now on Apicho, the eldest unmarried daughter who seems to be always on the point of getting wed but always just failing for some reason to pull it off.

We eventually discovered the reason for No. 3's extreme and obvious poverty. Poor Zenába had produced five girls, including a pair of twins, and only one boy, the second youngest child. Yaman (in full Ali Aman Shah) was one of our best boy friends, a bright, intelligent boy full of life and fun and knowledge, and good at all boys' games, but he was only ten or thereabouts, and not yet able to help his father in the heavier work of irrigating, wall building, ploughing, etc., and poor Ali Akbar looked worn and frail with six to provide for single-handed—not to mention the rare extravagance of the cat. Yaman manfully did all he could, and in addition when he could be spared from home trudged four mountain miles to Báltít to attend the school there with the Mir's grandsons and a few other ambitious boys. A great little fellow, with (as far as we could see) a hard enough life before him.

Yet No. 3 was one of the most cheerful and most hospitable houses round.

We supposed that Apicho's prospective bridegroom was as poor as she, and when the two families came to tot up the necessary wedding feasts they just couldn't face it. Certainly it had missed fire twice after we had heard that the date was fixed (you can in certain circumstances get from the Mir a special licence to marry at irregular dates). Meantime no one seemed unduly cast down, and Apicho continued to grow her hair so as to be ready. Sometimes it stuck out all round her head in about a hundred tiny plaits, on other days she had a wonderful, if somewhat shaggy, mane of frizzy hair about 5 inches long. She was a dear.

The small boys and girls have the centre of their heads close shaven (a cleanly and sensible arrangement) with just a neat fringe left all round to show below their caps; married women wear, hanging down beside their faces, two plaits which are knotted up into two balls to be well out of the way. It is a most becoming style of hair-dressing. The plaits softly frame the face and the two balls dance merrily about. When a girl reaches thirteen or fourteen and marriage beings to loom ahead, she starts growing her hair in some variety of bob as a practical preparation for the state of matrimony.

We went off to one of the deep open reservoirs hoping in the good light to get a photograph of the cattle being watered at the usual time. But, alas! the nice bright day must have modified their time-table, for not the ghost of a beast turned up. On the way we saw a pretty young woman whom we knew, doing some washing. She was squatting in the sun on a stone sofa beside a pool which was still covered with thick ice and dipping the clothes in through a hole she had broken for the purpose. She then laid the wet garment on the stone and whacked it with a thick wooden beater. Further on, Najat of No. 1 was washing some tattered pieces of felt, probably to pluck down for shoddy. She had flung them into shallow water and was vigorously trampling them while chunks of ice clattered round her ankles. A hardy folk the Hunzukuts.

As we came back we found a large group of women and children on the main road, and one of the wee girls had a "doll." This consisted simply of one piece of stick with some rags hung round it and two cross sticks for arms which were jointed on and neatly attached to a piece of string so that they waved about when you pulled. They made it "dance" for us with much amusement and laughter, but we could not detach the doll and its owner from the crowd to get a decent photograph.

The snowfall, skimpy as it was, broke the Great Cold, and the milder weather made photographic work a good deal less painful: giving films and prints ten changes of water when there are large icebergs floating in your buckets and there is no means of heating the dark-room is not enticing. I basely sent some of my own off to Kashmir to be dealt with there, but nothing would induce DL to risk the perils of the road for his. It takes weeks and weeks to get them back so that my lazy method had its own drawbacks, and anyhow no D. and P. people, however good, give your photos the same affectionate attention as you do yourself.

The breaking of the cold while we still had a good hoard of firewood left, meant that we could now afford to be more luxurious and keep a fire going in the dining-room. This also meant that I had a room to click the typewriter in even when DL was working with an informant in the study, and that he could have another big table to spread out maps on.

A minor advantage of the cold weather was the possibility of hanging meat and so gaining respite from the daily hen, which as an article of diet is a thing you can get tired of. The sheep are lean and minute, but tender enough when sufficiently hung. Without being great meat-eaters, DL and I could polish off a leg of mutton in one sitting.

As we were slaying sheep for home consumption we thought it would be instructive to study the local methods of butchering, so Levy Kalbi, who was on the job, was instructed to call us before cutting up the next beast. I didn't specially crave to see the killing, but our folk evidently thought there was no good shirking any part of the rite, and when we went out there was the luckless animal with its legs tied and its neck nicely arranged on a stone.

They did the job neatly and humanely. I don't think the poor beast had an idea what was going to happen. He probably thought, if a sheep thinks at all, that he was merely going to be shorn. Anyhow, they sliced his throat expeditiously with a cry of "Bismilláh, ar Rahmán ar Rahím"—in the name of

1. Gohir Nímo of No. 9 reaping.
(See p. 134)

PLATE XVII

2. Family group of No. 1A. Aliko (seated in background) watches Sóni proudly rocking his first grandson. (See p. 161)

God, the Merciful, the Compassionate—then they let the blood drain out, washed the neck carefully, and got busy with the skinning. Kalbi is a clever, neat-fingered fellow, as indeed all Hunzukuts seem to be, and in ten minutes had coaxed the skin off whole (without slitting it down the tummy) as easily as you peel off a pair of silk stockings. There were only the holes at the neck and at the four "elbows" and a little slit at the tail, so that with a stitch at the tail and four ties at the legs the skin would serve as a water bucket or a bag for flour.

He then hung up the carcase and cleaned it—a wonderfully unmessy business—while we noted down all the words for its various innards. It would have been much more instructive and enlightening if either of us had ever seen a sheep killed at home or had known the English words for all the curious things it has inside it. There was not, even round the kidneys, one ounce of fat.

As usual out here, you do not pay a person in cash for performing a service of this kind; there is some recognized perquisite. In this case Kalbi considered that he would be handsomely remunerated if he might have the guts. We did not covet them ourselves, and gladly acquiesced. They are much valued. They will give you strings for your zither (many people, including Kalbi, make beautiful zithers for themselves), and for your bow; they serve as thread to sew your long boots and your skin sack, and you put them to a hundred other uses. Others of our retainers laid claim to the wool, the skin, and various other items. Later Kalbi gave us a demonstration of skin-curing and -kneading.

The long native boots are extremely comfortable-looking, like long-legged moccasins, and their construction is an elaborate art. Ibex skins are preferred, but ibex have nearly been killed off and other leather has to be substituted. The soles may be made of cow-hide. Boots are precious things, so however cold it is you take them off when you come to a very rough piece of ground or want to walk through water. At best the unlined boot is not over-warm, and really luxurious people wear woollen socks or stockings inside if they have them. The women can knit excellently well, but it is very rare for anyone to have enough wool to spare for superfluities. The preciousness of boots accounts, I think, for a fact which puzzled us at first: you never see children, sporting as they are in every possible respect, sliding on the ice for fun. Boots are too valuable, and barefoot sliding would be a bit severe. Also, as David remarked, sliding and snowballing are games for such as can go home and change their clothes and get warm beside a nice big fire. These poor mites have at most one warm *choga* (and possibly a share of Father's on occasion) and a tiny fire at mealtimes only. Anyhow, they don't slide.

The bright weather of February 1st did not last, and though the cold was broken we reverted to gloomy grey weather and the ceiling of snow-cloud overhead. We knew that a week or two would bring the great festival of the Bopfau, or Barley Seed-Sowing, and we feared that it was going to take place in semi-darkness. But everyone assured us: "Oh no, it will be bright for the Bopfau." The great week drew near and we had heard no word from the Mir confirming his earlier invitation to come and stay at Kerimabad (his garden and rest-house in the park below the Fort at Báltít) for the occasion. We were beginning to fear that he had forgotten us and were wondering whether we could without offence remind him. Just as we were nearly in desperation and terribly afraid that we should wake some morning to be told that everything was over, a kind message came from him to say that he hoped we would come over on Wednesday afternoon. He himself would be away at Áltít, engaged with the preliminary ceremonies, but everything would be ready for us and we need only bring our own bedding. Now we knew that the GREAT DANCE was bound to take place on the Wednesday afternoon, and we feared that this meant that he did not specially want us at it—in which case, of course, there was nothing to be done.

We had a glorious ride over to Báltít on the Wednesday afternoon (of February 6th) in perfect weather, exactly as predicted. Various grandees had been told off to welcome us, a nice fire blazed in "our" beautifully furnished sitting-room, and the Mir's pet cook-for-European-guests, Mirza Hasan, was waiting with his best bedside manner to offer us tea. It was then about three-thirty. We were gratefully drinking tea and thinking that after all if we were not to see the dance, there were compensations in a quiet afternoon, when Mirza Hasan came in with a most courtly grin to say that if we had finished we ought to mount at once as the Mir had sent word that all was ready and they were waiting our arrival to begin.

So we gulped the rest of our tea, leaped into the saddle again, and set off for Áltít, only a mile and a half away. As someone else has already remarked, however, mere miles in this sort of country are a misleading form of reckoning, since they all stand on their hind legs. Kerimabad and Báltít Fort are perched on the brink of a great cliff about 600 and 1,000 feet respectively above the Áltít level. The ground on which they stand appears to be the ancient outpouring of the mighty ravine behind, whose glacier provides all the water for the central part of Hunza. The ground that forms the Báltít spur is not honest rock but finely powdered crumbly earth well strewn with boulders, and the zig-zag road that leads down it is not the kind of thing you would choose for a brisk canter. We scrambled down it with such reasonable caution as haste permitted, forded the torrent at the bottom—very small, of course, at this season—and made towards Áltít Fort. A fine stretch of open and (relatively) level ground lies on the landward side of the Fort, which in its turn is perched on a mighty rock cliff that falls a sheer 500 feet or more into the Hunza river, presenting a most inhospitable face to the Nagir enemy across the water. This open stretch of country explains the fact that Áltít was inhabited long before Báltít, and still remains the ceremonial centre for old-time festivals.

A lovely long polo-ground—the biggest in the Agency, except perhaps the one at Gilgit itself—flanked on both sides by a row of poplars and, of course, by low stone walls (you can no more have a polo-ground in these regions without walls than you could have a billiard table without cushions), leads towards the Fort. Even from the landward side the Fort rises up most impressively from the great rock on which it is built, and the village huddles round it close and tight. We skirted the polo-ground by a narrow path with high field walls rising on our left and passed the field in which to-morrow the Bopfau ceremonies were to take place. As we drew near, the various princes and princelings came out courteously to welcome us, the less important ones, of course, coming farthest, then the grandsons in reverse age-order, and lastly Ghazan Khán himself, the heir and "Prince of Wales." Just outside the Fort there is a fine pond outlined with poplars, the main "road" (say 4 feet wide) on the left of it. The hall-doors of the houses open straight on to this track, their front-door steps being tree trunks with notches cut in them in which the foot is planted sideways as you mount.

Prince Ghazan Khan led us through a narrow alley between the town houses to where the Mir himself was standing to greet us. As always he made us feel more than welcome, and took us to a nicely carpeted balcony where chairs stood ready. The balcony was only a few feet above the courtyard, and we had a perfect view. You must try to imagine a "courtyard," with no straight walls or edges, shut in by irregular tiers of houses piled on top of each other, mounting the rock to the towering Fort above, their flat roofs and roofed balconies all projecting higgledy-piggledy as the haphazard contours of the rock dictate. Every roof and point of vantage was packed with people till, as usual, you felt sure the beams were bound to crash. Everybody was in their gayest and brightest dress, and every single face just radiant. There never was a people anywhere with such a gift for looking happy as the Hunzukuts.

In the courtyard the musicians squatted at the base of the walls: three pipers, three men with pairs of kettledrums, and three big drummers, all of them clowning and play-acting vigorously as they played. Dancing of the more or less ordinary type was going on, varied by the singing of songs—all unfortunately in Shina, not Burushaski. The Hunza people say they have no songs of their own. DL conscientiously recorded the words of these songs later, but as in the case of the Tumushelling chant it is doubtful whether after centuries of being mangled they will yield any intelligent meaning.

Presently the GREAT DANCE came on. The most glorious

piece of dancing either of us has seen. Oh, for a Philip Thornton to record the music and interpret the movements! It consisted of twelve acts with twelve separate tunes, through all of which, however, the same *time* was preserved (the only thing about a tune which I am competent to recognize!). The light was too weak for my 6.3 lens, so I had to leave all thought of photography to David, and in compensation I concentrated as best I could on memorizing the various figures of the dance. It wasn't possible to make courteous conversation to our hospitable hosts and at the same time overtly take notes, and when I set myself to write down the detail immediately on our return to Kerimabad I found to my disgust that I could reconstruct only ten out of the twelve acts.

The eight pairs of dancers, all old or middle-aged men, dressed in gay shirts, homespun *chogas*, and long soft native boots, each clutched a bright strip of barbaric-looking Bukhara silk thrown behind his shoulders (over the right and under the left arm), a foot or so of the silk dangling out beyond his hands. The figures of the dance were very varied; some of the most interesting and striking were these: The dancers formed a circle, doing a dignified slow polka on their flat feet three times round, then faced inwards and danced towards the centre with their arms stiffly stretched out in front. When they had nearly met they all flung their arms suddenly over the heads with a well-synchronized shout of Ha-Ha-Ha! Then all bent slowly forward and dabbled the ends of their scarves on the ground as if dipping them in water.

Again they all circulated, waving their arms and scarf-tails gracefully, then sat down on the ground with legs stiffly out in front pointing to the centre. Then they leaned forward and again dabbled the scarf-ends on the ground beyond their toes. Then they leaned back almost to the point of losing their balance and flung their arms up with the same shout. Next they leaned slowly back till they lay flat on the ground and rolling from side to side they gently flogged the shoulder of first one and then the other neighbour with their silken scarves.

Throughout a couple of other figures the dancers crouched

on their hunkers and waved their arms and leapt frog-like along.

A very quaint and effective act consisted of the dancers turning back to back in pairs, each leaning heavily against his partner, and dancing with all his weight on his heels. They danced round the circle three times like this (it must be particularly difficult for the ones who have to dance backwards). All were raising and flourishing their arms alternately and making great byplay with the outward-facing dancer of the other pair. The semi-final act had no small resemblance to our Sir Roger de Coverley. The circle halted facing inwards and the two leaders of the teams of eight signalled across and danced to meet each other, overshooting and passing back to back. As they passed, they halted a second, leaned heavily back against each other's shoulders and raised first one hand, then the other with their waving scarves, and each then flourished off to take the other's place. When all eight pairs had similarly changed places the dance was at an end.

The team work was admirable throughout. There was not at any point the slightest hitch, such as invariably wrecks amateur lancers or quadrilles at home. I could not extract from my adjacent prince any information as to the length of time they had spent rehearsing; he implied that they just "remembered" from one year to the next; but such faultless co-operation must have followed very strenuous rehearsal both of dancers and musicians.

Seeing so many of the dancers very elderly, I asked the Mir was there no fear that the skill and knowledge of the dance would die out. He assured me that every year a couple of younger men are drafted into the team so that the tradition may not be lost. The dance, in very much its present form, has been performed uninterruptedly for six hundred or seven hundred years, and probably immeasurably longer.

It seems likely that it originated in some imitative-magic rites designed to benefit the crops: dabbling the ground may be preparing it for seed: the cry with high-flung arms may be intended to encourage the growing ears to tower to heaven: the crouching springs may imitate the springing of the shoots:

the flogging may portray the threshing and the back to back scene with waving arms might well represent the winnowing. None of the present-day Hunzukuts attach the slightest magical value to these things, and it is hard to believe that they themselves at any period ever did so, for a less superstitious people can never have existed. But they love dancing and music and *tamashas*, they love any pretext for holiday-making and dressing up, and they may well have borrowed the Bopfau Dance, minus its magic implications, from some people amongst whom the magic was still believed to be potent.

The wise Mir fully realized the psychological value of periodic festivals, and though the keeping up of all the ancient ceremonial often imposed a good deal of hard work and fatigue on himself, he devoted thought and care to preserving the old traditions and preventing the ceremonial's being curtailed or scamped.

When the dance was ended the performers turned and all saluted the Mir; then one by one they came forward and took his left foot in their two hands and stooped over it with the gesture of kissing and then faded out backwards.

The next item on the programme, the Seed Sowing itself, was scheduled for noon on the following day (Thursday, February 7th). We determined to ride down to Áltít bright and early, partly to avoid crowds in narrow tracks, and partly hoping for photographs in the new-found daylight. We overshot the Fort and scrambled out on to the edge of the river cliff—not without some risk to our necks—in attempts to get good pictures of Áltít Fort in profile.

There is a nice little old mosque not far from the Fort where chairs had most thoughtfully been placed in case we should like to rest a while before the show began. We presently installed ourselves here to watch the crowds pouring in from miles and miles away; people on foot streamed across the countryside, all very gay and merry, and as much interested in us as we in them. When a group of horsemen arrived, men of consequence from distant villages, they did not ride straight in, but halted at the end of the polo-ground till they were observed from the Fort; then the band struck up a wild tune and the party galloped hell for leather down the field, providing a fine spectacle for the pedestrian crowds.

As noon drew on we went along towards the pond and took our stand where DL thought his prospects of cine-photography were best. It was his first serious attempt to use his cine-camera, and everything seemed unpropitious. The only point of view from which it was possible to command the path of the procession faced straight into the eye of the sun while the path itself was in heavy shade. I posted myself as well as I could to try to shade his lens, and as a matter of fact the film has not turned out too badly. We were both so much preoccupied throughout the day with the unwonted problems of the cine, and the endeavour not to appear rude or ungrateful, that I realized too late that I had entirely forgotten to take ordinary snapshots of separate figures, etc., as I should normally have done. It is particularly disappointing for the chance was unique, and there would have been ample opportunity if I had not let my wits go wool-gathering.

Noontide came; music was heard inside the Fort, and out came the band in necessary single file carrying on their usual byplay with vigour and evident enjoyment. Next followed "The Great" (viz. headmen, officials, and the like) in single file on foot, but carrying "horses" in their hands. The horses were wands made of a few dark red willow twigs, bent over in a circle at the top not unlike one of the toys a bishop has to play with. A striking personage was a man bearing two huge loaves of barley bread on his back. They were about the size of millstones and looked about equally digestible. Next came a sturdy fellow bearing shoulder high an ancient iron platter hung with chains, on which was piled a white cone called the *chopan*, crowned with a pear and a bunch of maidenhair. The *chopan* is concocted of several favourite Hunza foods, *maltash*, of course, a mulberry preserve called *bing*, and other ingredients kneaded together and coated thick with flour. This dish was escorted by a man drowned from head to foot in flour, whose face was like an over-pierrotted pierrot; lastly came a man carrying a dish of burning incense.

Next appeared a lot of men bearing white and red pennants

and one carrying the Hunza standard (rather a new invention this, I fancy). The standard is a large triangle of white with two pairs of horizontal red stripes, an open hand in red, and a bow and arrow in green: a handsome and effective national flag.

After the standards came the men of the Royal Family, including Hari Tam of three or four (but not the new baby), the younger members leading the way, and lastly Sir Muhammad Nazím Khán himself, mounted on his snow-white Badakhshani stallion. The horse wore a scarlet saddle-cloth heavily embroidered in gold, and from a broad gold collar round its neck there dangled a large "feather brush" of pure white yak's hair. The Mir, looking as always every inch a king, was robed in bright green velvet cloak with massive padded gold embroidery. He had on a fine silk turban of pale blue. All the people entitled to a place in the procession, from the Mir downwards, were wearing bunches of large-leafed maidenhair in their caps. Gathering this fern, which as far as we could learn grows only in one spot in Hunza near Áltít, and collecting the willows for the "horses" provide exciting tasks for the boys for a day or two preceding the feast, while women of the Diramiting clan are busy baking the barley mill-stones and compounding the *chopan*.

Before the procession ultimately emerges many elaborate traditional ceremonies take place in the ancient rooms of the Fort, which is still used for these occasions though no longer inhabited. The detail and significance of these ceremonies (which we were not invited to witness) were fully investigated by DL and I shall not here anticipate his account of them.

The procession passed along the narrow track till it reached the Bopfau field, 6 feet or so above the path and supported by the usual revetting wall. The younger and more active scaled the wall, but for the Mir himself a ladder had been placed at an angle of 45 degrees, bridging the water-channel at the base of the wall, and I followed the royal lead up the ladder. The Mir then took his seat on a chair beneath which a carpet had been spread (chair and carpet being doubtless modern innovations). Chairs had been set for us also and the crowd formed a circle round. A large skin sack was then brought containing sections of a roasted ox. These were emptied out on to a skin tablecloth on the ground, while hundreds of thin bread pancakes were spread on another skin. The Master of the Ceremonies, a fine old man with a white beard dyed orange, took an adze and hacked the joints of meat into neat little chunks. A dish of bread and meat was brought to the Mir to handsel, and he duly tasted a little of each.

A piece of meat was then folded into several flaps of bread and the name of a village was called out. The little parcel was promptly passed back over the heads of the crowd to the authorized representative of that village who was present to receive it. A portion of the royal food was thus distributed to every village in Hunza. Bundles of new arrows and bundles of arrow heads wrapped in red handkerchiefs were then emptied at the Mir's feet. These he distributed to all the people about to take part in the archery.

The stage was now set for the essential part of the Bopfau ceremony. The Mir and Royal Princes stood up and formed a semi-circle facing east, holding their joined hands out cup-wise in front of them. A small bag of seed-grain had been brought adorned at the mouth with a bunch of maidenhair. From this, grain was poured into their hands, and on top of the Mir's handful was placed a microscopic bag made from the skin of a sheep's heart and filled with gold dust. The officiating greybeard intoned a prayer of blessing, and at a given signal the Mir and Princes flung the grain back over their heads and the people crowded in to catch it in their hands. Those lucky enough to secure any, promptly rubbed it between their palms and ate it. He was doubly lucky who secured the bag of gold, but we heard that he was expected to distribute it in alms, so the concrete advantage was slight.

The grain-throwing was three times repeated, and we all moved off to another part of the field, where a little heap of manure had been spread out. Two yoked oxen were now driven forward drawing an old-style plough (rather perfunctorily attached for it came adrift and had to be readjusted).

Then the Mir, still wearing his royal robes, ploughed three parallel furrows and formally initiated the Barley Sowing of the year. In theory no true Hunzukuts will sow his barley till this ceremony has been performed, but we were told that in fact anyone who is ready earlier and thinks the time is ripe has not the slightest hesitation in going ahead with the good work. Never was a people so admirably full of common sense!

The Bopfau field was now deserted for the polo-ground; the crowd helter-skeltered down the wall, bringing the stones down on their heels in clouds of dust: the one and only time when I saw Hunza folk knock even one stone from its place without halting to replace it. We descended by the ladder with greater dignity and proceeded to the raised dais reserved for "The Great" on such occasions. Directly opposite the Grand Stand at the farther side of the ground was a little pile of earth about 2 feet high, and piled as steep as it would stand, on the side of which was fixed a target of brittle wood covered with a thin plaque of beaten silver. The mark was about 2 inches by 2½, and much the shape of an egg in profile.

Before the archery began all the Mir's horses in fine trappings were galloped down the field—the band thumping and piping as they came. Then the archers rode by carrying their immense bows of spliced wood faced with plates of ibex horn and strung with plaited leather. There were about thirty of them, including Prince Shah Khan ("Little Lord Fauntleroy") on a small pony with a full-sized bow nearly as long as himself. From the far end of the ground they came hurtling along one by one, coaxing their horses into a steadier gallop as they neared the mark, then flinging down the reins and firing as they passed. Some arrows flew a bit wide, but by far the greater number buried themselves to the feathers in the little earthen mound. A few horses sheered off, not permitting their riders to take a shot, and one fine animal, seeing the mound stuck as full of arrows as it could hold, decided that the game was a steeplechase and cleared the mound in a magnificent leap, evoking much laughter. One man, a very William Tell, split the target through the very centre to thunderous applause.

Lord Fauntleroy came along riding full gallop as if born in the saddle and got his arrow well into the mound of earth, to his father's justifiable delight: "the boy is only learning," he modestly explained.

There were three courses of archery, at each of which the mark was won. The archer who strikes the target is entitled to pocket it for his reward, but on the two last occasions it was only grazed; I suppose that William Tell was debarred from further competition. If the targets had not been hit they would have fallen as perquisites to the bandsmen. After the archery there was going to be polo, but the Mir thoughtfully suggested that this was a thing of which we had seen enough for life, and perhaps we should like to ride home before the crush. It was by now two o'clock, and we had had nothing to eat since a very early breakfast, so we gratefully made our adieux. DL was fairly weary: there are few things more exhausting than wielding a 16 mm. cine-camera in adverse circumstances at eye-level.

We scrambled up the crumbling cliffs to Kerimabad again and found that the invaluable Mirza Hasan was awaiting us with a welcome spread of tea and cakes. He had observed us zigzagging up the hill. You can't, of course, easily arrive anywhere in Hunza unobserved if you come by the one and only road. Dádo got busy packing up our kit, and we made ready to start back on the road to Aliábád. Before we left, the Mir himself returned, and we were able to thank him once again, and congratulate him on his royal weather. He was delighted that we had taken the whole affair so seriously and done our best to put its main features on record; as far as he can grasp what DL's work is all about, he feels proud and happy that Hunza customs are considered of so much interest and importance. He said he thought he remembered one British officer having attended the Bopfau many, many years ago, but he could not recall the name, and we have not been able to trace any record left by this predecessor. It would be extremely interesting to have an earlier account of it all.

The two glorious days of Bopfau weather were almost a miracle: a very suitable miracle for a Chief traditionally supposed to be able to control rain and sun. It is said of the Mir's grandfather, Ghazan Khan, that he was so skilled in the art that he could cause rain to fall when wanted and ride unwetted through it! On the second afternoon, as we were riding home, the clouds and mists were darkening in again and robbed us of some superb photographs we had marked down for taking on the homeward way. Some cold days ensued—an unpleasant jar after we had begun to shed cardigans and blankets. Still . . . the Great Cold was definitely over, and the sound of flowing water was a delight to the ear after the ice-bound months. An even greater delight was the sight of people working in their fields again, and all our jolly children friends romping about. Some of the women and children living quite near we had not laid eyes on for months.

Everyone was frantically busy. When the women weren't actually carrying manure out to the fields in their baskets and dumping it at regular intervals or squatting down to spread out the heaps evenly over the surface, they were sitting in groups here and there spinning for dear life in the welcome daylight and chattering like magpies, exchanging the gossip of their homes after the long seclusion. When I came upon any little lot I hadn't seen before, they hailed me eagerly: "We *have* missed you!" they shouted. And I laughed and said: "But I have been there all the time and *I* have gone out every day; it is you who have been hiding in your houses, crouching over the fire!" "That's true," was the laconic answer, "it was winter." It was fun to be amongst them all again and find them as natural and friendly and as merry as ever, and so very much neater and cleaner than I should be if I had their work to do and only icy water to wash in.

By the third week in February we could with a microscope begin to detect the first shoots of the winter-sown wheat, and even imagine a slight flush of green on the bare white twigs of the poplars, though the leaf buds had not yet begun to swell perceptibly.

I passed Kaníza's house one day as they were all busy dumping manure and noticed a strange girl helping. I knew that the married sister in Báltít had generously taken over Kaníza's twin sister. "Is that Kaníza's twin?" It was—twice as big and flourishing as our little Kaníza. By way of making conversation I asked the mother: "Isn't it strange that Anjír should be so much bigger than her twin?" "Not really strange," she said quite simply, "there is food in Báltít." Yet when my photographing was done they pressed me to come in. I made to squat just anywhere on the woman's platform, but they must needs find a rug for me to sit on. They were cooking lentils in a big stone pot on a tripod over a tiny fire, and they produced a dish of boiled potatoes and wanted to share it with me. I took a tiny taste for friendliness, but excused myself from eating more with the phrase I had found gave no offence, "I came, having just eaten." These people's hospitality just left me gasping. That dish of lentils and potatoes was probably the only serious meal of the day for five or six of them. And if I had so little, should I want to stuff any of it into over-fed foreigners? I trow not. We were not conscious of being exactly over-fed in Hunza, but by contrast with what our neighbours—much better folk than we—existed on. . . .

Another day I met on the narrow track a perfectly strange lad with a lump of dried apricots in his hand (rather like a lump of the all-glued-together dates you see in a grocer's shop) which he was eating as he walked along. We greeted each other "Jú na!" This is the old-time native greeting, still much more in use than the formal "Salam aleikum" of Islam, which the women scarcely use at all. When you do say "Salam aleikum," the correct Hunza reply is "Salam aleikum." At first, of course, we used to answer: "W'aleikum as salam!" as is usual amongst Muslims elsewhere; but it came to sound stilted and highbrow to our own ears, as I do not doubt it did to theirs. Immediately the boy held out his apricots for me to take some. I tugged a small one off the corner and popped it into my mouth, where it lasted me like chewing-gum for half an hour. These apricots are very good and most sustaining, far tastier than the dried apricots we buy at home, but for serious eating they need to be steeped overnight and then make a delicious dish.

A month later, by the third week of March, we were well

into the Spring. The winter wheat formed a bright green carpet on the shelf-like fields, about three-quarters of our Aliábád ground being given over to it.

The barley which the men had sown after the Bopfau, just the other day it seemed, was showing green over the most of the rest, and would presently outstrip the wheat and ripen first. The only brown fields left were those that were being prepared for vegetables and potatoes. No leaves were yet showing anywhere, but fat red apricot buds looked promising.

As autumn drew in we had begun to feel a little disappointed in our Hunza friends whose marvellous field-walls we had always admired so much with not one single stone out of its place. There were breaches here and there, sometimes quite big ones, and paths were often blocked by a fall of stones, and no one seemed to bother. This puzzled us as out of character, but as soon as the last fear of frost was over, every spare moment was spent by men and boys restoring the countryside to its normal state of faultless tidiness. We now saw the reason of the apparent neglect. The frost and ice simply tear the walls to pieces, and to repair them during winter would be sheer folly. We might perhaps have divined this; but now at any rate we knew.

One early day in March we saw Khano on the mountain side walking slowly and with circumspection. This was so strange a sight that we went over to investigate. "What are you carrying so carefully under your *choga*?" "My first kid," he said, opening his cloak to display the tiny head with triumph. "That's the mother there. I'm expecting four to-morrow. I do hope they won't get born at night in the byre. I'd rather they came when I'm out with them alone." "How do you happen to have so many goats?" we asked. "Oh, I'm herding for the Yerpa now. He's no boys of his own, you see." How crazy it would be to call a lad like that "uneducated" because he doesn't happen to have learned to read or write! He is proudly able to act as accoucheur to his goats, which few of our youngsters at home would feel equal to. We enquired later of Dádo and the rest what sort of wages Khano was able to earn, and their view was that he was probably not given any wage in our sense of the term, but that he would certainly be getting one or two free meals a day, and thus sensibly reducing the rationing problems of his own home. Hunza sheep lamb twice a year, but the goats have kids once only, in the Spring. Khano's promotion to wage-earning status was a little sad for us, for we saw him much more rarely after that.

One fine morning early in March the apricot trees that line the Dála just in front of our rest-house were suddenly invaded by the whole Dastagul family armed with long sticks, to the end of which a sharpened piece of curved iron had been attached. With infinite care they inspected every branch, and wherever they detected the nest of an insect they snipped down the twig on which it rested. These nests were small, cocoon-like things only about an inch long, with a nasty little grub inside. The nests clung very tight to their hospitable perch, and it was often necessary to cut quite a biggish spray in order to secure them; each was diligently collected and borne home to the fire. We were not qualified to identify the pest on which war was being waged, but it was reported to devour both leaves and fruit if not destroyed. All through the country every single apricot tree is scrupulously examined and cleared—there must be thousands. We certainly did not later see a single one that seemed to be suffering from insect attack.

About this time we made another addition to our retainers—a dear old grey-bearded man with the jolliest bright eyes and a merry, happy smile, but not a tooth in his head, was roped in to work at Wakhi. The Wakhis, as I have said, are immigrants into the north of Hunza from the Wakhan districts of Afghanistan. They have settled in various places above the level at which the Burusho themselves care to live. Hunza men will tell you that they cannot induce their womenfolk to live where the apricot will not ripen. I suspect, however, that the men are just as unwilling to forgo their trees and wheat and fruit, but Adam-like prefer to blame their mates. The higher villages of Hunza are therefore inhabited almost wholly by Wakhi-speakers. Being unaccustomed to wheat, apricots, or

's Fort at Báltit, six hundred years old. Mountains in background 23,000 ft. concealing great glacier that waters all the oases of central Hunza. (*See pp.* 105, 106)

PLATE XVIII

trees of any kind, they do not miss them, and in compensation enjoy opener valleys and wider pastures.

Wakhi is an Iranian language, and, dearly as we both loved Burushaski, there is no denying that it was refreshing to revert to a tongue which has one form of plural instead of thirty-eight, and which cares no more about genders than English, less in fact, for it has only one word for "he" and "she." Charming old Farághat is a khalifa, or lay priest. He can read, and perhaps write a little Persian (a *very* little), but his mind is grammatically quite untrained, and one tense or case suits him for any purpose just as well as another. It is natural that at his age he is resistant to new ideas, but how resistant was almost incredible. After weeks of patient work he was no nearer appreciating the need for collecting the various tenses and participles than he was on the first day, so progress was slow. DL's patience amazed me. There would, of course, have been no use showing impatience, for it would have merely served to scatter such ideas as the nice old fellow had, and he was doing his best. There are some strange and wonderful consonant combinations in Wakhi, and Khalifa Farághat's lack of teeth did not make them any easier to diagnose: is it sh-kh-th, or th-kh-sh? It was clear that the hope of extracting any intelligible text of even the simplest form from Farághat was nil, and the Mir very kindly promised to fetch down from up-country a professional Wakhi story-teller to supplement. We awaited his arrival with eagerness. Picture our dismay when he proved to be an equally kindly, equally aged, equally toothless, equally futile old bird. Farághat had brought with him his youngest son, an extraordinarily handsome little fellow of nine or ten, so that the child might not miss his daily lessons, and as they sat about together pouring over a tattered, well-thumbed primer of some sort they made a touching picture.

It would be very unfair to generalize about Wakhi racial character from two such elderly men, but the impression these two left on us of kindly slow-wittedness confirmed DL's impressions of ten years earlier, when he had been travelling through their districts and had tried to get informants to work with. They are the greatest possible contrast to the alert, intelligent Burusho: possibly there is more than sugar in a diet of apricots!

Quite suddenly after the first lovely rush of water the channels went silent again. Not that they were ice-bound, but it seems that the first warmth of the year melts all the recently fallen snow off the top, which gives you your first rush. After that comes a pause before the sun has gathered heat enough to melt the older, hardened snow and make an impression on the glaciers. This arrangement of Nature's suits the peasants well. The first rush waters their new planted barley and springing wheat; the pause gives them time to clear out all the silt and sand that is cluttering up their channels, and to repair the walls. They find the silt a useful top-dressing for their fields. All the menfolk worked hard to get their irrigation works into trim before the real water flow began. Meantime all the *pferis* near us were empty, and poor Sagi had to go a mile or more to draw water for baths and washing up, in addition to his usual pilgrimage for our drinking water. So we installed an assistant for him.

Among the enlivening sounds of these early Spring days was the tootle-tootle of boys' whistles. At a certain moment when they consider the degree of sap flowing in the willows is right for their purpose, they cut themselves sections of various lengths. With great ingenuity they coax off the bark in great flute-like pipes and make an extraordinary variety of whistles with many notes. The deepest notes are achieved by inserting a finer pipe into a larger one, and thus providing a lining to the latter as it were. The same procedure that yields a whistle will also supply a squirt, a pop-gun, or a pea-shooter, and these various toys diversify the day.

Despite the pleasure which water, work, and sunlight bring, the season of Spring awakes no poet's raptures in the Hunza heart. "Starvation Springtime" would have given Keats an odd title for an Ode. Many weeks before the new barley was ripe for cutting every household round us had already run out of every sort of flour, many also out of potatoes and apricots.

The most cautious rationing had not been able to spread last year's supplies over the whole twelve months. Perhaps not all, but certainly many families were surviving on such edible weeds as they took from amongst the barley, and such small greens and turnip tops as were available in the women's vegetable plots. I had heard the phrase "Starvation Springtime" without fully realizing its import. One day passing along near No. 6 I saw Afiato's wife out on the roof, and shouted up: "Jú na, Bibi, the days are bright again; may I come some day and make a picture of you making bread?" "Come and welcome, Mother, but bread I cannot make till the new harvest. We have had no flour left this many a day. Have you not noticed the little children crying? They are hungry, poor mites, and they are too small to understand." Now that my attention was called to it, I did notice that we occasionally heard a wailing of small children such as had not been before. The bigger children and the grown-ups made no complaint, just tightened their belts and went on working—and smiling.

I had taken a photograph one day of Dirzi Nazar's wife, carrying a basin of greens up on to her roof to cook. It was rather a jolly photograph with Raka rising just behind Jamáli's head. When it was printed I went along as usual to give her a copy. She was nowhere about, but Nazar was on the roof doing the best he could with a dish of green stuff. He came down politely in answer to my greeting. I handed over the photograph. He was pleased. "Come along here, girl, and see what you look like!" he called to her. For a moment or two they lingered over the picture; suddenly Nazar burst out into uncontrollable laughter of so infectious a quality that it was some time before I could find voice to ask what the joke was. "Excuse me, Mother dear, but it really is so funny to have a lovely picture of the mountains and your wife and your house —with no bread in it," and off he went again in delighted appreciation of the irony of the situation. A few weeks later the mulberries ripened to vary and supplement the scanty diet of green food, and Nazar sent along a platterful for us. I could hardly *bear* to accept them; yet to refuse would have wounded the generous givers. How petty a return was a small cash gift to the child who brought them!

At last, as March drew to its close, the apricot buds were reddening and swelling, and the most glorious season of the year from the scenic point of view was at hand. No one who has not seen Hunza, its fields carpeted with new green, its orchards clothed with blossom and the snow mountains towering behind, can form even a feeble picture of its loveliness. The sad thing was that we were going to have to forgo the sight.

The next door valley of Yasin is the home of the only extant dialect of Burushaski, and if our work on the language was to be at all complete we must go and spend some weeks there, making a study, however sketchy, of "Werchikwár." Many reasons made it advisable to devote April and May to the job, of which one was that we should thus pass through Gilgit while the annual Jalsa was on. Every year all the Chiefs and Governors of the Agency gather in Gilgit for a kind of Chiefs' Conference *cum* Ascot week, over which the Political Agent presides, and since Major Kirkbride had hospitably invited us, this would give DL an opportunity of meeting old friends of his official days whom he could not hope to visit in their own provinces.

When I say "next door valley" I refer to the geographical position of Yasin on the map. The great ranges that intervene between Hunza and the Yasin valleys are, however, impassable even for goats, and in order to reach Yasin—only some fifty miles distant as the crow flies, if any crows do fly over—we should be obliged to travel down the Hunza river to Gilgit (a four days' march at our modest pace) and five days' up the Gilgit river to our goal. With much reluctance we prepared to mobilize and bid Hunza a temporary farewell.

First, however, there were the celebrations of Nauroz to see, which, owing to the unexplained originalities of the Hunza calendar, fell some ten days before the correct date of the Spring Equinox. Again, as for the Bopfau, the Mir worked magic on the weather, and after several cloudy, gloomy days the New Year ushered itself in with glorious sunshine and bright skies.

Thanks to the good offices of the invaluable and versatile Mirza Hasan, we had secured two excellent ponies for the Yasin trip, and we decided to try them for the first time on this New Year ride to Báltít. DL's was a handsome brown, guaranteed to be up to his weight, which though not considerable was nevertheless somewhat greater than that of the average Hunza rider. It was accompanied by the owner, Haiyáto of Hasanabad, one of the cheeriest-faced men I have ever laid eyes on. My white one, known as Busho (the cat), was escorted by a willing and obliging lad whose actual name I have forgotten since the temptation to christen him Ernest was immediate and irresistible, so obviously full was he of the importance of being earnest. It was a great delight to feel a real horse, in contrast to a "tat," between our knees again, and we set off in high spirits for Báltít. Instead of making for Kerimabad, the Mir's hospitable gardens and European rest-houses, we mounted direct to the old Fort, which is perched on the perilous-looking brink of a great ravine with a magnificent view up and down the Hunza valley. Steep though the road is, our new mounts pluckily carried us up to the very gate. Dismounting here a rough spiral ramp led us to the "basement" of the Fort, which rises four storeys high. You enter a dark sort of hall with a square hole in the roof through which leads a rude wooden stair whose banisters are just plain poplar poles polished white by centuries of use. This lands you on an open lobby without parapet or railing, when another wooden stair (minus banister) conducts you to an open balcony, that serves as a spacious ceremonial reception-room. A low wall, not over 2 feet high, does nothing to impede the view—one of the finest views that any palace of kings can boast. At the back of this balcony is a handsomely carved pavilion under which stands a roomy "throne" covered with a purple velvet, gold-embroidered cloth. For the moment we were conducted further into a magnificent sitting-room with a fine bow window offering not only the distant scene but a more immediately amusing view of the flat roofs of the capital huddling as close together as they can and stepped up the steep hillside. Each, of course, with its square smoke-hole in the centre.

The Mir was dressed in khaki uniform and was wearing his K.C.I.E., lots of gold lace, etc., and a fine gold skull-cap as the foundation of a silken turban. It is only on state occasions that he abandons the native woollen head-dress of the country. He was also wearing a magnificent old sword in a gold embroidered, purple-velvet scabbard, whose name is Sháhmár, "The King Slayer." After tea and smokes he adjourned with David to the outer balcony to receive his guests, all the headmen and officials of the country who had come from near and far to do homage and wish him a Happy New Year, and must be feasted with bread and meat. When the men had withdrawn the Queen and her ladies came in to join me, and we had an entertaining and amusing time. I had hoped to get some photographs of the royal group, but the indoor lighting was difficult; DL had taken the exposure meter with him, Dádo had removed my climbing stick (marked in feet) which I usually measured with, and the presence of so many grown-ups all offering good advice as to how the little princes and princesses should stand and comport themselves produced a strained atmosphere. In all the cirumstances a better photographer might have failed to get results!

Presently the outside ceremonies were over, the ladies said good-bye, and discreetly vanished before the Mir returned. After another go of tea, the Mir showed us a fine collection of old matchlock guns and swords finely damascened and overlaid with gold and silver wherever these could be got to stick. We then set off downhill to the polo-ground in advance of the Mir's party, and as we threaded our way through narrow lanes between the houses that seemed piled on each other's backs, Qudrat Ullah diverted us for a few moments to introduce us to his people. We were met at the front door by a large cow, a very nice cow, who was shooed back to her proper quarters while we were ushered up a ladder on to an open roof-balcony to meet some of the most beautiful women you can imagine, beautifully dressed, not a bit shy, and most cordial. No ladies in Hunza affect seclusion except the immediate royal family. In addition to Qudrat's mother, a delightfully gracious woman, and his pretty young wife, we met Dádo's wife—also very pretty, but a shade more embarrassed. The families are in some way inter-related. We got some photos here, the outdoor setting being more favourable, but dare not linger lest the Mir should be waiting for us.

We had only just got planted on the grand stand by the polo-ground when we saw his procession winding down the hill, the bodyguard in smart uniforms carrying the standard and the Mir with a white satin, gold-embroidered robe over his khaki, mounted on the Badakhshani stallion with the same handsome trappings as at the Bopfau. When he had taken his seat, up rushed a huge deputation from one village after another, shouting the equivalent of "O King, live for ever! May your New Year be blessed!" It was rather impressive. There was no mistaking the genuine affection and loyalty in voice and gesture.

After this followed the usual polo, archery, and dancing. Lord Fauntleroy again made excellent showing with his bow and arrow, and the youngest son of Ghazan Khan actually hit the mark, to his grandfather's pride and pleasure. The elder royal grandsons were not present; they were down in Gilgit doing their Scouts' training. We left about four, but the Mir settled down to see the daylight out at the sports and to preside at another bigger feed to The Great of the land. He was an amazing man for nearly seventy, and apparently entered into these shows with as much zest as the people themselves.

Chapter 25

LEARNING AN UNKNOWN LANGUAGE

BEFORE we quit Hunza for our trip to Yasin, I may perhaps interpolate—for language lovers only—a few notes on the more technical side of our work.

People at home, whose idea of learning a new language—if they want to do anything so eccentric and unusual—is to buy grammar and dictionary, instal a set of Linguaphone records, attend classes, or hire a teacher, often ask how you can tackle the problem of learning an unwritten language where such aids do not exist and whose speakers are what the Germans call *analphabetisch*. It may be of interest to them to know how DL has usually set about it, though other pioneer language workers have doubtless evolved other methods.

You first select a few intelligent men who speak their language well and clearly, and work with them until you light on the one best suited to your purpose. You then annex him to the household at a fixed, generous salary, so that he will always be available when wanted, whether at home or on tour. I may mention incidentally that in our life the language hobby involved a considerable regular outlay in wages, pony hire, travelling expenses, etc., for such language retainers, of whom we often had two, three, or four in tow at once, and such a post with us was much coveted.

As long as he was an official, David had, of course, to fit this private amusement of his into the nooks and crannies left by his work, which naturally took unquestioned precedence, and was often so exacting as to leave no time at all save for meals and a minimum of essential exercise, so that these costly informants might be unused for days or weeks.

Having picked a suitable and congenial man—there is no

use trying to work if it can be avoided with a person you dislike—the game begins. In our regions it was usually possible to find a man with some smattering of Hindustani, Persian, or Pashtu, which helped to speed up the preliminary stages. You get him in, squat him on the floor, and by means of your medium language get hold of a few everyday words:

father	mother	grandchild	good	bad
grass	tree	wheat	arm	leg, etc.

then the primary colours: *black*, *white*, *red*; the numerals, pronouns, and a few simple time-expressions.

Oddly, many non-European languages have only one word for *blue* and *green*, but you take refuge in *blue as the sky*, ''*blue*'' *as grass*. Again, oddly as it seems to us, many have ambiguous time-expressions that look indifferently before and after (like the French *tout à l'heure*) so that *yesterday* is the same as *tomorrow*, i.e. one day before or after to-day.

The next most urgent item is, of course, the verb. You choose the seemingly simplest verbal idea ''to have'' but immediately strike a snag. *I have a stick* seems straightforward enough to an English mind, but you extract only ''the stick is with me,'' ''the stick is beside me,'' ''the stick is in my hand''; there is, in fact, no verb ''to have.'' So you take *to go* and try to get the forms of the present tense: *I go*, *thou goest*. . . . Bearing in mind that your man has no idea of grammar, you will not be surprised or daunted by arriving at something of this sort:

I'm off	we're making a move
thou goest	you are clearing out
he's starting	they flee

You're an old hand and you guess at once that the verb is not bedevilled, but that you have got a clue to six verbs instead of one and to the future as well as to the present tense. Pursuing the past tense of a verb which lets its action be graphically illustrated you may extract something like:

Yesterday I smote	We had beaten
thou hast hit *or* banged	you thrashed
he struck	they whacked *or* belaboured

again with a merry assortment of different roots and a confusion of various shades of past-ness. All these various things you ultimately succeed in pigeon-holing.

According to the intelligence of your man—and many of these untutored folk are quite as intelligent as the average headmaster or Oxford don—and the amount of time you have to spare and the intricacy of the language (Burushaski being at least ten times as difficult as Shina or Khowar) your rate of progress will vary. In any case, you will find that, however bright and willing your informant, he is wholly unused to sustained concentration, and must immediately be released at the first sign of weariness or boredom. Also that you must spend many hours working through and sorting your notes and tabulating your results before the next interview, if this is to be profitable.

It was DL's practice to escape at the first possible moment from the thraldom of the intermediate language. First because translation from another tongue is always liable to distort and colour the speaker's own idiom, and secondly because both your and your informant's knowledge (especially his) of the second language is imperfect and often inaccurate, and the amount you actually have in common very limited. It is therefore at best an untrustworthy crutch.

You then bid him think over some short narrative—a fairy tale, an anecdote of real life (a wedding, a funeral, or a raid)—and be prepared to tell it to you very slowly. It is not the affair of a day to train him to speak at a pace you can carefully record, and at first if he has outstripped you and is asked to "say that again" he will repeat himself in totally different words till your text is an agglomeration of bewildering anacolutha.

Having got a first short text on to paper phonetically—without being at all clear of its meaning or the right division of words—and having deciphered of it what you can, you read it aloud to him next day, making corrections as required, and if *he* can understand it, you have made your first step forward. The more unsophisticated he is, the more enchanted he will be to hear his own words again verbatim, and you are half way to making a philologist of him; you have, at any rate, enlisted an interested collaborator. But you yourself have not got one word in ten, perhaps not one in fifty. You then work painstakingly through the text, getting a rough translation by means of the medium language, asking plural forms and other verbal tenses and acquiring in the process a mass of extra material in your notes.

As the days go on, your man becomes more and more helpful, he gets to know something of your grammatical wants and will now volunteer the plural forms, or stop his tale to interpolate: "he went, he goes, he will go, he has gone," or the like; or he will offer an equivalent expression, no longer as an anacoluthon, or digress to tell of some native custom, the details of some cooking process or some current superstition.

It is no easy task to keep your notes in such form as to be readily available for reference; it is still less easy to keep at command—in your head and on your tongue—all that you have already learned. Here, of course, the whole-time philologist has untold advantage over the busy man who can only snatch odd moments before or after a hard day's work, and sometimes after long blank intervals, for the pursuit of this most exacting of hobbies.

I never lost my admiration of the determination with which DL would give all his leisure to these exhausting séances. It might be half an hour before breakfast; it might be a pause between the reception of two official visitors; it might be a few minutes' interval while an important paper was being fetched from the office files, or a draft despatch typed for signature. Even on tour, when each day meant a mountain march of eighteen to twenty-five miles, in heat or cold, in rain or sun, over difficult and often dangerous country, plunging through banked-up sands by the river-bed, skirting precipitous cliffs along a rock-cut track eked out by the frailest of wooden bridges, or across the dreaded face of a stone shoot where the perpetual trickling of surface pebbles was an ominous reminder that any moment loose boulders might bombard the treacherous track; when each arrival at the rest-house of the day was the signal for visits of courtesy by some local headman or royalty, for the reception of petitioners and the sympathetic hearing of complaints; no sooner had these matters and a cup of tea been disposed of, than out came pen, paper, and writing-board and one informant or another was on the floor beside the Sahib's chair. If we were passing through a district whose speech might be some variant of the "classical" Shina of Gilgit, some local man would be fetched in to throw light on the local patois and its divergence from what it was convenient to take as the norm. These extra séances by the road yielded, for instance, seven different methods—all instructive and all mutually illuminating—of conjugating the transitive verb in Shina.

Whether the locality had fresh local matter to offer or not, there was always some language-informant in our train, and in defiance of fatigue or headache, work could be and was pursued.

As knowledge accumulated, the word for word translation of texts was no longer necessary, and difficult passages were explained and commented on in the language itself, so that the last shred of possible misunderstanding and obscurity arising from the intermediate language was eliminated.

The problem constantly arose at every stage, whether with limited time at your disposal and limited endurance at the informant's, it was better to linger over a seemingly insoluble riddle or to pass on. DL found that in practice, though it went against all military principle to leave a fortress untaken in your rear, this sometimes fell of itself, if you ignored it and continued your campaign. In other words, that a tangle of to-day, which seemed only to grow worse as you wrangled with it, might unravel itself by some new turn of phrase acquired to-morrow, or a week hence—or a year.

Lest all this sound too easy, let me make it more vivid by an analogy. Suppose yourself shipwrecked on the coast of France, where the community are illiterate fishermen and peasants, and there are neither books nor schoolmasters. You get down to acquiring spoken French. There may be a couple of sailors among the foreshore folk who have, like yourself, a limited knowledge of Dutch. You set to work:

u(n)	deu(x)	troi(s)	quatre	
cinq	six	se(p)t	huit	neuf

Having got the simple numerals you proceed:

u	nenfant	une	femme
deu	zenfants	deu	femmes
troi	zenfants	troi	femmes
quat	trenfants	quatre	femmes
cin	kenfants	cin	femmes
sé	tenfants	sé	femmes
hui	tenfants	hui	femmes
neu	venfants	neu	femmes

It will take a little time to work out the true initials of the nouns and the finals of the numerals, to discover the secret of the vowel—the *h* mute you will never reach for it is an orthographic fiction—and to formulate the rules of liaison.

You will not at once discover when the adjective precedes and when it follows its noun, nor which inanimate objects will be considered masculine and which feminine—why, in fact, *un couteau* but *une fourchette*, *un sofa* but *une chaise*—what principles govern the use of *du* and *de*, *beaucoup de* but *bien des*.

And when you turn to verbs it will take perseverance to disentangle the four "regular" conjugations and the handsome varieties of the "irregular." The uses of *me* and *moi* may hold you up a bit, and the idiomatic vagaries of *en*, *y* and *que*. By the time you have entirely reduced to order, say, the verb *s'en aller* and can account to your own satisfaction for n'est-ce pas? jusqu'a ce qu'il ne vienne, a moins qu'il ne soit, si j'etais que de vous, vas-y, ne voilà-t-il pas? and have recorded verbatim all the folk-lore, local history, and gossip that you can track down, your hair may well be turning somewhat grey. Yet French is a language closely allied to our own, of familiar structure, full of cognate roots and basing on Latin which we know; the Frenchman's customs and modes of thought are akin to ours; his religion and morals are variants of our own. Try Burushaski.

I am conscious that in writing of all we heard and said I may have seemed to imply—though I trust not with the unblushing disingenuousness of some travel-writers—that conversation always flowed smoothly and easily. This was not wholly the case. The worst brick I heaved was when I saw a relatively strange woman clearing up after a day's work and breezily accosted her: "*Jú na*, sister, I see you are sweeping up the threshing floor with your little bastard." In extenuation I may remark that the words for "broom" and "bastard" differ only in ending in *s* and *sh* respectively, and that the *s*-one turns its *s* into *sh* in the plural. Any offence that might have been given was quenched in the delighted laughter of the people with me, but I was afraid to talk of brooms, whether singular or plural, for many a day.

Even at the end of fifteen months of strenuous practice in talking (and several years of preceding hard work), neither of us had acquired the skill or fluency in speaking that would have rewarded the same effort and goodwill expended on a language like Persian, German, or Shina. The most confirmed language-smatterer could not truthfully say that Burushaski is an easy language to "pick up." It may amuse the reader to know something of the snags that it holds for the unwary—and the wary, too.

Burushaski rejoices in four noun categories, roughly corresponding to "genders" in Greek or Latin, but not, as will be seen, based on sex-distinction. If, however, we think of the gender eccentricities of French and German we may indeed question whether grammatical gender in the European languages is really sex-linked as our terminology implies. Professor Meinhoff has other theories about its origin.

Be that as it may, Burushaski divides its nouns into names denoting human male and female—which is straightforward enough—but treats the names of all non-human, living animals as belonging to Class 3, cows and bulls, cocks and hens, mares and stallions alike, while including in the same class the names of a large number of inanimate concrete objects. Class 4 comprises the names of all abstract things—heat and cold, kindness and dreams—of all inanimate objects of indefinite shape and form (such as flour, water, cloud, and sand) besides a distressing number which might seem to belong equally well to Class 3 but just don't.

Amusing facts are that the same word in Class 3 denotes an *apple*, but in Class 4 an *apple tree*; in 3 the belly of a living animal or person, in 4 of a dead one, and that while the singular *foot* belongs to 3 the plural *feet* belongs to 4—explain this last phenomenon who can.

These categories might matter little, but that adjectives have inflected forms that must agree, and that in certain forms the verbal endings, in others the verbal prefixes, vary according to the class of the subject, or it may be of the object. The word "is," for instance, may be: *bai*, *bo*, *bi*, or *bila*, according to whether the subject is Class 1, 2, 3, or 4.

As if this were not enough, some of the commonest actions of everyday life require to be expressed by a totally different verb according to the class to which the object belongs. There is no one imperative for "Give me!" It will be *jar jao*, *jar achi*, or *jar aghun* according to what is to be given. So with *bring* and *eat*.

Nor does this exhaust the vagaries of the noun. A large number of nouns denoting relationship, parts of the body, or any object intimately associated with its owner, do not exist at all in an independent form. The attitude of mind underlying this phenomenon is not illogical. A *mother*, a *hand*, a *set of bed-clothes* cannot be conceived *in vacuo*; they must belong to somebody. A set of seven prefixes gives the clue to whose they are, and none of these "starred nouns" (as we called them for convenience) can be used without the appropriate prefix. There are therefore seven words for *mother*: mine or thine, his or hers, ours, yours or theirs. If all the prefixes conveniently ended in a consonant, or if none of the starred roots began with a vowel, the two component parts of the starred word could be simply juxtaposed. This is unfortunately not the case. All the prefixes end in a vowel, and when the hypothetical root-word has an initial *a-*, *i-*, or *u-* this blends with the vowel of the prefix to form a new combination, so that in practice you are confronted with four times seven possible pronominal prefixes for starred nouns.

Add to this the fact that there are thirty-eight possible endings for the plural, and you know most of the worst about the Burushaski noun.

It would be too much to hope that the verb would be any

simpler. Nor is it. The actual conjugation shows a gratifying regularity in the final inflections for tense and person. A proportion of intransitive verbs, however, demand a set of pronominal prefixes (the same possible twenty-eight as those required by the starred nouns) which vary according to the subject; some transitives require these prefixes to denote their direct object, others again to denote their indirect object.

A very large number of verbs or verbal participles, moreover, enjoy a separable prefix of their own after which the pronominal prefixes are infixed, not without suffering phonetic modification in the process. The sort of way this works out may be shown by one example: "Having gone" is represented by:

nán (if it is I who have gone)
nukón (thou)
nín (he)
numón (she)
nimén (we)
namán (you)
nún (they)

The perfect tense of *to come*, "I have come, etc." is:

daiyaba
dukówa
dibai, dibi, dibila
dumóbó
dimébán
damábán
duwán, dubien, dibitsan

paradigms displaying a logical symmetry but not to be commanded at a moment's notice. DL and I used to say that given a pencil and paper and twenty spare minutes we could say a great many things in Burushaski with commendable accuracy, but to keep a brisk dialogue going without blundering required more mental agility than perhaps we had any right to hope for in middle life.

Lest all this should seem too childishly simple: a transitive verb can be formed from almost any intransitive by a simple lengthening of the vowel in the first root syllable and the

Old Fort at Áltít, centre of ancient ceremonial. (*See pp.* 106, 227)

PLATE XIX

prefixing of an *a*; a further lengthening of the vowel will convert the same transitive into a causative. If the three verbs are clearly said one after the other, the difference is easy to distinguish, but I know no form of conversation in which the speaker wants to perform this feat. When one verb is heard alone in the quick current of colloquial speech I defy the beginner to be always certain which vowel-length has been employed.

Another bewildering trick of Burushaski speech—the importance of which I must confess we did not at once discern—is that almost any word may mean its exact opposite if pronounced with lengthened vowel and a different tone of voice. If you ask what sort of a horse a would-be seller has brought, the answer *yashkian* may mean either "a very suitable, satisfactory beast for you to ride," or alternatively "a miserable nag you could not be seen on." You need to know. It is best to go and look. *Caveat emptor*, anyhow! Similarly, if I asked Zaidu how much flour we had left in store and he replied *kaman*, this might be interpreted "a good deal, quite enough for the present," or "just a little," or "very, very little indeed."

This playing on vowel length, quality, and tone is carried to amazing lengths. The only kind of parallel I can think of in English is a child's use of *tiny* as less small than *teeny-weeny*, or the onomatopœic *squeak* denoting a thinner, less important sound than *squawk*. The Burusho can imply admiration, ridicule, contempt, degrees of size, importance, loudness, and what not by skilful sleights of vowel play. The only mild approach we can make to this in English is when by our intonation and expression we can say: "He's a fine fellow, he is," and give it to be understood that the remark is ironical. But *we* use this phonetic irony with extreme economy, whereas it is lavishly employed in Burushaski.

A particular snare into which I was apt to fall—though on paper I could have passed a stiff examination on the facts—lay in this: prefixes apart, Burushaski has no one word for *brother* or *sister*. If said by a boy, *acho* means "my brother"; if said by a girl "my sister." This form of the word means, in fact, "another child of my father and mother, of the same sex as I myself." A second word denotes a boy's sister; a third, a girl's brother. Just to prevent your feeling too sure of things, a boy will address a much older sister out of deference as "my brother." When chattering to my children friends I often provoked delighted chuckles by inadvertently saying the equivalent of: "is that little boy your sister?"

The same sort of differentiation is carried into several other relationships. It does not simplify the tracing out in haste of complicated family genealogies which was one of David's little tasks. My *cousin*, if our two fathers are brothers, is usually described as *my brother* or *my sister*, unless it is necessary to be more explicit; whereas a cousin not reared in the same house has a name to him- or herself. An *uncle* who is my father's brother is *big father*, *little father*, or *middle father* according to his relative age, while my mother's brother is an uncle.

One relationship word the Burusho have for which we might well devise an English equivalent. If young Mr. Smith marries young Miss Jones, what relationship exists between the parent Smiths and Joneses? (Amongst us, carefully dissembled hostility, of course.) Burushaski has a special and convenient term for what is amongst them this very real tie of friendship and alliance between the houses. If the Jones family are extra busy or short-handed, the Smiths will come along to lend a hand, or vice versa.

It is a common error of the uninitiate to take for granted that people of a primitive material culture will have a limited and easily mastered vocabulary. As all serious language-students know, the reverse is the case. Burushaski would no doubt be found to lack our large supply of terms—mostly non-English—to express philosophical ideas or aesthetic appreciation, though it would from its own rich resources be perfectly capable of creating them without borrowing at second-hand, if anyone could spare time from the urgencies of living to indulge in the futilities of philosophy or aesthetics; but it is rich beyond belief in verb-concepts and in concrete words denoting crops and buds and fruits at every stage of growth, implements of every kind, fields of every shape, size, height, and aspect. Domestic animals are differentiated by separate words to the *n*th degree. A mere *sheep* scarcely exists. A convenient word, for which there is no English equivalent, means "one head of small cattle, whether sheep or goat"; after that you must be more specific and make it clear whether you wish to designate the female lamb not yet weaned, the ewe who has not yet lambed, the ewe who has been once to the *tér*, or the ewe who has been twice, the unweaned male lamb, the one-year old castrated ram, the entire ram who has not yet sired, and so on almost *ad infinitum*. And a queer fool you seem if you fail to distinguish animals so different. Similarly with all other stock, the goats having special extra titles according to whether their horns spread out or more conveniently turn in.

There is, of course, no general *basket*: the large, open-ribbed one that carries dry leaves or straw is a totally different object from the small round basket with a handle in which you take a few eggs or apricots, or again from the shoulder-basket that serves all the purposes of our wheelbarrow. These explicit words save all need for circumlocutions like soiled-linen basket, picnic basket, wastepaper basket of ou rclumsier analytic speech.

Every peg and hook and gadget that forms a component part of loom or lathe, mill or sluice, has its own appropriate technical name for which no other name will do. The haughty armchair ignoramus who discourses about the limited vocabulary of the agriculturist would probably be surprised if he worked a while on a farm, at the manifold resources of a whole stratum of the English language that lay outside his ken and confounded his reckoning.

The rich variety of nouns in Burushaski is nothing, however, to the wealth and flexibility of its verbs. The Burusho would seem to think primarily in verbs, the precise meaning of which is a more elusive thing to grasp. Our simple adjective *cold* is, for instance, represented in Burushaski by the past participle of a verb meaning *to cool off, to become cold*. A verb that one day you pin down to meaning "to turn off" the water from a field, staggers you the next by obviously meaning "to turn on,'' till you discover that it ''diverts the flow of water'' whether in one direction or another.

All technical terms, be they verbs or nouns, are capable of vivid metaphorical application, humorous and pointed when you are sufficiently *au courant* to appreciate the intended allusion. Such metaphorical uses are improvised as required with an originality and freshness that an American might envy.

A tiresome person may be ''a wasps' nest'' or ''a painful disease,'' an over-strenuous worker ''an earthquake,'' an only child ''one torch-splinter,'' a loutish person ''a pumpkin,'' an inexperienced fellow ''a green apricot,'' a short-handled spoon ''a tadpole,'' and so forth.

Clocks and watches are, of course, unknown where work is simply from dawn to dusk, yet the complicated exchanges of water at midnight or 3 a.m. are faultlessly concerted. Our day appointments would be defined ''when the sun is one lance-length above the hill'' or ''when the first shadow falls on such and such a spot.'' Dádo had had experience of European time in some earlier service, and was thrilled to possess the watch that DL gave him. He used to come to the study every evening to set it by our little clock. He always held it upside down, and in order to compare it with ours (which was naturally right side up) he went through the oddest neck contortions to get his head upside down. But the idea of time had enslaved him; he was more rigorously and unforgivingly punctual than any servant we ever had, and it was impossible to bear the reproach in his eyes if we waited to wind up a paragraph after dinner was on the table. When I was typing in the dining-room he would appear at the door and say politely but firmly: ''I must come to lay the table in another three minutes, Mother.'' Sometimes, just to tease him, I would say, ''Well, you can't, for I'm going to finish this, and it will take at least ten minutes.'' ''Oh, Mother *dear*, then dinner will be late!''

Burushaski has no expressions for East and West or North and South except the learned words of Arabic; Hunza thought runs ''up river'' and ''down river,'' ''uphill and downhill.'' One day in describing a house I said: ''You know So and So's, it is on the Dála." "No, no, it is on the Middle Channel." For a moment I was puzzled, for the house, in fact, sat exactly on the upper bank of the Dála, but of course watered its fields and drew its water from the channel *above*: the essential fact to a Hunza mind.

Though their technical vocabulary is so exact, the Hunzukuts are only human, and occasionally like ourselves take refuge in "thingumabob," "what you may call it," and "bandobast." They have coined an invaluable word which for fun I wrote "Alice." I found it was quite in order to say: "We are nearly out of charcoal, tell Zaidu to do Alice," viz., to make the necessary arrangements for getting more, or "the Alices are coming, tell everyone to get the Alices," which would mean that the So and So's are coming, tell everyone to get ready whatever is necessary. I hoped to import "Alice" into my home-speech as maid of all work, but here she awakens thoughts of Wonderland and the Looking Glass and proves a plant too delicate to rear in another atmosphere.

The weather in Hunza also provides some entertaining idioms. It is natural to say "the rain is falling," but the Hunzukuts not illogically also say "the sun is falling" where we would say shining, and where we put a thing *in* the sun to dry he puts it *on* the sun, that is, on the patch of warm sunshine.

In the main, Burushaski is innocent of the elaborate circumlocutions of ceremonial speech in which Persian, for instance, is so rich. The humblest peasant addresses his King as "thou," but one foreign courtesy-word has crept in. One day I excused myself to the party of women amongst whom I was sitting by saying: "I must now go home. My husband will be ready to eat bread." "She has said 'my husband,' " they chuckled. "Well, isn't the Colonel Sahib my husband? What should I have said?" "You yourself should say 'my spouse' (*jama'at*) though we might say 'her husband.' "

After this I was careful in talking to man or woman, however humble, to enquire after the *jama'at* and not crudely after the wife or husband, and found that this was more acceptable. I noticed, too, that when I asked: "Are you well?" the return question would sometimes be couched in the ungrammatical form: "Are your name well?" but this was chiefly used by the children as more respectful. I was told it would be unsuitable for me at my age to use to anyone, even to the King. Otherwise in Hunza spades are spades.

DL's original vocabulary (vol. iii of the book already alluded to) comprises some 3,000–4,000 words. From our first day with the Hunzukuts to our last, we were recording new words without ceasing, or registering new meanings for words we thought we knew. Far from having "completed" a vocabulary of Hunza Burushaski after a hard year's work DL felt he was just beginning it. Ten years more could have been profitably spent on the task if we had had them to spend. At least no language enthusiast can complain that the field is bare; there are ample gleanings left for him or her. A rich harvest indeed awaits the reaper—but labourers to date are few.

Chapter 26

DIGRESSION TO YASIN

WE had intended to start on Friday, March 20th, but after a couple of hellish days packing, clearing up correspondence, developing, printing, washing photographs, and tidying the house so as to leave all in order for our absence, we found that we must postpone till Saturday. This apparently unimportant alteration in our plans caused evident jubilation amongst the servants. "Why are you all so pleased?" I asked Zaidu. "Well, you see, Mother, it is said not to be lucky to start downstream on a Friday; upstream is all right, but not down." I said that if they felt like that they should have told us and we should have gladly changed the day to oblige them. "What should you have done if we had insisted on starting on a Friday?" "Oh, we'd have managed all right. We'd have said good-bye and left our own houses and camped on Thursday night in your compound, and so we should not have had to *begin* the journey on Friday." Wonderful people! The few superstitions they half-heartedly indulge (which we suspect they have caught in this mild form from their superstition-ridden neighbours, the Shins) they are always prepared and able to outwit.

We got off at nine on March 21st in lovely weather, at once warm and cool. Quite a large crowd assembled to say good-bye and see us start, our friends shouting: "Come back soon. We shall miss you." As we rode through Murtazabad we saw the first occasional fruit blossoms and felt sad to be leaving Hunza behind in apricot time. Slight steam was rising from the sulphur springs by the river as we passed. Later, in Nagir, we saw the first wasps of the year and the first butterflies—a copper-coloured fritillary and a tiny blue. The road was a very different proposition from what it had been as we travelled up the previous July. From richly watered Minapin we looked across the river to the Hunza village of Hindi with new eyes, for various fields were pointed out as belonging to one or another of our acquaintances. "Hindi is a fine place," they told us; adding without conscious irony: "There's hardly any water, but otherwise . . ." From the Nagir side the Hindi road looks pretty terrifying (as, of course, the Nagir road must also look from the Hunza side), but we were assured that it was really a better road; its only drawback is that there are fifty recognized spots on it subject to rock bombardments: a mere nothing amongst these ever-crumbling hills.

The onward journey was uneventful. At Sikandarabad and Chalt all the apricots were in full bloom—a glorious sight. After Chalt there was one part of the road completely buried under an avalanche which we had some difficulty in coaxing our horses over, we ourselves scrambling across on foot. A good deal of intermittent rain for a couple of days and a horrid ride in driving wind and sand on the last lap rather spoiled our ride to Gilgit. Just before we reached the Gilgit river we were staggered by a magnificent view of Nanga Parbat filling a whole triangular gap in the nearer mountains. Often as we had ridden this stretch before, we had never happened to see her like this.

In Gilgit (2,000 or 3,000 feet lower than Hunza) all the apricot blossom was already over, though a few peaches and apples were still in flower. We had a delightful (but from the work point of view wholly wasted) ten days in Gilgit. Nothing could have exceeded the kindness of Major and Mrs. Kirkbride, who put us up in the Agency House. It was odd to be quartered in the guest room of what had been for four years "our" house, and odder still, but delightful, to attend the Jalsa as guests and spectators instead of responsible hosts. The British officers as new friends and our old friends the Chiefs all treated us with the utmost kindness, and the ten-day holiday was extremely pleasant.

On April 4th we resumed our pilgrimage to Yasin. We imagined we had forgotten the road. Far from it: every detail came back afresh as we rode along, and a host of vivid memories crowded in on us. It was yet early in the season; the river flowed graciously along, clear as crystal and a miracle of blended colours, which would put a peacock's tail to shame. When we returned a few weeks later, after the first melting of of the snows, it flowed sullen, swollen and strong, the more familiar thick, opaque, grey-muddy mixture. Quickened memory set me to watch for a lovely bush of "crow's pomegranate" at the foot of a rock by the roadside. We had seen it one year covered for the 6 feet of its height from tip to toe in yellow blossom, flame- and scarlet-flecked. As we had ridden nearer half the blossoms suddenly took wing: a swarm of "painted ladies." Alas! we were now too early,the painted-lady bush was not in leaf; as we returned, her blossoming was over. It was a sight too lovely for recapture.

We made the four-day ride to Yasin in six stages, partly in order not to arrive too tired for work and partly because DL seized chances of picking up some supplementary information about Shina dialects when we halted. The river junctions on these upper reaches of the Gilgit river are great, wide, open amphitheatres, possibly once the meeting place of glaciers, anyhow the greatest contrast to our narrower, wilder, more forbidding Hunza ravines.

On April 11th we set out on the last stage from Gupis to Yasin, having given two days in Gupis to Kuhi Shina. At the great bridge over the Yasin river we were met by Rajah Khan Sahib Mir Baz Khan, one of our good old friends, and found that he had staged a ceremonial welcome for us with bands and *feux de joie*, and decorations over the gateway of the rest-house. We made enquiries for a Yasin ex-retainer, Muslim by name, with whom DL had worked in olden days. To our great joy he was still to the fore, somewhat older and maturer, now a Levy too; but he had not forgotten his earlier lessons in language work, and was immediately booked to start work on the morrow.

A couple of hundred years ago Yasin was conquered by a royal Khushwaqt family from Chitral, and since then Khowar has been the language of the upper classes. Indeed, the passing traveller might well be unaware that the language of the people remains their original Burushaski, though most of the menfolk are of convenience or necessity bi-lingual. We had known Muslim as a Khowar speaker; it was a pleasant surprise to find that, as he put it, "Burushaski is my mother and father tongue," and that he spoke nothing else in his home and among his friends. To distinguish Yasin Burushaski from its sister speech of Hunza it is convenient to call it Werchikwar, as the Khowar-speakers do.

The Yasin country is opener and far more plentifully watered than Hunza, but higher lying with a longer, severer winter. We had snow still on the ground on April 14th. The different conditions are reflected in the architecture. All the houses are one-storeyed only, and none of them have the delightful upstair balconies that are such a cheerful and sociable feature of the Hunza house. With ample land and water the Yasinis are able to grow more wheat than they can themselves consume, and sell their surplus to Gilgit in exchange for tea and sugar, luxuries unknown to the Hunzukuts. On the other hand, their summer season is too short to allow of any second crops. We found the peasant people extremely kind and friendly, and if we could have made a longer stay among them we should have been able to feel thoroughly at home. Their women are also free and unveiled, and I think good-looking, but all the younger ones affected a dark brown face cream of some kind which was said to be protective to the skin but was extremely unsightly. As we walked about making what observations we could, we found them very ready to try to understand our exotic Burushaski. David got as far as speaking in Werchikwar, but I with less ready linguistic adaptability firmly imposed on them the speech of Aliábád and Báltít. Despite dialectal differences we could hear one party of boys shouting delightedly to another: "They speak our language!" (which was scarcely true).

It was wonderful, after the precipitous Hunza country, to be able to walk up and down gentle slopes of natural grass and skip across moss-and-fern-lined streams amidst a wealth of tiny flowers.

There was no advantage in my also trying to slog at Werchikwar as we were not staying long enough to turn it to account. So we had decided beforehand that I could best employ working hours in trying to work out the major differences between Hunza and Nagir Burushaski which are perhaps too nearly identical to be styled separate dialects, but yet naturally show some distinctive variations. To this end we had borrowed from the Mir of Nagir a morganatic brother-in-law of some education, Ali Ausat by name, a young man about the same age as Qudrat Ullah, and annexed him—at a salary, of course.

The two had travelled together in our train since Aliábád with instructions to talk together about everything under heaven, and make notes of all the points, however trifling, in which their speech differed. While DL toiled away with Muslim in one room of the spacious rest-house, I set up my writing table in another, and got the two young men in to help me to set on record whatever observations they had made. Each day I suggested one set of things for them to work out together before the morrow—household utensils and field implements, irrigation terms, the vocabulary of relationship, etc., etc., and we then ran through their comparative lists with ample digressions whenever any point of interest challenged attention. It proved a most amusing game, and their good-humoured wrangles over which of two forms of expression was the more classical Burushaski were a constant amusement to all three of us. I hope it will prove that we covered most of the vital points; it is for DL to work out the material in due course.

Superficially the main items that leaped to the eye (or ear) were: first, that the Nagir vocabulary has been far more deeply interpenetrated—or corrupted—by Shina than Hunza Burushaski, but that on the other hand Nagir has been more conservative in preserving full verbal forms and un-telescoped vowel sounds. Nagir preferring, as it were, "I shall" to "I'll," "he does not" to "he doesn't," "we will not" to "we won't," and the like. The differences, however, between the Hunza and Nagir speech proved (as we already knew) to be trifling compared with those between Hunza Burushaski and

Werchikwar, where the two forms constitute different and independent dialects. It was, however, extremely interesting to find that in some important points Werchikwar and Nagiri were closer than Werchikwar and Hunza Burushaski. Since there are no historical records of Burushaski a hundred or two hundred years ago—what would we not give for them!—these dialectal variations are doubly valuable to anyone attempting to understand the direction in which the language has developed and is developing.

After strenuous mornings at these tasks, we spent the afternoons exploring the country on foot or on pony back, and getting what contacts we could with the people. Just behind the bungalow we succeeded after some hunting in re-finding the boulder on which the carved initials "W.H. '70" form a humble memorial to the luckless Hayward who was murdered by his treacherous Yasin hosts. Newbolt's fine poem "He Fell Among Thieves" gives the poetical version of his death. The prose one seems to be that by the somewhat indiscreet display of gifts which he had with him (intended for bestowal on chieftains in Chitral whither he was bound) he excited the cupidity of the Yasini Chief, who could not bear to see these treasures carried beyond his borders. Human life was held of little account in these regions before the coming of the Pax Britannica, and the obvious thing was to murder the gift-laden guest and annex the spoil. Hayward's tent was therefore quietly surrounded. He realized his danger, and sat on his camp bed, revolver in hand, and loaded rifle by his side, determined to sell his life as dear as might be. But the plunderers had no mind to take unnecessary risks. They bided their time till he grew drowsy from fatigue, cut the tent-ropes, and murdered him at their convenience like a rat caught in a trap, without speechifyings on either side. A tragic, sorry tale.

Yasin houses tend to be grouped in fives and sixes within a walled enclosure. We halted to admire some carving on a wooden lintel, and the owner of the house, Arab Khan, forthwith invited us to come straight in and see some better carvings inside. This gave us a wonderful chance to see a Yasin interior just as it is in normal life. Cows, calves, hens, and chickens shared the one main living-room with men and women in a promiscuity unthinkable in Hunza, though it is true the large animals were in theory confined to one end of the room by a small partition a couple of feet high. None of the human occupants showed the least shyness or embarrassment. They showed us fine, well-smoked carvings on the handsome square pillars of the house. The idea of the greater ornamentation of the inside of their dwellings has probably come to them from Chitral, and possibly the longer winter with the longer spell of enforced leisure may be a factor too. I wish we could have stayed longer than the short three weeks we had allowed ourselves, learned to speak Werchikwar, and settled down really to making friends with these hardy kindly folk, less radiant that our Hunzukuts, but in many ways akin in temperament and not behind in goodwill.

We returned again another day to Arab Khan's house to try some interior photographs, and were shown an interesting collection of utensils: a wooden bucket hollowed in one piece from a tree-trunk, and provided with a square lip and a wicker handle; some delightful wooden spoons with the handle rising sharp from the side, such as Hunza calls "Wakhi spoons," wooden ladles all in one piece, etc. A nice old woman was teasing wool from a small but highly ornamented *pfurukus* beside her. The house possessed no cupboards like those roomy ones that are a feature of every house in Hunza, and all the family kit was either lying about or slung over rails above the partition.

The space seemed greater than in the Hunza house (partly owing to the lack of cupboards and the fact that the byre formed part of the room), but the general effect was much untidier and grubbier. The sleeping platforms appeared to be shared by the hens and chickens and a layer of straw was spread under the blankets. The hospitable folk kindly put out the fire to get rid of the smoke in the interest of DL's photographs. The room had two semicircular fireplaces, the one just behind and at a slightly higher level than the other. The floor similarly rose by one low step, and a door at the back of the upper compartment seemed to lead into a store-room. A certain delicacy—to which the true anthropologist should be a stranger—prevented our intrusively examining everything in as much detail as we should have liked. While we were within we saw many pairs of bright young eyes peering at us and our strange antics through the "vulture smoke-hole" above our heads. When David pressed a rupee into the hand of the old lady who had so hospitably done the honours of the house, she received it with much pleasure and genuine surprise.

One day we devoted to the exploration of the Naz Ber, a great nullah which runs up behind the village of Yasin. At this time of year, with grass and willows and flowing water, the steeply rising valley was romantic and picturesque, but it must be bleak and desolate for the greater part of the year. Such women and children as we met were friendly and unafraid, though we may well have been the first white people they had ever seen.

As we left Yasin on April 28th heavy clouds hung over the mountain tops and robbed us of our parting view. Half way to Gupis we noticed the first house with a wicker, mud-plastered grain bin on the roof such as are common in Gilgit, but are not seen either in Yasin or Hunza. Next day we got a rarely beautiful view of the rocky promontory of Róshan towering above the river, with a ruined fort on top, like a finer, larger, and more impressive version of one of the robber castles on the Rhine, and a better sight than we had ever had of the curiously twisted vertical streaks in the mountain above that are known as "The Snake and her Babies" about which the obvious local legend runs. Below Róshan there is a huge, lofty pocket of boulders—a weary thing to toil across—reported to have been pitched there from his shoulder basket by an ill-tempered Div. The Gilgit-Yasin road has some fine old native rope bridges to show, and Haiyáto obligingly stepped down one to pose for us. We now got into the region where every large forked tree is made to serve as a store for a stack of maize-straw, a familiar Gilgit sight, unknown at higher levels.

Passing through a gorge in which wild almond trees were growing in profusion, our Hunza men fell out to cut themselves a supply of polo-sticks, for which almond wood is reckoned the best of all. They had noted the spot on our upward march. A few "crow-pomegranates" were in flower, lovely little bunches of tiny yellow bells with yellow tongues, shading off into orange and flame and even scarlet. The painted ladies were hovering round, but the largest swarm I counted was a beggarly dozen. The blossoms are guarded by the most savage thorns.

All this downward ride to Gilgit we enjoyed perfect weather, bright and sunny but not over-hot, and indescribably lovely views. Rounding a corner on a shelf-like track I spotted the first and only live snake I have ever seen in these parts lurking in two inches of shade cast by a big boulder. Haiyáto bravely seized it by the tail for me, swinging it gingerly, but it was extremely active and sat up half its own length so that he prudently judged it better dead than alive, though I don't for a moment suppose it was a poisonous type. He lashed it so vigorously against a rock that its head was crushed beyond hope of recognition.

Near Gakuch we came upon a lot of gold-washers at work by the river-side. They turned out to be people from Yaghistan. Gold-washing is considered rather a base occupation, and gold-washers enjoy no social prestige. A whole family working hard all day in a favourable spot—that is a sandy backwater well out of the main current of the river—may salvage as much as eightpennyworth of gold. Wherever we came to habitations, the young green of crops and willows was refreshing to the eye.

The great boulder-estuaries from the side gorges that had been dry as we marched up, were now seamed with water-channels. We were still able to take short-cuts by fording these, but it was evident that in a very short time they would be impassable and travellers would have to stick to the higher, longer road and Government bridges. Amongst the boulders the tamarisks were out but not yet in blossom; instead, there were some lovely brooms with tufts of butter-golden blossom edging the fields and jolly blue clumps of small wild iris dotted here and there. Such people as we met on the roads all had sprigs of spring blossom in their caps.

Before getting into Gilgit we halted at the Wishing Boulder

to let our followers try their luck. There is a curious mark on one side of it rather like the impression of a giant's open hand. The story runs that if you take so many paces from it with closed eyes, turn and approach again, and finally succeed in placing your hand in the mark, your accompanying wish will be fulfilled. Futile attempts to earn their wishes provoked much mirth and chaff. About four miles before Gilgit, where the Kargah and Naupor Nullahs debouch, there is a fine tongue of smooth-faced cliff, on which, a hundred feet or so above the nearest accessible ground, some unrecorded artist at some date unknown carved a handsome figure of a standing Buddha. We reckoned it must be about 30 feet in height. Having during four years in Gilgit omitted (as one does) to take particular heed of this really remarkable monument, we now took some pains to visit it. Unless the light happens to strike the figure at a certain angle it is by no means easy to descry. Later inhabitants, knowing nothing of Buddha or his history, call the figure a Yakhshini, and tell of a man-devouring ogress who had her dwelling here. A passing saint was called on for assistance, and succeeded in pinning her to the rock. He said she would be unable to escape again as long as he was alive, and that if, when he died, the people would bury him at the foot of the rock, all would be well. He was then about to resume his peregrinations. The people were grateful for their deliverance, but prudently considered that they might not know the moment of his death nor where to find his honoured and valuable carcase. To avoid future disappointment or disaster they therefore prudently slew their benefactor and buried him forthwith. The Yakhshini is still there to attest the truth of this moral tale. On the near-by spur to which we laboriously scrambled we found a lot of well-built ruined walls on a site commanding a fine view. They suggested an ancient fortification or perhaps a monastery such as abound on similar but more inaccessible heights in Tibet. On a bare mound above the adjacent village of Naupor, the ruins of an ancient stupa were unearthed a few years ago. The top, stone-built chamber in which some manuscripts were found is now exposed to view. It would be interesting to know the history of the stupa and

1. DL taking photo of Mir Muhammad Nazím Khán on the mountainside at Báltít.

PLATE XX

2. View of Áltít Gort from same spot, looking up Hunza River. (See p. 227)

the ruins, but the manuscripts threw no light on the matter. So far as they have yet been examined they appear to be comparatively commonplace copies of already well-known sacred writings of latish date. They are now lodged in the Srinagar Museum, which is permanently closed.

Our return to Gilgit coincided (somewhat unfortunately we ungraciously felt) with the Jubilee celebrations and perforce we spent another very pleasant (but time-wasting) holiday with our most hospitable friends the Kirkbrides. It was May 13th before we were able to disentangle ourselves from Gilgit and its seductions and set our faces once more towards Hunza. The very horses seemed to scent that they were heading home and gave us of their best. The weather was now very definitely warming up, and we marched early to avoid the greater heat. Nomal and Chalt provided us as usual with loathsome milk tasting of Tom Cat. This indescribably vile flavour is due to some wild herb that grows in these neighbourhoods at certain seasons. I am not botanist enough to know its name, and it is not a plant of which I covet seeds or slips. It is mercifully unknown in Hunza.

As we rode through the rich, well-watered string of Nagir villages we were escorted for part of the way by various Nagir princes sent by their father to show us courtesy. Green crops, shady walnut trees and masses of blue iris and wild rose made the road enchanting, its loveliness enhanced a thousandfold by the bleakness and barrenness of the great mountains. I confess I always covet these lovely villages for Hunza, the more so that the Nagirkuts are far more slack and slovenly in their cultivation than "our" people. All the irrigation water, coming straight from the melting glaciers of Rakaposhi, was now milky and unappetizing. The Nagir people, though not actively uncivil, never volunteer a greeting as you pass and never throw you a kindly smile even when they speak. We noticed, too—and how it shocked our loyal Hunza folk—that the Nagir princes also were allowed to ride past unsaluted and apparently unregarded. The Mir of Nagir had been pressing in invitations to us to visit him—as soon as he had convinced himself that no great harm seemed to be accruing to Hunza from our presence there. It was tantalizing to delay our return to headquarters; on the other hand, since in common courtesy the visit must some time be paid, we had promised to visit Nagir before returning to Aliábád, so we remained on the Nagir side of the river and proceeded to that gloomy, sunless capital.

At Minapin, the last stage before Hunza or Nagir, as the case might be, we were met by a laughing, bright-eyed boy, too genial to be a Nagir product: it was Haiyáto's son (one of three) who had come the fourteen miles to meet his father, explaining "I was heartsick for you and the horse, my father."

Ernest, Dádo, and Qudrat Ullah had never been in Nagir before, and were much amused at seeing Hunza from across the water. Everything *did* look odd, Aliábád beacon-tower very imposing above the empty, graveyard hill. Nagir is more spacious and richer than I had remembered. The fields are all slightly sloping and the revetting walls not nearly so high or so well-built as those of Hunza. The houses, like the Gilgit houses, are mainly built of sun-dried brick, and looked tidy and neat. Upper balconies are rare, and it seemed to me that the smoke-holes were much smaller and usually at one side of the roof, but the roofs appeared to have a parapet of a foot or so all round. The villages, so familiar in profile from the Hunza side, are much deeper than their appearance from the distance would suggest. The path from Sumair onwards up the Nagir gorge was very narrow, crumbly, and in poor repair, but looking at the texture of the cliffs it was not easy to see how anything radical could be done to improve it unless the course of it were entirely altered and carried much higher up and over the top of various bluffs and crags: an expensive engineering feat. Presently we came to an ugly *zhingát* on a long stretch of steep, almost fluid rubbish-heap slope—a place well remembered in my nightmares—across which the track, such as it was, was a bare 18 inches wide, and not even level at that. It is a good quarter of a mile; we took it on foot at the double, and were thankful to reach comparative safety at the other side, and see our horses and men follow without mishap. There is no shame in funking these things; the natives like them as little as we, and are as frank about it. Familiarity with a *zhingát* breeds caution, not contempt. As we rode in we saw Ali Ausat at the nicely carved door of his house, rather grubby but pleased to see us, passed the miserable apology for a hospital which contrasts ill with the well-built one at Aliábád, though the two Mirs got the same grant from Government for the purpose of building them, and on past a fine, large, shallow pond. On our right was a steep green slope with jolly poplars and a lot of grass, and then we reached the polo-ground. Here the Mir came himself to meet us from the shelter of a roofed summer-house where he had been waiting. Another mile of almost perpendicular zigzag, which the ponies could only just manage, brought us to the familiar old polo-ground (now disused for play), with its lovely double line of poplars. This peculiarly steep and horrible approach is new, and the Mir is very proud of it. From the top there is a magnificent view with the pond below looking like a lake and the Mir's palace picturesquely perched on a steep hill-face with fine windows looking out not at any view but straight into the terraced hillside opposite. Mir Sikandar Khan looked shrunken and frail compared with ten years ago, but very brisk, and was apparently able to ride up his new road without a qualm.

He himself received us most hospitably and kindly, but his people serve him ill. Immediately on our arrival a shindy broke out with talk of grass- and fodder-shortage, though grass and fodder are plentiful in Nagir, and we found the rest-house dirty and unswept, bathroom and utensils uncared for, and a general atmosphere of grudging incompetence pervading it.

We dined with the Mir that evening and duly entertained him in return, while I paid a visit to the ladies and met the numerous little princes and princesses. The Queen of Nagir, a fine, handsome woman, not a day older than when I had last seen her eleven years ago, is a sister of Khan Sahib Mir Baz Khan of Yasin, and I was able to bring her first-hand news of her brother and his family, in which it is fair to say she did not seem over-interested. But she is a gracious motherly woman, and very intelligent—she even followed my Burushaski (Hunza variety) with ease. The brightest moments of my call were provided by the charming little prince, Shaukat Ali, son of the Mir's eldest son, who unhappily died young during our time in Gilgit. The boy is therefore his grandfather's next heir. He is a most intelligent, well-mannered lad, and manfully upheld the conversation whenever it threatened to flag.

Two of the royal ladies were Hunza princesses married across the border, one a daughter, one a granddaughter of the Mir.

In his day the Mir of Nagir was a mighty hunter before the Lord, and one of the best polo players in the Agency. He told us he had shot three thousand head of big game in his life. He has now been forbidden by the doctors to attempt over-strenuous physical feats, and indeed it is obvious that he would no longer be able for them, but he still has the regal carriage of younger days. His sons used to tell us that they dreaded hunting expeditions with their father because he appeared impervious to fatigue, and quite indifferent to such trifles as food or sleep. His reception-room is hung with lordly trophies of the chase: local ibex, markhor, and several magnificent heads of *bara singh* bagged in Kashmir.

He is justifiably proud that his six sons form a polo-team equal to any other in the Agency.

We had feared that decency would compel us to spend at least three days in Nagir, but since *one* day easily exhausted all our conversational resources—the Mir has nothing like the wide range of interests nor the intellectual curiosity that distinguished his Hunza colleague—and since his ungracious underlings raised one difficulty after another about supplying our very modest needs (we had sent straight through to Hunza all our spare kit and animals so as not to impose any avoidable burden) though offered as of course more than adequate payment, we decided to curtail our visit and the Mir greeted our decision with unconcealed relief, though he "only wished we could stay a year." So the 18th saw us pack up and thankfully make our escape.

We had not been reckoning on any language work in Nagir, for we had secured as much material as we could hope for from Ali Ausat during our time in Yasin, so we lost nothing of that sort by cutting short our Nagir visit. We gained one valuable piece of information: the Nagir women *do* wear trousers! The trousers-for-women fashion in these parts is new: that is, it has been going only for the last four or five generations, introduced we were told from Chitral, and my Hunza women friends had assured me that the Nagir women were so backwoodsy that they had not yet adopted it—which I now know to be a libel. The little girls wear cotton caps and fringes like our Hunza ones, but the women cover all their hair in black woollen Salvation Army bonnet-like caps (a type of headgear of which I saw only one specimen surviving in Hunza). What the Nagir women and older girls look like I cannot say, for when they sight a man they crouch down with their backs turned and either pull a cloth over their faces or bury their heads in their arms. Give me the Maulai variety of Islam every time!

After I got back to Hunza and the women crowded round to ask "all about everything," I got a lot of fun by demonstrating—with only a mild amount of legitimate exaggeration—how the crouching and face-hiding ought to be done; but I cleared the Nagir women's character on the trouser question. Certainly half the charm of our delightful country is the freedom of the women and girls. They come up to the roadside or out on to the roof to greet DL just as naturally and frankly as to greet me. They are not brazen-faced or forward, just unafraid and perfectly unselfconscious.

They have one charming custom which I have not heard of elsewhere, and which could only exist amongst free women. When the Mir or any distinguished traveller (such as we!) is passing, the women and girls crowd on to their house tops and silently wave their hands. Not in a stiff Heil Hitler salute nor with our undisciplined exuberance, but with a quiet, graceful circular motion from the wrist, the two hands moving opposite ways outwards from the breast. It is the most gracious and dignified gesture of welcome and goodwill I have seen. We knew it from official days of old, when it might well have been merely a command performance; but it warmed our hearts when it greeted us as private individuals.

To revert to our homeward journey: After descending the

Mir's famous new road on foot (it was so steep that our people voluntarily carried the loads down and loaded the animals below) we rode as far as the perilous *zhingát*, then dismounted and scooted across it in undignified but prudent haste. It was actively streaming pebbles, and at the safer spots where a bush or an apparently well-rooted boulder sheltered the track, we halted, looked, and waited to make sure that nothing larger was coming and then ran for it. A biggish stone or boulder takes three to four seconds after it is sighted to reach the track, and you must use your judgment and gamble on your chances. We felt a little anxious till we saw that all our people and kit were safely over too. Under a small new half-built mosque we halted in the shade to drink some thermos tea. The owner of the land, an intelligent man, courteously came up and offered to spread bedding for us to sit on; there were some children about but they were shy and churlish and unresponsive to our advances. The ride through the villages was pleasant; there are lovely big trees in Nagir (such as Hunza cannot afford), and lashings of water. The fact that the Nagirkuts don't level their fields completely, but allow them to be on a fairly steep slope, seems to entail a much more elaborate system of ridging and much more trampling through the crops to direct the water. We wondered whether it really saved trouble after all.

Presently we came to the long Shayár *zhingát* just opposite Aliábád, though so many dusty miles away by road. We had had it under observation for many months from our windows, and knew that in fact boulder bombardments down it were rare, though very thorough and impressive when they did occur. Still, it is always a nasty business. Like the other one, it was trickling actively, but the surface of the track across it was wide and fair, so we rode at it as always before. We were about half-way across when Haiyáto looked up and saw puffs of dust above us indicating the marksmanship of falling stones. He shouted "Ride for your life, Sahib!" and stupidly got so excited as to frighten the horses, who, without any additional incentive, are always nervous and jumpy on these mountain shoots. I know few feelings more unpleasant than the trembling between your knees of a frightened horse. We put the animals into a quick trot—anything faster only invites stumbling—and got happily across without accident, though some quite nasty rocks were falling at intervals. All the rest got over safely too. We were not sorry when this bit of the road, was behind us. These two Nagir *zhingáts* are to my mind the ugliest bits of road in the Agency. They don't look nearly as sensational as the many *peris*—which can, of course, be dangerous enough at times—but a firm shelf, however high and narrow, is preferable to a shifting surface.

Somewhere below us under the cliffs on the Nagir side of the river gorge, but out of sight of the road, is the Hakúchar spring, where Hunza and Nagir royal ladies occasionally go into camp together for a few days. It was pleasant to think that the young princesses, married across the water into the related family of the hereditary foe, are able to meet their own womenfolk in privacy from time to time. When such a party is arranged five large tents are pitched there for them.

It was very hot slithering down the powdery spiral descent to river level, riding along the sea-beach to the bridge and then mounting the long Hunza zigzag to Murtazábád, but once there we came again into the welcome shade of apricots and *gindáwer* (jujube trees, I think). I very much wished that some of our own family could have been with us to see our arrival "home." Never in the days when DL was Political Agent and was popularly believed to have money and offices in his gift did we get such a reception. Though we were forty-eight hours ahead of our programme, the news that we were coming had got all round the countryside. Our easily identifiable little procession had, of course, been seen crawling for hours along the Nagir mountain side. Four miles out from Aliábád, on the hither side of the great Hasanabad Nullah, the advance guard met us: two small boys of six or seven had pattered out on their bare feet to be the first to welcome us. A few hundred yards farther on another little pair; next the three levies, who were, of course, to a small extent in our pay (they got the princely sum of nine rupees a month every third month when they came "on duty"!), and then at the bridge at the bottom of the nullah there was a whole horde of our boy friends of every sort and size. I felt so sorry for the wee-er ones who had footed it out so far, that I hoisted them in turn on the back of my saddle to everyone's amusement. As we rode up the hill, zigzagging by the path, the whole herd scooted up by cracks in the cliffs and other impossible short-cuts and waylaid us again and again with shrieks of delight like a sort of Hengler's Circus. Every few yards new ones added themselves in with cries of greeting: "You've come back! Are you well? Had you trouble on the journey?"

I was terribly afraid that my small pillion-riders might slip off to glory—and their mothers might not have been pleased—so I clutched their fat little dusty paws round my tummy, reflecting happily that coat and jumper would in any case be going to the wash to-morrow. Suddenly at the top of the hill I missed the last little one and spun round anxiously to ask Ernest what had happened. "Oh, that one was my kid; I lifted him down and packed him home"—so that was all right, but he might have mentioned it.

As we climbed the last barren steep into the outskirts of Aliábád, everyone rushed to the door of the house or the edge of the field or the corner of the roof, men, women, and babies, to shout a welcome and enquiries after our health and the fortunes of the journey till we grew hoarse with answering and retorting with enquiries for them and theirs. Presently we descried a mob of more small boys ahead and heard bursts of cheering and laughter. The youngsters had somehow got hold of a big drum and a pair of kettledrums and set up a lusty banging in excellent imitation of the regulation "welcome tune" of the professional musicians. As we drew nearer in, our small girl friends turned up in groups of four and five, and by the time we got to the big open slope beside the Sarkári Fort we looked like a modern version of the Pied Piper of Hamelin with at least two or three hundred laughing, dancing, shouting boys and girls in front and behind and around us. We were very proud that after two months away we remembered all their faces and most of their names (and the ones whose names you didn't remember you could conveniently call

The road-cum-waterchannel on which our nearest neighbours lived.

(*See p.* 114)

PLATE XXI

"grandson"), and were able to ask after the other members of their families and the sore leg or hurt finger, and congratulate Shamúli on having grown two new front teeth and been promoted to trousers in our absence. I noticed that small boys and girls who in their baby days are clad merely in a shift, don their first trousers with their second teeth.

Our miniature escort swarmed into the verandahs and all round the house, and the difficulty was to coax them to run home after we had many times said a pointed "Good-bye for the present." It was the greatest fun, and we would not have missed it for anything. The luck of arriving prematurely had forestalled any formal grown-up reception, and this was a much more delightful and spontaneous welcome home. And these are the people of whom a recent traveller writes that they are "quarrelsome and grasping and out only for what they can get from the traveller." There are various types of traveller. The only comfort is that people who read a superficial travel book forget ten minutes after they have laid it down whether the author was writing of Hunza or Honolulu. The same writer says that no one in these regions cares about clean drinking water but all drink from ponds that have been fouled by the animals watering, whereas as I have already recorded the Hunzukuts most scrupulously roof in their drinking tanks and approach them down steep steps to prevent any animals possibly getting near them. It is grievously unfair to libel in print a people who have no opportunity to protest and correct mis-statements of fact.

We found the bungalow just as we had left it, but without the two months' dust we had fully expected. After tea and a rest we quickly shunted chairs back to their accustomed places, I got out tablecloths and rehung curtains, and we had our cosy camp-home looking like itself before dinner.

Chapter 27

THE FIRST OF THE HARVEST

THE first few days after our return we spent in picking up threads again, and very jolly it was to make the tour of the dear, familiar farmsteads and be shown the new kids and lambs, the new stone shed, etc., to comment on the progress each field was making—in some, little knobs were forming on the barley stalks, where presently the new ears would come, in some few, the ears were already taking shape—to see how far the new fields had progressed towards completion, and what jobs were now in hand. We were touched to find that it was not only our more immediate, better-known neighbours who seemed glad to see us, but even the more distant, rarely visited families flocked to the doors and came out to kiss our hands till the greetings became almost monotonous: "We have missed you. You were long away. We are glad you are back. Are you well?" Old men tottered up to talk to us, young mothers brought new babies to be introduced; Baby Faqér laughed and crowed and "knew his grandmother" (he was a very bright and intelligent little chap for only five months), and little Afrots had not forgotten how to shake hands and say "How do you do?" performing these feats to the admiration of crowds from the three adjacent house-roofs and a large passing party in the lane.

Bare fields that had been lying fallow were being got ready and dotted with manure dumps for the independent millets, sand was being dug from the silt traps to add to the beasts' bedding, whence it would duly reach the fields, and women were fetching baskets of earth from the "Mir's Stables" to add to the banked soil round their potatoes. The whole countryside was a hive of industry. We missed the larger animals and learnt that they had already been taken up to the *tér* for the summer, while the tiny lambs and kids who were being carefully shepherded about to get what scanty grazing they could find without trespassing into the springing crops, demanded the unceasing vigilance of their small guardians.

The most noticeable new phenomenon was the constant stream of people, men or women, stooping under huge bundles of greenery till they looked in truth "like trees walking." We had come back to find the poplars well clothed and bushy (for poplars), giving an unwonted air of luxury to the landscape, but now they were being ruthlessly stripped to provide fodder for the animals, half starved throughout the winter on a diet of dry leaves. Poplar, willow, and *gindáwer* are all laid under contribution, but the new fodder has to be very carefully issued at first lest the poor beasts should perish of its unaccustomed succulence. I stood one day watching and photographing a minute human insect at the top of a 50 or 60 foot poplar skilfully stripping it of its spring glory and leaving only the tiniest green tuft at the top. A whole handsome row were about to be similarly shorn. In a moment of thoughtlessness I said to the peasant at my side: "They look so lovely, it does seem a pity. . . ." He turned on me almost fiercely: "What, Mother? Would you starve our beasts for the sake of a poplar tree? The leaves will come again next spring. There is no cure for a dead sheep." I stood rebuked.

No. 3 had been laying out a new vegetable plot. Apicho showed me the various beds ready for beans, scarlet runners (which here have yellow flowers), marrows, and greens, but confessed that manure was their great problem. They have only one cow, poor devils, and with the best will in the world one cow cannot produce enough.

The end of May is the season when new saplings of poplar, willow, etc., are planted, and we occasionally met people carrying off bundles of them to set in place. The mills were in action again, and such fortunate folk as had a little grain still left from their emergency store—not, after all, exhausted by weddings or funerals—were carrying pathetically small bags of it to be ground. But "Starvation Springtime" was still ruling the land, and we noticed the children looking very thin and peaky, and a few with sores on their faces—hunger sores. We had often remarked on the complete absence of skin diseases amongst these cleanly folk, and the hunger sores rapidly disappeared with the coming of more food.

The opening of June saw weeding being very intensively carried out, not only for the sake of the growing crops, but for the weeds' own sake; those which were dubbed "crows' vegetables" were thrown to the sheep and goats, while sorrel and the like found their way into the family cooking-pot. Irrigation questions were now serious, for the crops must not be starved of water at the critical moment, and we used to meet bands of Aliábádkuts armed with shovels walking out the eight or more miles to the highest point of the Dála to guard and govern the controlling sluices. The potatoes were now beginning to flower and the mulberries to show signs of ripening, and the air was rent by shrill boy and girl noises designed to scare the birds off the mulberry trees. Every boy was armed with his catapult bow, made and strung of course by his own hands. I asked Yaman how many birds he had killed with his little stones: "Seventy-two, so far this season, Mother, but I'll get lots more." "What do you do with them?" "Oh, I take them home and put them in the pot, but there's not much meat on them." Our first impression of Hunza had been that, except for magpies, it was an entirely birdless land; this was a mistake. Migratory birds came in flocks at various seasons when any sort of likely food was going. Their various species I was not ornithologist enough to know; to me, as to A. J. Balfour, each was just "an average small bird," and the Hunza terminology was no great help to identification, for they were known as "mulberry birds," "barley birds," or the like, according to which crop they threatened. We now also for the first time saw shorn goats. Whereas the Hunza sheep are robbed of their wool just whenever wool is needed, so that you never see a really generous-looking ample fleece, the goats are shorn only once a year, in early summer. If you think of it, goat's hair would be too wiry to spin at all unless it were a decent length.

Windy weather was knocking down unripe mulberries in alarming quantities, which were incontinently guzzled by the goats and sheep.

By June 9th ripe mulberries were reported from Ganesh and Hasanabad, some hundreds of feet below us, but we had to wait another three weeks for ours.

One afternoon we were out on the hillside and stopped to watch a group of boys playing a complicated game of *bada bada* with a lot of small stones cast into twelve little holes in the ground. It was roughly equivalent to some of our games of marbles, and thinking of a large consignment of these which we had brought with us for future gifts we ruefully realized how useless marbles would be in a country where there are not six inches of smooth, level ground. As we sat trying to master the rules of *bada bada* Gulo crept up alongside me and slipped her hand confidentially into mine, whispering "Our pussy cat has had a confinement," using for fun the same term as she would have applied to her mother, and not the word suitable for cats. "There are three kittens, and they opened their eyes yesterday; do come and see them!"

When the game was over we accordingly started crosswise downhill to No. 3. I halted at the door to make sure that Zénába was prepared to endorse the impulsive invitation. She was sitting crouched by the hearth boiling the greens for dinner and jumped up with delight to bring us in. We squatted down on a sleeping-bench, from the back of which the children produced a round fruit basket in which the cat was cosily curled up. She was evidently accustomed to seeing her babies tenderly handled, for she let us take them out without other comment than a loud purr. Dear little furry things they were, about the size of small mice, and Gulo bubbled over: "She made first the black one and then the white one and then the yellow one—and that was all." Meantime, in addition to Kaníza and Apícho, a strange young man had drifted in to see what was going on, and presently Father arrived and we all chatted together very gaily. Laughing somewhat apologetically, Zénába confessed that she had drawn on the emergency reserve to make some *daudo* (a sort of porridge with butter) for pussy to keep her strength up—and this in one of the poorest houses, where they have had no bread nor butter for themselves for weeks. *Daudo* is one of the nourishing dishes you make for a human mother, and the cat was such a pet that the kittens were considered as a birth in the family, one of the emergencies budgeted for. There is as little need in Hunza for an R.S.P.C.A. as for an anti-litter crusade. Everyone is devoted to his animals, and the children have pet names for every lamb and kid. You will often see a boy or girl carrying home a tired animal slung over the neck like a fashionable lady's fur. Only people who have lived in the East can realize how amazing was this affectionate care for a pet; or how still more amazing this happy family life where father could come in and find his wife and daughters entertaining two strange men and be obviously delighted to see the guests. At least, if this sort of thing is possible elsewhere in the East, I have not heard of it.

When we passed next day we heard that a strange cat, which must be the only other one in Aliábád, for in general everyone is too poor to keep either cat or dog, had come in while the mother was mouse-hunting and had killed two of the kittens. Yaman, the only brother of our most beloved young friends, and most intelligent of informants, lifted a pathetic little white body with his toes from the field to show us. The children were half horrified and half amused at the kittens' fate.

There were a few wild flowers these June days amongst the scanty grass of the *toqs*: red bladder campion, stitchwort, and an occasional starved-looking forget-me-not. The children were much amused when we told them what the English call it, and that sentimentalists amongst us use it as a love-token. After that, one or another would run up to us offering a tiny blue flower and saying, "Don't forget me!" Some future linguist, language-hunting like ourselves, may be puzzled to hear of *je til akol* growing in Hunza fields and rack his brains as to how the idea came to the Karakoram. On principle we have tried to avoid poisoning the ground for future workers by importing European ideas, legends, or phrases, and in this connection the forget-me-not, the "one little pig" and Afrot's *How do you do?* are the only sins on my conscience.

Men left at home in the village were now making pilgrimages towards the *tér* to fetch down the manure that their brothers up on the mountain side with the animals have been scrupulously collecting. They usually arrange to meet half way, the village brother taking up any supplies the other may need and the brother of the *tér* bringing down not only manure but butter and *brús*, a kind of preparation of dried curd not unlike cream cheese. The lads up at the *tér* have rather a jolly time. They take up only their oldest clothes, for the life is rough and the work is hard. Anywhere that there is a scrap of suitable ground they plant a little barley, harnessing themselves to the plough so as not to put work on to the horses or oxen they may have with them, who are considered to have earned a holiday. Each day at dawn they loose their animals, but keep a careful eye on them, and sometimes have hair-raising adventures in rescuing a beast which has fallen down a cliff. There used to be considerable danger from wild animals, but nowadays there are few of these surviving. Any family that lacks a spare son to take the animals up entrusts them to the care of some other, after a rather touching little ceremony in which the beasts are solemnly committed to the care of their new master, who is at the same time given a certain amount of grain with him as part of his fee. Milking, making butter, collecting the manure, tending the barley (if any), cooking their own food, corralling the animals at night, etc., occupy the herds the greater part of the time, but they find leisure enough for various games and feats of skill.

Every now and again they decide to supplement their scanty rations—the village can spare little enough to send with them—by the sacrifice of a goat and a feast of meat. The donor of the beast plays for the evening the rôle of Mir, appoints another as his Wazir, and they play-act their several parts with gusto. It is frankly admitted that the animal sacrificed to make this holiday usually is one of those whose owner is not present. When eventually the boy returns, minus one of the animals for which he was trustee, he formally announces the regrettable "loss" to its owner. The nature of the catastrophe is fully understood but not crudely stated. A wise owner is expected to reply: "It is God's will. Accidents will happen. After all, they are beasts of the mountain and the wild." He is reckoned a churlish fellow who institutes enquiries and demands compensation, though no one denies his right to it. The liberty to indulge in an occasional free feed is, we understood, sparingly taken and not abused.

With luck a she-goat will yield enough milk while up on the summer pastures to make two *maltash*, i.e. two birch bark parcels of butter for storage. If the goat is a trustee goat the herd is expected to hand one *maltash* to her owner and to keep the balance as his fee. Sheep's milk is poor in fat content and yields little butter, so it is usually devoted to making *brús* and *rakhpín*, a kind of hard, dried curd which has great lasting qualities and the appearance of a cake of soap.

The day that the herds return from the mountain with their charges is a festive one for the villages. Large parties go out to meet the returning absentees. Before finally leaving the *tér*, driven down by cold and the advancing autumn snows, the herds bake some special little cakes to bring back with them, and crowds of dancing, shouting boys and girls fall on their elder brothers demanding their share. Trust the Hunzukuts to stage a festival on the slightest provocation.

Our Ernest of the white horse reappeared unexpectedly from the *tér* in the middle of the season and walked over from Hasanabad to call on us and bring an offering of *brús* for DL and of wild mountain flowers for me. He had given his animals into a friend's charge, and taken a couple of days off because he was a member of the Hasanabad polo team and was wanted to play in an inter-village match. These matches rouse as much interest as Arsenal *versus* Chelsea, and a good player who is also the possessor of a good pony can ill be spared. I duly took a photo of him and The Cat, he no longer in the rôle of the humble *sais* but of the gentleman polo player. Stout fellow!

These early June days were the time for apricot and mulberry grafting. The cultivated fruit shoots are grafted on to wild trees. We watched the process, about which the Hunzukuts have little to learn. Each graft was given a double lashing of bark from mulberry root. We returned later and found them

1. Rakapóshi in summer from Aliábád. Apricot trees in foreground. (See p. 80)

PLATE XXII

2. The sole type of wheeled vehicle in Hunza; a barrow used only in levelling fields.

(See p. 211)

all thriving. The field walls looked very jolly at this season with wild flowers of the rock-garden type growing in the crannies between the stones and fostered by the seepage from the irrigated fields above. Amongst them was a wild mint and a wild thyme, the flavouring qualities of which are known and appreciated.

On June 12th we saw some people hungrily eyeing their barley and reckoning that it would be ripe for cutting in another fifteen days. It was said to be good this year in spite of an abnormally cold, late spring. Some rain showers that we had were welcomed though they temporarily cooled the air. But as clouds and rain continued, anxiety began to be felt lest the wheat should be late and delay too long the planting of the buckwheat-on-wheat. The barley is subject to a disease called *tam*, which stripes the leaves an ugly yellow and produces a milky liquid in the ears. Few plants were attacked this year. The disease called *matèl* (rust?), which makes black ears, attacks only wheat and millet, and if the cold and rain persisted it might be expected to set in. We were doubly anxious that this year's crops should be good: unselfishly for the people's sake; selfishly lest a bad year should be attributed to the maleficent influence of two crazy people learning Burushaski—though indeed these highly rational people would be unlikely to indulge any such fantastic association of ideas.

We saw some people one day collecting the under-bark from red willow trees; they use it for dyeing the leather of their native boots and skilfully chip it out from the living tree without injuring the willow.

Now that the people were really within sight of food they frankly confessed to being desperately hungry, and the strain of unremitting work—weeding, ploughing, manuring, grafting, irrigating from dawn to dusk on empty tummies—was showing in drawn, thin faces, but appeared powerless to damp their spirits or fray their tempers. It was dreadful to look on and be helpless to feed the multitude with loaves or fishes, while we lived—sparingly enough by home standards but—riotously compared with these much more deserving neighbours. We saw one day a group of men sitting pensively under a mulberry tree silently munching unripe fallen fruit, but the most pathetic sight was groups of little girls crouched beside a water-channel scooping out sand and mud and forming it into various types of breads and cakes which they pretended to "bake like Mother." They knew nothing of modern psychology, and were unaware that we interpreted their poor little mud pies as wish-fulfilments.

Cuckoos and larks were now filling the air with welcome, strangely home-like sounds.

One day the news of the Quetta earthquake reached us by telephone and spread dismay in twenty homes which had sons in British service there. How to get news? Mercifully the suspense was not prolonged. Thanks to the humane arrangements which allowed survivors to telegraph free, a telegram was telephoned through from one of the Hunza men to say that he and all his compatriots had escaped, owing to the fact that they were all employed by officers of the Staff College. It would be blasphemy to suppose that those were all unrighteous on whom the Tower of Siloam fell, but we could hardly resist a suspicion that the God of Earthquakes shared something of our feeling for the folk of Hunza.

It was the very end of June before the Barley Harvest was in sight, but as the time approached nearer and nearer, by painfully slow degrees, we saw women and girls devoting all their spare time to making new caps for the jollifications of Ginâni, and the men, who are not a whit less vain, were already sporting bright new shirts in anticipation. We came on Kaníza and Apícho putting the last touches on a cap made of some scraps of Tootal material which I had given to Kaníza to dress the new doll that Yaman had made for her. They were weaving the braid edging straight on to the cap, stitching it on as they wove. The method was interesting: six long coarse crimson threads are made fast by both ends to the edge of the double cap—outside, and slightly padded lining. The stitcher holds the cap inside out. The braider sits near and takes the six long loops of equal length, passing three over the fingers of the right and three over the fingers of the left hand; then she slips the left-hand loops on to the right-hand fingers, deftly lifts the original right-hand loops off on to the left fingers carefully crossing each pair of threads as she does so. Widely drawing her two hands apart Apícho then drove the set of crossed threads down on to the edge of the cap, where Kaníza secured the twelve-fold plait with a large stitch. This was repeated *ad infinitum*, the braid only showing on the right side of the cap and the long ugly stitches on the wrong. The process looks rather like cat's-cradle. I had always wondered why, when they take such infinite trouble over the minute cross-stitch embroidery of their caps and the hand-plaited twelve-ply braid, they finished the cap off with these long stitches. I also wondered why it seemed impossible to detach the braid without its ravelling out. I now saw that braid-weaving and stitching were part of one elaborate process.

By July 1st the luckier folk were already cutting their barley and clearing a field for their threshing floor without waiting for the formal harvest-initiation ceremonies of the Gináni, the date of which is naturally fixed by the Mir to suit Báltít, 1,500 feet higher, and consequently some days behind Aliábád. All our potatoes were by now in full flower and our wheat was turning "fox-colour."

On July 5th we rode over to Báltít for yet another of the Hunza festivals, and ye Gods! it was hot on the road—90 degrees in the shade—and we had to start at the very hottest time of day, about 2 p.m. The Mir gave us tea in his nice shady grass-grown apple orchard before we remounted and climbed up to the Fort. It is not easy to convey how steep the road is that in Báltít corresponds to the Mall. Your pony steps from one boulder to the next with a great lurch, his spine almost vertical, and for my part I could only just stick on by my usual technique of thrusting my stirrups back to the root of his tail and firmly gripping his mane with my right hand. The road runs between high stone walls and zigzags wildly. The little box-like stone houses of the capital are piled on top of each other in the craziest way—town-planning has to accommodate itself to the vagaries of a precipitous mountain side. They are indescribably picturesque, but you would not think them possible to live in, yet they provide a high degree of simple comfort. When you reach the courtyard the Fort towers above you like Bush House. Up the semi-spiral ramp outside and the two flights of ladder-like stairs, and out you come on to the great reception balcony with its incomparable view. The country looks its very best in July, every field green or golden with its crops and every fruit tree in full luxuriant leaf, apricots turning golden but not yet ripe.

There was a crowd of fifty or sixty on the balcony, and we chatted to the princes and others while DL endeavoured to find some spot from which he could command with his cine-camera the steep approach almost vertically below us up which the Harvest procession would presently be coming, without himself toppling over to certain death. The little parapet—not calculated for the convenience of camera men—just caught his shins in such a way as to encourage a fatal plunge. It is needless to mention that the sinking sun stared straight into his lens. The sun blazed relentlessly on the white mud floor of the balcony, the resultant glare alternating with inky shadows, while the table and chairs which had been hospitably provided for our convenience intruded with infernal incongruity into every foreground. If you escaped sudden death over the parapet to rocks 1,000 feet below, you might meet a less spectacular but equally fatal end by an unpremeditated dive down the trap-door. Photography in Hunza is fraught with danger and difficulty.

The Mir meantime had disappeared inside to robe himself before taking his seat on the throne under the carved verandah, where he would be well-nigh invisible to the camera lens. The cloth spread on the throne was the loveliest imaginable: a thick, bright sapphire-blue velvet with a border of apricot colour, or rather that delicate, yellowy, salmony pink which upholsterers call "apricot," though never was an apricot that shade. The whole border as well as a great medallion in the centre was embroidered in real gold, padded quarter of an inch thick: a barbarically lovely thing, bought, the Mir said, for Lord Curzon's visit twenty or thirty years ago, and as untarnished still as only real gold can be.

At last, when we were nearly grilled to death, we heard a

shout of "Here they come!" Far away, hundreds of feet below us, we could just descry a pair of horsemen scrambling up the road I have described. It was two of the royal princes, one of them Lord Fauntleroy, each with an armful of ripe golden barley. Soon they disappeared into the bowels of the Fort below us and presently their heads popped up through the trap-door. Someone whisked the barley from their arms and disappeared with it to rub the ears and toast the grains. The Mir appeared from an inner door. He was wearing a loose gown of pale blue silk all embroidered in gold and a pale turban also touched with gold. He greeted his people like a king and went over to his seat, quietly kicked off his slippers, and neatly slithered himself on to the couch-like throne in photograph-defying shadow, and sat cross-legged—the perfect picture of an Oriental monarch whose authentic ancestors were ruling Hunza while our Black Prince was fighting in the fields of France. He graciously signed for us to come near, and I let my chair be brought under the verandah, but DL begged to be allowed to stay out in the balcony where he could move about more freely.

Then came a henchman with ewer and basin and the Mir very sensibly spread a towel over his silken knees and velvet cloth while water was poured over his hands. Another minion then presented a priceless china bowl filled with sour milk, and the Mir taking a silver spoon lifted half a spoonful of the junket and held it out while the man sprinkled in three grains of toasted barley. This he ate—three times three grains in all—thus handselling the first fruits of the year's new harvest. Then the bowl was circulated to DL (with a fresh spoon) and then to me, and then in order of rank and precedence to the rest of the assembled company. It was a simple yet impressive little communion service. And throughout the country every family in like fashion ceremonially tastes the first grains of the new barley, and carries in the first-cut stalks solemnly to bind them round the *shiri dako*, the main pillar of the humble atrium, where they remain till in due course replaced a twelve-month later.

When the bowl and barley grains had made the rounds, in

was brought the largest wooden tray I ever saw, piled high with various foods: I noted a fresh cabbage, stacks of several kinds of bread, dishes of dried curds, mountains of rice with nuts and onions on top, and every sort of vegetable cooked in butter. The Mir sampled everything very sparingly, laughingly explaining that he must not tuck in now as he had to eat dinner with us presently. Then the royal tray was taken over and placed before the princes, while mountains of bread and meat were set in the centre of the balcony for everybody. The meat was hacked up as usual with an adze and the food quickly distributed and almost as quickly disposed of, no one going through the farce of having a delicate appetite. The beauty of this kind of feast is that there is no "clearing away," for in five minutes not one visible crumb was left.

Then all stood up and turned to the Mir with a bow and a curious gesture brushing down their beards or moustaches or whiskers with both hands (whether they had any such trimming on the face or not) and said in unison *mubárak manish!*—may it be blessed!—thereupon fading out one by one down the trap-door. When the road was clear we all climbed down too, and in the courtyard the Mir mounted his horse again for a sort of triumphal march home. He suggested our riding with him, but we explained that we should prefer to walk down if we might. He laughed and said: "So should I, but I must not!" The ascent of the Hunza Mall is all right, but riding down it is unattractive. We waited till he had plunged vertically out of sight and took our time to the descent on foot. There is a wonderful collection of old buildings, with balcony rooms propped on rudely carved pillars, a charming old, now disused mosque, also lavishly carved, and a wonderful old mill, all packed tight round the feet of the Fort for safety.

After we got back to the Mir's gardens we washed and changed, and dined with him in a roomy tent. The poor man had been having severe toothache for several days and no sleep at night, yet he manfully ate his way through dinner and kept the conversation going. Next morning we were awakened by a magnificent voice chanting the Call to Prayer before dawn. It was the only *muezzin* we ever heard in Hunza, but the Mir takes a pride in having every sort of artisan and artist in his service. I peeped out through the muslin curtain of our tent, but I didn't notice any great rush of the population to pray. There was polo at 6 a.m., to which we did not turn out.

After breakfast there was a great feast in the large courtyard outside the garden at Kerimabad where the Mir sat daily to hold public court. The large open space was packed with feasters. The Mir was seated under a verandah on another throne (again in heavy shadow), and strings of people came with huge baskets on their backs, laden with food. We were seated on the vantage ground of a rocky shelf in a great boulder that commands the courtyard and at the same time forms the foundation of a splendidly sited guest-house bungalow of comparatively recent date. Yesterday's performance was repeated but without the ceremonial of the toasted barley grains. Yesterday the guests on the Fort balcony had been only "The Great," but to-day the feasters were a more representative and larger crowd. The eating did not take long, and we then adjourned to see the usual kind of dancing.

After that lunch we said good-bye and rode home: again at the very hottest time of a ninety-in-the-shade day. But we were thankful to have seen the Ginãni ceremonial which was just over when we arrived the year before. We had now seen the Hunza year right through with all its festivals, and alas! packing and departure were beginning to loom large in our thoughts. We could not linger so long in Hunza as to risk having again to *walk* the Burzil—Fate and weather might not have been so kind the second time. DL had toiled with his two Wakhis through all the work he was likely to be able to extract from them, and we bade the dear old men an affectionate and thankful farewell. Khalifa Farãghat was the proud possessor of a pair of "old age spectacles" we had procured for him from the Agency Surgeon in Gilgit, which he said gave his eyes a new lease of life.

We had brought the faithful Muslim back with us from Yasin, having obtained leave for him from the Rajah, and David had been spending all his leisure from Wakhi and Burushaski on rounding off his Werchikwar, but we presently dismissed him too, to concentrate on our own windings up.

There was an unbelievable lot to do: specimens of plants and grains to be labelled and packed; photographs and manuscript notes of every kind to be sorted into order and well wrapped in waterproof paper; parting gifts to be thought of; arrangements for the journey down to be made in advance; the last lot of duplicate typescript, texts, etc., to be got off by different posts to the Bank lest one lot should be lost; specimens of such utensils and implements as we could hope to carry to be collected. We had reluctantly to abandon the hope of bringing home in triumph a stone *balosh* as too heavy for any load, and breakable withal.

Chapter 28

FINALITIES

OUR final weeks in Hunza were overcrowded with unavailing attempts to fill all the lacunæ of over a year's work, and working was not rendered easier by a temperature of 105 degrees in the shade, nor by the fact that we were both beginning to feel the strain of an intensive fifteen months at close on 8,000 feet (although we had not been consciously conscious of the altitude), and were undeniably somewhat played out.

We had to try to take all the photographs—moving or still—that had hitherto escaped us, develop and print the latter, and keep up to the end our practice of giving copies to the interested parties.

Two lines of enquiry in particular demanded attention. Until faith in the purely scientific and disinterested character of DL's intentions had been firmly established, he had refrained from any attempt to map in detail the inhabited country immediately about us, or to enquire too closely into the amount of land belonging to any given household. Such activities would inevitably have given rise to the fear that he had been sent to make a survey for Government as a prelude to land taxation. Now that such fears were unlikely to arise—and would not impede us greatly if they did—we toiled up and down the steep and rocky tracks, taking sights, pacing distances, measuring fields, and making calculations. A country harder to survey, even in the rough and ready fashion which alone was possible, it would be difficult to conceive. It was impossible to find even twenty yards of level ground in a straight line to make a base from which anything else was visible; pacing distance was almost otiose when spurs jutted and angles re-entered everywhere. There were no landmarks: every house was a rough replica of every other and not certainly identifiable from any distance, every poplar tree which from one point of vantage stood out in splendid isolation immediately fell into line with a dozen others when you walked a hundred yards. The whole habitable country was tilted at an angle of 45 or 50 degrees, and seamed with sunken rock-ravines; the river was perennially invisible in its gorge; tracks and water-courses were sunk between high walls, and not to be divined unless you were actually in them out of sight of everything: a heartbreaking, leg-exhausting task, the sketch map that DL coveted.

A second important task was an enquiry into matters of revenue and taxation. To have questioned the peasantry, except very casually and incidentally, would again have been to excite curiosity as to ulterior motives—the non-existence of which might well have seemed incredible—though we did manage to accumulate a good deal of information that was invaluable as corroborative material. The only way to get coherent information was to approach the Mir direct and beg permission to enlist the assistance of Prince Jamál Khán, now his grandfather's right hand in administrative matters, and then try to keep the boy's untrained attention from wandering off the point at issue.

All the while book-boxes had to be gradually packed and top-dressed with lighter material so as to make manageable loads, new boxes had to be conjured out of old to take the curious and unwieldy articles—from bows to winnowing forks—ultimately destined for some museum. The contents of each box had to be inventoried in detail, for Customs purposes as well as for our own reference, then strongly wired, then painted with name and numbers. Dádo and the rest helped manfully over all such tasks as they could tackle, but much could be done only by DL or by myself.

Finally there was one blind spot of language which cried out for—and got—attention, the Dumáki spoken by the alien Béricho, that minute language-island within the larger language-island of Burushaski itself.

During fifteen months in Hunza our solitude had been invaded only twice by a European passer-by: an inspecting engineer, Mr. Halcro Johnson of the Orkneys, had spent a night and explored some of the countryside with us, conjecturing about hydraulic pumps to lift water from the ever-changing bed of the river to the fields above, and Colonel Schomberg, ever entertaining, informative, and critical, had passed through on one of his endless wanderings in the wilds. As luck would have it, no less than two parties turned up in those last hectic days. Colonel Lang, Resident in Kashmir, made the pilgrimage to Hunza in company with Major Kirkbride, lunched with us on August 28th on the way up, and spent a night on the way down; our genuine pleasure in seeing these distinguished guests was slightly marred by pressure of work and less-even-than-usual ability adequately to entertain, for our supplies were sorely on the ebb. We gave them the one and only tin of sausages we had had!

It was many years since a Resident had found time or inclination to travel up to Hunza. Soon after the party had left us we heard the Mir's saluting gun (a new toy since our time) sending unwonted echoes through the immemorial silences, and that night the mountain side was magnificently starred with bonfires lighted high on almost inaccessible peaks and spurs. Impregnated as we were with knowledge of Hunza fuel-poverty, we could not but reckon the cost of such a gallant and loyal tribute to the King Emperor. Most probably the sheer delight in accomplishing the feat of carrying treasured juniper logs to such heights and setting them ablaze at the concerted moment, and the love of every Hunzukuts for a *tamasha*, prevented anyone but ourselves from indulging in such sordid reckonings. We wondered how much or how little Colonel Lang appreciated what those bonfires meant.

Our next visitors were of another sort. A couple of months before *The Times* had cabled me that one Peter Fleming, evidently a white-haired boy of theirs, was apparently missing somewhere in Central Asia on the way from Peking to Kashgar. They had had no news for months and were getting anxious. Could I make enquiries? Distances that look slight enough on a map in Printing House Square are more formidable in the mountains of the Karakoram. From Báltít to Kashgar is a month's severe marching in favourable weather conditions, and in others not marchable at all. The telegraph stops at Misgar, five marches up, and there is no telegraph office between Misgar and Gilgit. So far as we knew Kashgar had no wireless; anyhow, we had not. We had, indeed, seen a party pass, bound for the north, and said to be taking up a wireless *receiving* set to Kashgar, though they themselves preserved a hush-hush silence about the contents of their massive loads, far too heavy for pony packs, and as we thought far too unwieldy to be manhandled round the cliffs and over the glaciers of the route, so that we anticipated its almost certain non-arrival.

My only chance of getting news was to indent on the kind co-operation of the Mir. He has—by Central Asian standards—an efficient if unorganized news-service, which, however, conveys its news on foot, by word of mouth. He promised to keep me informed. At length he sent me word that there was a traveller, Temmelemming or possibly Semmelemming or possibly almost any other name, reputed to be heading for Kashgar, but still about nine marches out, travelling with a lady. As to whether he was a *Times* correspondent or not, there was no word. Newspaper correspondents are parasites of modern civilization, a human type unrecognized amongst the happy dwellers in the oases of the Tarim Basin or of Hunza. We had not then heard that Peter Fleming was crossing Central Asia under the wing of the famous international ski-ing and hockey champion, Mademoiselle Ella Maillart, and the fact that Temmelemming was accompanied by an unexplained lady suggested that he was not improbably some enterprising Swedish missionary touring with his wife. I cabled, therefore, to *The Times* with caution, anxious not to raise hopes that would be distressing to Fleming's people if he should prove to have perished. News of Temmelemming under a bewildering variety of aliases continued to come at intervals, and I duly continued to forward them to *The Times*. At last I was able to cable that the traveller was indeed Fleming, and had safely reached Kashgar—a stop-press scoop that fell a little flat in London, which had had a wireless from Fleming in Kashgar some weeks before. Meantime Fleming and the lady (whoever she might prove to be) were approaching Hunza, and we sent a runner out to meet them, bid them welcome, and invite them to look in on us at Aliábád.

They turned up on the morning of August 29th at eight o'clock, sunburnt, hatless, happy, and indomitable, and we had the honour of offering them their first English breakfast on British soil after the famous journey of which all the world now knows. It wasn't much of a breakfast, but it wasn't *tsamba*. They were an engaging pair of adventurers. If Fleming might have stood for the errant knight in search of a distressed princess to rescue, Ella Maillart was obviously quite as competent to do any rescuing that might be required.

Over a merry breakfast we learned Peter Fleming's indignation at the suggestion that he was lost at all. He had reached Kashgar ahead of his scheduled time. While we were still at table our merriment was enhanced by a cable that came for me, forwarded by post, of course, from Gilgit. Dated many weeks before, it came via the Dead Letter Office in Lahore, where it had been mouldering for some reason that we never fathomed. It announced Fleming's wireless from Kashgar, and reasonably suggested that I might cease to cable Temmelemming's progress. I felt that nothing but courtesy and cable-economy combined had prevented an exasperated Foreign Editor from qualifying my cables with some forcible adjective. I was now able to close the cable-correspondence with the triumphant news that Fleming and Maillart had just breakfasted with us in excellent health and spirits, and hoped to reach Srinagar in a fortnight or three weeks. I then air-mailed a letter enclosing the Dead Letter telegram to prove that I was not really the congenital idiot I must have seemed. The explanation was, I presume, accepted, for I never received either a dressing-down or a bill for my cabled futilities.

Meantime we adjourned from table to take photographs of each other outside. I had been boasting to Miss Maillart of the friendliness of Hunza women and their lack of camera-shyness.

She had a bobbed shock of dusty brown hair, long untrimmed, a horizontally-striped jumper of navy and white, loosish navy knickers, and long boots. She made an unheralded descent on a group of Hunza women in a neighbouring field—they fled in terror from the apparition. Unfortunately there was no time for me to round them up and woo them back, for the two newspaper colleagues had to hasten back to Báltít to join in some festivities in honour of the Resident. We later had the pleasure of hearing them both lecture in London on their astounding journey, and it was hard to identify the beautiful lady in evening dress graciously displaying lantern slides to the Central Asian Society and humorously making light of the hardships and perils of those seven famous months, with the tomboy figure of the Karakoram who had left so vivid a memory behind in Aliábád.

By mid-August the last batches of drying apricots had been gathered in, withdrawing those bright pools of colour which had so gaily painted roofs and boulder surfaces. But the independently sown millets were tossing glorious golden heads (*cha*) far more challenging to the eye than wheat or barley, or graceful tassels of golden rain (*bay*) lovelier even than ripening rice; the millets-on-barley, later sown, were still a brilliant green, and the sweet buckwheat-on-wheat was bursting out into seas of beautiful, sweetly-smelling pink. We were glad not to have had to leave without seeing and scenting sweet buckwheat once again, while the yellow ill-smelling blossoms of the bitter buckwheat were too unobtrusive to spoil the delicate sheets of green amongst which they hid or taint the general air. It was going to be hard to tear ourselves away from Hunza in her summer glory.

All our last comings and goings amongst the farmsteads were clouded by "that go-ey feeling" which schoolchildren know so well, casting the shadow of the prison house over the last precious hours of holiday.

After my first ill-advised distribution of a few Woolworth balls amongst the toddlers we had firmly abstained from any form of gift-giving. Now the moment had come when self-discipline could be relaxed. We got up from Gilgit two pony-loads of rock salt, a consignment of large, bright-coloured handkerchiefs, and a supply of the unspun, bright, Central Asian silks which go to embroider women's caps. Needles, safety-pins, thimbles, and multi-coloured beads I already had by me in large quantities, and I had the store-room full of carefully hoarded empty tins and containers, spare packing-cases and kerosene tins, while the dark-room offered rows of empty bottles and the six priceless petrol drums which had faithfully stored water for innumerable photographic washings.

Three of the petrol drums we set aside for the three headmen of Aliábád, to whose kindness we had owed carpeted stone sofas at "The Gate" for merry festivals, and many another gracefully offered courtesy. The other three we reserved for the trusty servants, Dádo, Zaidu, and Sagi. To Sagi, also, who had toiled so many weary miles and climbed so many thousand feet to fetch us never-failing supplies of drinking water, we gave a couple of spare buckets, which he had more than earned; packing-cases and kerosene tins were divided at their own discretion—and without quarrelling—between levies and servants. Since even two pony-loads of salt would go nowhere among two hundred households, we had reluctantly decided that we must confine our farewell largesse to the twenty houses of our more immediate and most intimate neighbours, which happened to stand geographically somewhat apart from the rest of the village.

With heavy heart I divided the salt into twenty equal shares, added needles, pins, and beads according to the numbers of the womenfolk, with a supply of silk for every house with a maturing bride, and supplemented all with a few empty tins or bottles. Then I tied this odd and heterogeneous offering into a coloured handkerchief, to be delivered by my own hand on our last evening.

For Ustád Nadíro, the master carpenter, to whom we owed more thanks than to any other single individual, DL had ordered from Bombay a saw and chisels, augurs and awls of Sheffield steel, and for Afiato, the peasant priest, also an outstanding benefactor, a pair of old-age spectacles to prolong his reading days. The tools came in the nick of time, and DL sent up a message to No. 8 that if the Ustád could spare time after dark to come and open a packing-case for him, he would be grateful. The old man sat down to the task, and as the tools came into view he lifted them out with the loving reverence of a good craftsman. "These are the things, Sahib." "And these things are yours, Ustád, old friend, with our thanks." A moment of dumb, delighted incredulity and the old man was on his knees raining kisses on an embarrassed hand. Long may Nadíro live to wield his English steel!

There was—I regret to confess—an almost inexhaustible supply of empty cigarette tins. They were known to be considered ideal receptacles for embroidery odds and ends. I let it be known that any little girl of embroidering age who cared to come might have one on application, and for nearly half a day I stood by the verandah distributing one each, while an orderly mob of well-loved eager faces surged round me. To their honour be it said that of many hundreds only one child attempted fraudulently to secure a second tin, and she, poor kid, must nearly have perished of the unanimous scorn poured out upon her. "A grasping people, the Burusho of Hunza!" Let anyone say that in my hearing and I shall make him eat his lie.

The children's joy in possessing these valued momentoes a little eased the pain of parting.

At last, on September 2nd, everything down to our last toothbrush was packed. We started out betimes to evade as much as possible of the heat of that gruelling road. The whole of Aliábád, great and small, young and old, men and women, was gathered on the open slopes by the Sarkári Fort to see us ride away, and the air was thick with cries of "We shall miss you!" We waved as far as possible to each, and shouted our good wishes and farewells as the band played us on our way. Dozens accompanied us, running alongside through adjacent fields for a full mile or so, then slipped away to resume the insistent toil of a summer's day which must be done though the heavens fall or Sahibs ride into the blue. The road plunged, steep and narrow, into the Hasanabad ravine, the last stragglers

1. Children watching water-hole (centre) to close it with the mushroom-plug (right) at given signal from father. (*See p.* 94)

PLATE XXIII

Two small Hunza princesses with pet puppy. (*See p.* 246)

3. Khalifa Farāghat teaching his son to read the Persian scriptures. (*See p.* 241)

dropped off, and left us with only the immediate followers who were accompanying us to Kashmir.

As we toiled up the hot, dusty, unending zigzag out of the gorge towards the Murtazabad ridge, we espied three forlornly idle little figures under a tree ahead. Girls seldom stray so far beyond the village boundaries as their brothers. "If it weren't so far out I should guess those youngsters to be Kaníza, Shamúli, and Nigín," said I, "but they couldn't possibly . . ." But they had. As we drew near we saw that all three were crying, but bravely battling for self-control and jerkily wiping their eyes with their cuffs: "We shall remember you! May your way be blessed!" they called in chorus. "God make you grow! And may you, too, be blessed!" we answered back. And our mutual "Khudayár! God be with you!" blended, as our ponies breasted the last inch of crest and vanished over the ridge. With instinctive delicacy of feeling the children had chosen a strategic spot where there could be no looking back, no lingering of farewell.

Valete, Hunzukuts nostri gratissimi!

INDEX

Agha Khan, His Highness the 31, 146, 149
agriculture 107, 135 *et passim*
Aliábád 73, 77, 274, 280 *et passim*
Áltít 105, 106
animals, love of 285–6
apricots 97, 179, 238, 302
aqueducts 69, 83, 105
archery 235
architecture 125, 132
  in Kashmir 35–6
  in Nagir 274
  in Yasin 268–9
Astor River 57, 58
Awantipura (Kashmir) 36

Baba Ghundi 148
Báltít, capital of Hunza 104
  Fort 105–6, 227, 245, 291
Báltistán 106, 164
Bandipur (Kashmir) 42
basket making 98, 163
Béricho (sg. Bérits) 164, 198, 200
Biddulph, Colonel 20
birds 284, 290
Bopfau (Barley Seed Sowing) 226–236
bread 86, 243
burial 170
Búbuli, Princess 105
Buddha 272
Bunji 60, 61
Burushaski, language 9, 19, 22, 24, 25, 71, 140, 254–62
  of Nagir 267
  of Yasin *v.* Werchikwar
Burusho 28, 68, 179
Burzil Chauki (11,100 ft.) 47, 49
Burzil Pass (13,775 ft.) 48–55
Burzil River 46
butter *v.* maltash

carpentry 129
catapult bow 143, 284
Chalt 65, 264, 273
Chilás 17
children in Hunza 73, 79–80, 94, 96–8, 101, 118, 128, 137, 145, 158–9 *et passim*
  babies Chap. 20
Chillum Chauki 54, 56
Chitral 19
  siege of 216
Colvin, Lt.-Col. 33
cooking 116, 172
crime 121

Dála (water-channel) 83, 93, 105
dancing 160, 199, 203
  Bopfau Dance 228–30
Darél 17
Dashkin 57
Diramiting 181, 233
Doian 57–8
dress 162, 221–2
  boots 225
  women's caps 174, 290–1
  woollen cloaks 168, 173
Dumáki language 164–5, 298

education 216–17, 239
Elliott, Sir Ivo 35
embroidery 143, 165–6, 173

festivals
  Harvest Initiation 291–5
  Harvest Thanksgiving Chap. 19
  New Year 244–5
  Seed Sowing 226–36
  Wedding Day 197–202
  Winter Solstice 201–5
fields 71, 79, 211–12
Fleming, Peter 299–301

INDEX

fodder 275, 283
fuel 91, 131, 299

Gakuch 271
games
  at mountain pastures 287
  children's games 134, 143, 144–145, 209, 217, 285; *see also* polo
Ganesh 105, 106, 285
Ghazan Khan
  Mir of Hunza, father of Safdar Ali and Muhammad Nazim Khan 237
  Prince, eldest son and heir of Sir Muhammad Nazim Khan; succeeded his father ("our" Mir) in July 1938 73, 108, 228
Ghulmit (Nagir) 65
Gilgit 15, 16, Chap. 2, 62–4, 244, 264, 273
Gilgit River 265
Gilgit Stupa 272–3
Gillan, Major and Mrs. 29, 57
Gináni (Initiation of Harvest) 93, 291–5
Godai 56
gold-washing 271
grafting 288
Grierson, Sir George 20
Gupis 265
Gurés 45
Gurikót 57

hairdressing 223
Hakúchar 279
Haramuk 43
harvesting 81, 102, Chap. 18
Harvest Initiation *v.* Gináni
Harvest Thanksgiving Chap. 19, 145
Hasanábád (village and glacier) 72, 208, 279, 285
Hattu Pir 58
Hayward 268
Hedin, Sven 24
Herwán (Kashmir) 36
Hindi 264
Hindu Kush 18
Hispar Glacier 105
hospitality 128, 151, 155, 217, 238, 243
houses 124, Chap. 17
Humáyun Beg, Wazir 121
Hunza *passim*
Hunza climate 80, 111, 194, 205, 212, 221
Hunza-Nagir 17
  Campaign (1891) 17, 120
Hunza Princes 71, 73
Hunza River 64, 72, 79, 105, 108
Hunzukuts (sg. and pl.), a person or people inhabiting Hunza (more correctly "Hunzu") 9, 68, 72, 81, 90 *et passim*
  origin of 106

Indus (river and valley) 59–61, 64
inheritance 120, 182
Institutet for Sammenlignende Kulturforskning 26
iron-work 163–4
irrigation 71, 83, 94, 105, 143, 284
Ishkoman 17
Ismailis (Maulais), Ismailism (Maulaism) 31, 67, 146, 147
Ivanow, Professor 31, 146

Jalsa (in Gilgit) 22, 244
Jamu (Hunza) 208
Jhelum River 33, 41
Johnson, Halcro 299
Jutiál 62

Kak, Ram Chandra 36
Karakoram 18 *et passim*
Kashmir 33, Chap. 7
  architecture 35–6
  Valley Food Control 34
  servants 41

INDEX

Kargah Nullah 272
Kashgar 300, 301
Kerimábád 227, 295
Khushwaqts 19, 265
Khowár language 19, 265
Kirkbride, Major and Mrs. 244, 264, 273, 299
Kiser 104 and footnote
Kishengunga River 45
Kuh Ghizr 17

labour
communal 83, 120
division of 103
land tenure 120–2, 182
Lang, Lt.-Col. and Mrs. 33, 299
leather 225
dyeing 289
Lecoq 24
Ledger, Major, I.M.S. 109
Leitner 20
Leverhulme Research Fellowships 28
litter 145, 146, 147
Loralai (Baluchistan) 15
Lorimer, Lt.-col. D. L. R. 9 *et passim*
language work 18–21, 25, 111–112, 140–1, 241, 248–62, 295, 298
photography 80, 175–6, 177, 188, 224, 232

Maillart, Ella 300–2
Malinowski, Professor 29
maltash (Hunza butter) 86–7, 89, 288
manure 101, 144, 145, 210, 237, 283, 287
map-making 297–8
marriage 146, 164, Chap. 22
wedding day 197–202
Martand (Kashmir) 36
Maulais *v.* Ismailis
Millar, Lt.-Col., I.M.S. 34
milk 86, 287–8
in Nomal and Chalt 273
mills 176–8, 283
mill-stones 67
Minapin 65, 66, 264, 274
Minimarg 41, 47
Minór (Gilgit) 62
Mir of Hunza, Sir Muhammad Nazim Khan, K.C.I.E. (1892–1938) 23, 29, 72, 77, 108–9, 120–2, 231, 233, 246, 291–4
Mir of Nagir, Sir Sikandar Khan 23, 65, 106, 273–6
Mir Baz Khan, Rajah of Yasin 265, 275
Misgar 300
money 123, 174, 225
morals 146–7, 190
Morgenstierne, Professor Georg 26, 27
Munda languages 24
Murtazábád 70, 263, 279
music 172, 198–9, 202

Nagir 65, 72, 105, 180, 273–8
Nagirkuts (people of Nagir) 180, 273
Queen of 275
women of 180, 277
Nagir River 105
Nanga Parbat 43, 56, 60, 80, 264
Naupor (Gilgit) 272
Nauróz (New Year) 244–5
Nilt 65
Nómal 373

old age 172, 183–5, 216

Pari 62
Partáb Pul 61
pastures 143, 207
mountain 287
Peshwári 46
photography 80, 175–6, 177, 188, 210, 219, 224, 232, 243, 292, 297

Pir Panjàl 33, 43
polo 56, 227, 288
population 124, 179, 185
Puniál 17

Quetta earthquake 290

Rakapóshi (Raka) (25,550 ft.) 65, 70, 80, 138, 273
Ram Ghát 58
religion 31, 54, 146–9, 180, 217
religious exercises 149, 186
Rice, Major, I.A.S.C. 42
Róshan 270

Safdar Ali, Mir of Hunza 120
Saiyyid Sháh Wali 65
salt 129, 211
sanitation 115–16
Seker (Gilgit) 62
Sháh Khán, Prince ("Little Lord Fauntleroy") 235, 236, 293
Shaukat Ali, Prince of Nagir 276
Shayár (Nagir) 278
Shimshál 121
Shina language 18, 165, 228, 265
Shins 169
Shiri Badat, King of Gilgit 206–7
Schomberg, Colonel R. C. F. 299
Sikandarábád 65, 264
smoking 172
spinning 99–100
Srinagar 32
Stein, Sir Aurel 24
stories 206, 213–14
Kiser 104
Princess Búbuli 105
Shiri Badat 206–7
Sumair (Nagir) 274
superstition 82, 147, 156, 161, 263
Swedes 155–6

Tangir 17
Tapkients clan 181
taxes 120, 149, 297
Thól (Nagir) 65
Threshing 81, 100–2, 136–7
threshing-floors 79, 142
Tishót 68
Tragbal Pass 43
trees 130–1, 240, 283
Tumushelling (Winter Solstice) 201–5
turning (on lathe) 170–1

Ulter Ber 105, 143

vermin 115

Wakhán 21
Wakhis 179, 240
Wakhi language 21, 240–1
wall-building 95, 211
washing 223
water storage 96, 115, 212
weaving 165–9
with feathers 222
weddings 197–201
weeding 134, 243
Werchikwár language 20 and footnote, 244, 266
wheelbarrow 211–12
wine-making 194–6
winnowing 102
women
in Hunza 81–2, 99, 102, 117, 118, 122, 146, 155, 191, 277, 286 *et passim*
in Nagir 180, 277
Wreford, Captain and Mrs. 33, 34
Wular Lake 41–2

Yághistán 17
Yakhshini (ogress) 272
Yasín 17, 244, 265–70

Ziárat (Baluchistan) 15

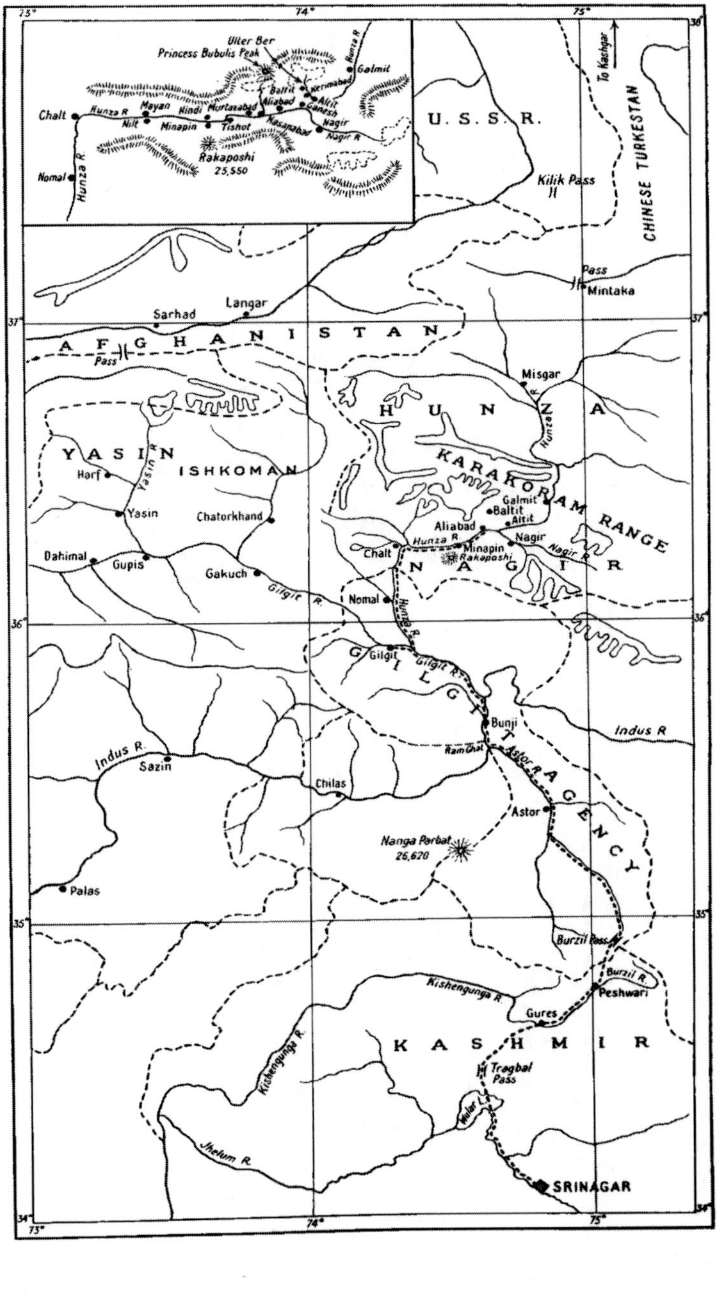

73°
74°
75°
36°
37°
35°
34°
Ulter Ber
Princess Bubulis Peak
Hunza R.
Galmit
Baltit
Kerimabad
Altit
Aliabad
Ganesh
Chalt
Hunza R.
Mayan
Hindi
Murtazabad
Nilt
Minapin
Tishot
Hasanabad
Nagir
Nagir R.
Rakaposhi
25,550
Nomal
Hunza R.
To Kashgar
U. S. S. R.
CHINESE TURKESTAN
Kilik Pass
Pass
Mintaka
Sarhad
Langar
A F G H A N I S T A N
Pass
Misgar
H U N Z A
Hunza R.
K A R A K O R A M RANGE
Y A S I N
ISHKOMAN
Harf
Yasin R.
Yasin
Chatorkhand
Galmit
Baltit
Altit
Aliabad
Nagir
Hunza R.
Chalt
Minapin
Rakaposhi
Nagir R.
N A G I R
Dahimal
Gupis
Gakuch
Gilgit R.
Nomal
Hunza R.
Gilgit
Gilgit R.
G I L G I T A G E N C Y
Bunji
Indus R.
Indus R.
Sazin
Ram Ghat
Astor R.
Chilas
Astor
Nanga Parbat
26,620
Palas
Burzil Pass
Burzil R.
Kishenganga R.
Peshwari
Gures
K A S H M I R
Kishenganga R.
Tragbal Pass
Wular L.
Jhelum R.
SRINAGAR